Cacti Beginner's G

Second Edition

Leverage Cacti to design a robust network operations center

Thomas Urban

BIRMINGHAM - MUMBAI

Cacti Beginner's Guide

Second Edition

First published: March 2011

Second edition: December 2017

Production reference: 1221217

Published by Packt Publishing Ltd.
Livery Place
35 Livery Street
Birmingham
B3 2PB, UK.

ISBN 978-1-78829-918-3

www.packtpub.com

Credits

Author
Thomas Urban

Reviewer
Glyn Astill

Commissioning Editor
Vijin Boricha

Acquisition Editor
Divya Poojari

Content Development Editor
Deepti Thore

Technical Editor
Nilesh Sawakhande

Copy Editor
Safis Editing

Project Coordinator
Shweta H Birwatkar

Proofreader
Safis Editing

Indexer
Pratik Shirodkar

Graphics
Tania Dutta

Production Coordinator
Arvindkumar Gupta

About the Author

Thomas Urban is the owner of Urban-Software.de, a software and consulting services company providing add-ons, plugins, and services for the Cacti Performance Monitoring systems. He has been in the consulting business for more than 5 years and has been creating web applications for over 20 years building reporting interfaces, network management software, asset management sites, and much more.

He is a part of the Cacti community and is known as Phalek in the Cacti forums, where he is among the Top 10 contributors.

He started writing the first Cacti Beginner's Guide for Cacti 0.8 back in 2011. The second edition is his second official effort.

I would like to thank my wife for putting up with my late night writing sessions and for making sure that I never ran out of coffee on the countless evenings I spent sitting in front of the keyboard instead of with her and the children.
I would also like to thank the Cacti community, especially the developers, for creating the Cacti 1.x release and making sure that Cacti still has its place in the performance monitoring world.

About the Reviewer

Glyn Astill has over 15 years experience in system administration, software development, and database development on both Windows and Linux systems. During this time, highly available and high performance Linux database systems have been a major focus.

He currently works for LexisNexis Risk Solutions as a Senior DBA. Prior to joining LexisNexis, Glyn worked as a developer and DBA for seetickets.com, a UK ticket agency, where he was responsible for designing and supporting database systems capable of sustaining periods of very high load during popular ticket on-sales.

I want to thank my wonderful wife Elizabeth and my amazing daughter Ruby for supporting me.

www.PacktPub.com

For support files and downloads related to your book, please visit www.PacktPub.com. Did you know that Packt offers eBook versions of every book published, with PDF and ePub files available? You can upgrade to the eBook version at www.PacktPub.comand as a print book customer, you are entitled to a discount on the eBook copy.

Get in touch with us at service@packtpub.com for more details. At www.PacktPub.com, you can also read a collection of free technical articles, sign up for a range of free newsletters and receive exclusive discounts and offers on Packt books and eBooks.

https://www.packtpub.com/mapt

Get the most in-demand software skills with Mapt. Mapt gives you full access to all Packt books and video courses, as well as industry-leading tools to help you plan your personal development and advance your career.

Why subscribe?

- Fully searchable across every book published by Packt
- Copy and paste, print, and bookmark content
- On demand and accessible via a web browser

Customer Feedback

Thanks for purchasing this Packt book. At Packt, quality is at the heart of our editorial process. To help us improve, please leave us an honest review on this book's Amazon page at https://www.amazon.com/dp/1788299183.

If you'd like to join our team of regular reviewers, you can email us at customerreviews@packtpub.com. We award our regular reviewers with free eBooks and videos in exchange for their valuable feedback. Help us be relentless in improving our products!

Table of Contents

Preface

Cacti is a performance measurement tool that provides easy methods and functions for gathering and graphing system data. You can use Cacti to develop a robust event management system that can alert on just about anything you would like it to. But to do this, you need to gain a solid understanding of the basics of Cacti, its plugin architecture, and automation concepts.

Cacti Beginner's Guide will introduce you to the wide variety of features of Cacti and will guide you on how to use them for maximum effectiveness. This book is designed in such a way that you can explore it chapter by chapter or skip any chapter without missing a beat. If you are a network operator and want to use Cacti for implementing performance measurement for trending, troubleshooting, and reporting purposes, then this book is for you. You only need to know the basics of network management and SNMP.

What this book covers

Chapter 1, *Installing Cacti*, acts as a quick installation reference for users new to Cacti.

Chapter 2, *Using Graphs to Monitor Networks and Devices*, teaches you how to add devices and graphs; then we will see how to display them.

Chapter 3, *Creating and Using Templates*, explains how to create host and graph templates and how to apply them to the devices.

Chapter 4, *User Management*, gets us introduced to the Cacti user management and explains the Realm and Graph permission settings. It will also provide information on how to utilize the new user groups functionality for multi-customer environments.

Chapter 5, *Data Management*, explains how Cacti provides the ability to create own data input methods to query for information.

Chapter 6, *Cacti Maintenance*, serves as a guide on how to backup and restore the Cacti data as well as provide some information on log file management and data housekeeping.

Chapter 7, *Network and Server Monitoring*, provides some extended information on how to use Cacti for network and server monitoring. It will provide information that goes above plain SNMP monitoring.

Chapter 8, *Plugin Architecture*, provides information on the new integrated plugin architecture and how to download and install new plugins.

Chapter 9, *Plugins*, provides information on the commonly used plugins and also introduces the reader to plugin programming.

Chapter 10, *Threshold Monitoring with Thold*, provides an introduction to the Cacti threshold plugin, Thold.

Chapter 11, *Enterprise Reporting*, provides some information on the reporting solutions available for Cacti. It concentrates on the graph reporting solutions, Nectar and CereusReporting.

Chapter 12, *Cacti Automation for NOC*, introduces the Cacti command line interface to the reader. It will also provide an overview of the integrated automation functionality for automated device/graph management.

Chapter 13, *Migrate Cacti to a New Server*, introduces various steps to migrate Cacti to a new server and the steps to prepare the required files, before transferring them.

Chapter 14, *Multiple Pollers with Cacti*, introduces you to remote poller concept that allows administrators to spread the polling of devices to multiple systems.

What you need for this book

You will need the Cacti software with version 1.x, two CPUs with 1 GB of RAM, and 20 GB of hard-drive each with CentOS 7/Windows as an operating system.

Who this book is for

If you are a network operator and want to use Cacti for implementing performance measurement for trending, troubleshooting, and reporting purposes, then this book is for you. You only need to know the basics of network management and SNMP.

Conventions

In this book, you will find a number of text styles that distinguish between different kinds of information. Here are some examples of these styles and an explanation of their meaning.

Code words in text, database table names, folder names, filenames, file extensions, pathnames, dummy URLs, user input, and Twitter handles are shown as follows:

An example for such a naming standard would be "_customername_user".

A block of code is set as follows:

```
// Realm Id can be: 0 - Local, 1 - LDAP, 2 - Web Auth
if ( ( $realm_id < 0 ) || ( $realm_id > 2 ) ) {
    // The realm id will be local unless a valid id was given
    $realm_id = 0;
}
```

Any command-line input or output is written as follows:

```
cd /var/www/html/cacti/cli
```

New terms and **important words** are shown in bold. Words that you see on the screen, for example, in menus or dialog boxes, appear in the text like this: "Select **LDAP Authentication** from the **Authentication Method** drop-down box."

 Warnings or important notes appear like this.

 Tips and tricks appear like this.

Reader feedback

Feedback from our readers is always welcome. Let us know what you think about this book-what you liked or disliked. Reader feedback is important for us as it helps us develop titles that you will really get the most out of. To send us general feedback, simply email feedback@packtpub.com, and mention the book's title in the subject of your message. If there is a topic that you have expertise in and you are interested in either writing or contributing to a book, see our author guide at www.packtpub.com/authors.

Customer support

Now that you are the proud owner of a Packt book, we have a number of things to help you to get the most from your purchase.

Downloading the example code

You can download the example code files for this book from your account at http://www.packtpub.com. If you purchased this book elsewhere, you can visit http://www.packtpub.com/support and register to have the files emailed directly to you. You can download the code files by following these steps:

1. Log in or register on our website using your email address and password.
2. Hover the mouse pointer on the **SUPPORT** tab at the top.
3. Click on **Code Downloads & Errata**.
4. Enter the name of the book in the **Search** box.
5. Select the book for which you're looking to download the code files.
6. Choose from the drop-down menu where you purchased this book from.
7. Click on **Code Download**.

Once the file is downloaded, please make sure that you unzip or extract the folder using the latest version of:

- WinRAR / 7-Zip for Windows
- Zipeg / iZip / UnRarX for Mac
- 7-Zip / PeaZip for Linux

The code bundle for the book is also hosted on GitHub at `https://github.com/PacktPublishing/Cacti-Beginners-Guide-Second-Edition`. We also have other code bundles from our rich catalog of books and videos available at `https://github.com/PacktPublishing/`. Check them out!

Downloading the color images of this book

We also provide you with a PDF file that has color images of the screenshots/diagrams used in this book. The color images will help you better understand the changes in the output. You can download this file from `https://www.packtpub.com/sites/default/files/downloads/CactiBeginnersGuideSecondEdition_ColorImages.pdf`.

Errata

Although we have taken every care to ensure the accuracy of our content, mistakes do happen. If you find a mistake in one of our books-maybe a mistake in the text or the code-we would be grateful if you could report this to us. By doing so, you can save other readers from frustration and help us improve subsequent versions of this book. If you find any errata, please report them by visiting `http://www.packtpub.com/submit-errata`, selecting your book, clicking on the **Errata Submission Form** link, and entering the details of your errata. Once your errata are verified, your submission will be accepted and the errata will be uploaded to our website or added to any list of existing errata under the Errata section of that title. To view the previously submitted errata, go to `https://www.packtpub.com/books/content/support` and enter the name of the book in the search field. The required information will appear under the **Errata** section.

Piracy

Piracy of copyrighted material on the internet is an ongoing problem across all media. At Packt, we take the protection of our copyright and licenses very seriously. If you come across any illegal copies of our works in any form on the internet, please provide us with the location address or website name immediately so that we can pursue a remedy. Please contact us at `copyright@packtpub.com` with a link to the suspected pirated material. We appreciate your help in protecting our authors and our ability to bring you valuable content.

Questions

If you have a problem with any aspect of this book, you can contact us at
questions@packtpub.com, and we will do our best to address the problem.

1
Installing Cacti

So, you have decided to install the Cacti tool. Throughout this book you will learn how to use Cacti and learn new things about it. This book will build up your knowledge, from chapter to chapter, as you complete the tasks. As you go through the book, you will see different information boxes and tips, and I encourage you to read through them as they provide valuable information. At the end of each chapter you will see a summary of what has been covered in the chapter and what you will learn in the chapter to follow.

Let's get on with setting up Cacti 1.x. Take a look at what we will do next. In this chapter we are going to cover:

- Installing the prerequisites for Cacti on a CentOS 7 system
- Installing Cacti on a CentOS 7 system and Windows 2012 R2 system
- Compiling and installing the Spine poller
- Upgrading an existing Cacti installation
- Running Cacti for the first time
- A quick overview of the Cacti web frontend

Here we go...

Preparing the system - basic prerequisites

In order to install and run Cacti, we need to make sure that all system prerequisites are met. Here we'll give an overview of the different components needed.

Web server

As most of Cacti is built as a web interface, a web server is needed. This can be Apache's HTTPD or Microsoft Internet Information Server if installing on Windows, but, in fact, any PHP-capable web server can be used to run the web interface. For optimal support, the use of Apache or IIS is suggested.

PHP

Cacti has been built with the PHP programming language, and therefore needs PHP to be installed on the system. Most Linux distributions already have a base PHP environment installed but some might need additional packages for Cacti to function properly. In particular, the LDAP, SNMP, and MySQL extensions should be installed. Be aware that Cacti 1.1 does not support PHP 7.1.

MySQL database

Cacti uses the freely available MySQL and MariaDB database engines for its database server and they are available for most operating systems. One should note that the database server does not need to be installed on the same host as Cacti. For best performance and to avoid stability issues with the Spine poller, MySQL version 5.6 or MariaDB 10.x should be used.

NET-SNMP package

The NET-SNMP package provides the SNMP binaries used by Cacti and supports SNMPv1, SNMPv2c, and SNMPv3. The NET-SNMP package also provides the SNMP daemon for Linux.

Installing Cacti on a CentOS 7 system

You're now going to install Cacti from source on a CentOS 7 system. You'll use CentOS 7 as it's 100% binary compatible with Red Hat Enterprise Linux 7, but in fact you can follow most of the installation process on other Linux distributions like Ubuntu or SUSE Linux as well. By installing from source you'll get some insight into the inner workings of Cacti, and it will also provide you with a system that most Cacti and plugin developers are used to. There are differences between a source installation and a yum/apt installation, but they will be described later on. Let's get started.

Preparing the system

Assume that the CentOS system has been installed with only the "Server" package selected and there is no graphical user interface installed.

This is the default installation for a CentOS system with no manual package selection.

Time for action - installing the missing packages and preparing the system

The default CentOS installation is missing several important packages. This section will show you how to install all required packages on your CentOS 7 system as well as the latest MariaDB 10.x version:

1. Set up the MariaDB repository for installing the latest MariaDB version. You can get the latest repository from https://downloads.mariadb.org/mariadb/repositories/:

```
echo "# MariaDB 10.1 CentOS repository list - created
2017-02-08 16:11 UTC
# http://downloads.mariadb.org/mariadb/repositories/
[mariadb]
name = MariaDB
baseurl = http://yum.mariadb.org/10.1/centos7-amd64
gpgkey=https://yum.mariadb.org/RPM-GPG-KEY-MariaDB
gpgcheck=1" > /etc/yum.repos.d/MariaDB.repo
```

2. Now we can install all required packages for Cacti:

```
yum -y install mariadb-server php php-cli php-mysql net-snmp-
utils rrdtool
php-snmp gcc mariadb-devel net-snmp-devel autoconf automake
libtool dos2unix wget help2man
php-posix php-ldap php-mbstring php-gd
```

```
root@localhost:~                                                    —    □    ×
libsepol               x86_64       2.5-6.el7                         base        288 k ^
libss                  x86_64       1.42.9-9.el7                       base         45 k
lm_sensors-libs        x86_64       3.4.0-4.20160601gitf9185e5.el7     base         41 k
mariadb-libs           x86_64       1:5.5.52-1.el7                     base        761 k
xz-libs                x86_64       5.2.2-1.el7                        base        103 k
zlib                   x86_64       1.2.7-17.el7                       base         90 k

Transaction Summary
================================================================================
Install  18 Packages (+48 Dependent packages)
Upgrade   5 Packages (+39 Dependent packages)

Total size: 82 M
Total download size: 77 M
Downloading packages:
No Presto metadata available for base
warning: /var/cache/yum/x86_64/7/base/packages/kmod-20-9.el7.x86_64.rpm: Header V3 RSA/SHA256 Signature,
key ID f4a80eb5: NOKEY
Public key for kmod-20-9.el7.x86_64.rpm is not installed
(1/89): kmod-20-9.el7.x86_64.rpm                                      | 115 kB  00:00:00
Public key for krb5-devel-1.14.1-27.el7_3.x86_64.rpm is not installed  ] 4.0 MB/s | 9.4 MB  00:00:16 ETA
(2/89): krb5-devel-1.14.1-27.el7_3.x86_64.rpm                         | 651 kB  00:00:02
(3/89): httpd-2.4.6-45.el7.centos.x86_64.rpm                         | 2.7 MB  00:00:03
(4/89): krb5-libs-1.14.1-27.el7_3.x86_64.rpm                         | 740 kB  00:00:02
(5/89): krb5-workstation-1.14.1-27.el7_3.x86_64.rpm                  | 772 kB  00:00:02
(6/89): libcom_err-1.42.9-9.el7.x86_64.rpm                          |  40 kB  00:00:00
(7/89): libcom_err-devel-1.42.9-9.el7.x86_64.rpm                    |  31 kB  00:00:00
(8/89): libdb-devel-5.3.21-19.el7.x86_64.rpm                        |  38 kB  00:00:00 v
```

3. At this point you should also take care of updating your packages to the latest version. The following command will do this for you:

```
yum -y upgrade
```

4. The next step will start the required MySQL/MariaDB server:

```
systemctl restart mariadb.service
```

5. Cacti 1.x requires the `timezone` tables within MySQL to be populated. The following commands allow you to do so:

```
mysql_tzinfo_to_sql /usr/share/zoneinfo >
/tmp/mysql_timezone.sql
mysql -u root mysql < /tmp/mysql_timezone.sql
```

6. The `timezone` settings for Cacti are very important, so you will need to set your current `timezone`. The following command will help you to do so:

timedatectl set-timezone Europe/Berlin

7. Now that you have set your `timezone`, installed the MySQL/MariaDB server, and upgraded your system, you will have to set some special configuration parameters for MySQL/MariaDB. Edit the `/etc/my.cnf` file:

vi /etc/my.cnf

8. Change your `[mysqld]` section. Make sure to change the time zone setting to your actual `timezone`:

```
[mysqld]
datadir=/var/lib/mysql
socket=/var/lib/mysql/mysql.sock
symbolic-links=0
max_heap_table_size=90M
max_allowed_packet=16M
tmp_table_size=64M
join_buffer_size=64M
innodb_file_per_table=ON
innodb_buffer_pool_size=450M
innodb_doublewrite=OFF
innodb_additional_mem_pool_size=80M
innodb_lock_wait_timeout=50
innodb_flush_log_at_trx_commit=2
collation_server=utf8_general_ci
character_set_client=utf8
default-time-zone='Europe/Berlin'
innodb_flush_log_at_timeout=3
innodb_read_io_threads=32
innodb_write_io_threads=16
```

9. As you have already learned, the `timezone` setting is very important in Cacti. You already changed it for the database server and your system, but PHP also needs to be aware of your `timezone`. Therefore, you will now edit the `/etc/php.ini` file. While doing so you will also enable error logging for the syslog system, which will help you find issues with custom plugins. Now edit the `/etc/php.ini` file and set the following lines:

```
; Log errors to syslog (Event Log on NT, not valid in Windows
95).
error_log = syslog
```

```
...
[Date]
; Defines the default timezone used by the date functions
; http://php.net/date.timezone
date.timezone = Europe/Berlin
```

10. The next step will enable the web server as well as restart the required MySQL/MariaDB server. Use the following commands to start these:

    ```
    systemctl start httpd.service
    systemctl restart mariadb.service
    ```

11. Now that the web server is up and running, you should enable the http/https ports on the CentOS firewall. The firewall-cmd command will help you with this task:

    ```
    firewall-cmd --permanent --zone=public --add-service=https
    firewall-cmd --permanent --zone=public --add-service=http
    firewall-cmd --reload
    ```

12. As you want to have both services started automatically after a reboot of the system, you should also enable both services during boot time. This final step will allow you to do so:

    ```
    systemctl enable httpd.service
    systemctl enable mariadb.service
    ```

13. As a final step you should set the SELinux system to permissive. On a CentOS/RHEL system this can be done by editing the file /etc/selinux/config and setting the SELINUX variable to permissive, which will become active after the next restart:

    ```
    SELINUX=permissive
    ```

14. Before continuing it is now a good time to restart the system.

What just happened?

You just gave the system a location to find the remaining packages needed for the Cacti installation and then installed them. You also enabled the web server and database server to start at boot time. In addition, you have also set some very important system settings and disabled the SELinux setting. You are now ready to start the next installation phase.

Downloading and extracting Cacti

Go to http://www.cacti.net and download the latest version of Cacti. In the top-left corner, under **Downloads**, click on the **Cacti** link. You can download the Cacti files from there. Please also make a note of the **latest stable version**. You will need this information in the following steps. For simplicity, we're assuming that your server has an internet connection.

Cacti version variable CACTIVERSION:

As the Cacti version may be different, we will use the CACTIVERSION or NEWCACTIVERSION variables during the different installation and upgrade steps to refer to the Cacti version. Check the current version on the Cacti website and change these variables accordingly.

Time for action - downloading Cacti

It's now time to download the latest Cacti version to your server. You will need your system username and password to login to your CentOS installation. If you have installed your CentOS system with the default settings, you should already have an SSH server running. If you're already logged in on the machine, you can ignore the first step:

1. From a Windows machine, log on to your system using an SSH client such as Putty. If this is the first time you are connecting to the server, Putty will display a security alert and ask you to accept the RSA key. After doing so, Putty will display a logon prompt where you can log on to the system.

2. Maximizing the window so long text lines do not break at the end of the line might make things easier.

3. You'll need to become the root user in order to be able to set up Cacti properly. Should that not be an option, performing these steps with sudo should achieve the same results.

4. Change to /var/www/html. This is the document root for Apache.

5. Create the CACTIVERSION variable and set it to the current Cacti version

   ```
   export CACTIVERSION=1.1.28
   ```

6. To download Cacti, you can use the wget command. Enter the following command to download Cacti:

   ```
   wget https://www.cacti.net/downloads/cacti-$CACTIVERSION.tar.gz
   ```

7. You should see the following output on your screen:

```
[root@localhost html]# wget https://www.cacti.net/downloads/cacti-$CACTIVERSION.tar.gz
--2017-12-19 08:33:11--  https://www.cacti.net/downloads/cacti-1.1.28.tar.gz
Connecting to 10.27.30.106:80... connected.
Proxy request sent, awaiting response... 200 OK
Length: 8953179 (8.5M) [application/x-gzip]
Saving to: 'cacti-1.1.28.tar.gz'

63% [============================>                  ] 5,699,341   1.87MB/s
```

8. You now have the `tar.gz` file on your system, so let's move on and extract it. The following command will extract the files and directories contained in the archive to the current directory:

    tar -xzvf cacti-$CACTIVERSION.tar.gz

9. Finally, you are going to create a symbolic link to this new Cacti directory. This will allow you to easily switch between different Cacti versions later, for example, when upgrading Cacti. To create a symbolic link, enter the following command to create a link named `cacti` which points to the `cacti-1.1.28` directory:

    ln -s cacti-$CACTIVERSION cacti

```
[root@localhost html]# ls -l
total 8748
lrwxrwxrwx. 1 root root        12 Dec 11 09:52 cacti -> cacti-1.1.28
drwxrwxr-x. 1 1000 1000      2826 Nov 19 15:27 cacti-1.1.28
-rw-r--r--. 1 root root_8953179 Nov 19 15:29 cacti-1.1.28.tar.gz
```

What just happened?

You downloaded the latest Cacti version to the root directory of the web server and created a symbolic link to the extracted directory. With the Cacti files in place, you are now ready for the next phase of the installation process.

Creating the database

The database isn't automatically created during the installation of Cacti. Therefore, you are now going to create it here. At the same time, a database user for Cacti should be created to allow it to access the database. It's also a good idea to secure the MySQL database server by using one of the included CentOS tools or the commands provided.

Time for action - creating the database

For simplicity, let's assume that you're going to host the database on the same server as Cacti:

1. Execute the following command to log on to the MySQL/MariaDB CLI:

   ```
   mysql -u root mysql
   ```

2. The default MySQL root account does not have a password set, so you can do it now:

   ```
   SET PASSWORD FOR root@localhost = PASSWORD('MyN3wpassw0rd');
   ```

3. You can remove the example database, as it is not needed:

   ```
   DROP DATABASE test;
   ```

4. Together with the example database, some example users may have been created. You can remove these with the following command:

   ```
   DELETE FROM user WHERE NOT (host = "localhost" AND user = "root");
   ```

5. On a CentOS distribution you can use the following command to guide you through the preceding steps:

   ```
   /usr/bin/mysql_secure_installation
   ```

6. Now that MySQL is secured, let's create the Cacti database. Enter the following command. This will ask for the MySQL root password which you provided in setup step 1 or step 5. When finished, you'll have an empty database called cacti:

   ```
   mysqladmin -u root -p create cacti
   ```

7. As the database is still empty, you need to create the tables and fill them with the initial data that comes with Cacti. The following command will do just that. Once the command finishes you'll have a working cacti database:

    ```
    mysql -u root -p cacti < /var/www/html/cacti/cacti.sql
    ```

8. Unfortunately, Cacti is still unable to access it, therefore you're now going to create a database user for Cacti. Enter the following command:

    ```
    mysql -u root -p mysql
    ```

9. You'll see the following on the screen:

```
[root@localhost html]# mysql -u root -p mysql
Enter password:
Reading table information for completion of table and column names
You can turn off this feature to get a quicker startup with -A

Welcome to the MariaDB monitor.  Commands end with ; or \g.
Your MariaDB connection id is 14
Server version: 5.5.52-MariaDB MariaDB Server

Copyright (c) 2000, 2016, Oracle, MariaDB Corporation Ab and others.

Type 'help;' or '\h' for help. Type '\c' to clear the current input statement.

MariaDB [mysql]>
```

10. Type the next few lines in the MySQL prompt to create the Cacti user and allow him to use the time_zone_name table of MySQL. Make sure to choose a strong password:

    ```
    GRANT SELECT ON mysql.time_zone_name TO cactiuser@localhost
    IDENTIFIED BY 'MyV3ryStr0ngPassword';
    GRANT ALL ON cacti.* TO cactiuser@localhost IDENTIFIED BY
    'MyV3ryStr0ngPassword';
    flush privileges;
    exit
    ```

What just happened?

You used some tools to secure the MySQL server and created a database. You also filled the Cacti database with the initial Cacti data and created a MySQL user for Cacti. However, Cacti still needs to know how to access the database, so let's move on to the next step.

If you are not using CentOS to install Cacti, you can use some MySQL internal functions to secure your installation.

Configuring Cacti

You need to tell Cacti where to find the database and which credentials it should use to access it. This is done by editing the config.php file in the include directory.

Time for action - configuring Cacti

The database and some other special configuration tasks are done by editing the information in the config.php file:

1. Change to the cacti directory:

   cd /var/www/html/cacti/include

2. Edit config.php with vi:

   vi config.php

3. Change the $database_username and $database_password fields to the previously created username and password. The content of the file should now look like the following:

```
/* make sure these values reflect your actual database/host/user/password */

$database_type     = 'mysql';
$database_default  = 'cacti';
$database_hostname = 'localhost';
$database_username = 'cactiuser';
$database_password = 'MyV3ryStr0ngPassword';
$database_port     = '3306';
$database_ssl      = false;
```

There are many other settings within this file that we will explain in later chapters, so leave them alone for now.

What just happened?

You changed the database configuration for Cacti to the username and password that you created earlier. These settings will tell Cacti where to find the database and what credentials it needs to use to connect to it.

Creating the poller cron entry and Cacti's system user

For the poller to work correctly, Cacti also requires a system user account. You are going to create one now and also set up the poller's cron entry. We are going for a one-minute-based poller interval to prepare for the one-minute polling in a later chapter.

Time for action - creating the poller's cron entry and Cacti's system account

Let's create the cron entry so the poller runs frequently:

1. To create a user called `cactiuser`, issue the following command as root. It will also add the user to the `apache` group:

   ```
   adduser --groups apache cactiuser
   ```

2. Change to the `cacti` directory:

   ```
   cd /var/www/html/cacti
   ```

3. Change the ownership of the `cacti` directory, the newly created user, and `apache`. You will also change the permissions of some special directories as well as enable the `apache` user group to write to the `rra` and `log` directory. The `setfacl` command is important for some internal Cacti processes to work properly and makes sure that the `apache` user is able to write to these directories:

```
chown -R cactiuser.apache /var/www/html/cacti/
chmod -R 775 rra/ log/ resource/ scripts/ cache/
setfacl -d -m group:apache:rw /var/www/html/cacti/rra
setfacl -d -m group:apache:rw /var/www/html/cacti/log
```

4. Add the poller cron entry. Edit the `cacti` file in `/etc/cron.d`:

```
vi /etc/cron.d/cacti
```

5. Add the following line to the file:

```
*/1 * * * * cactiuser /usr/bin/php
/var/www/html/cacti/poller.php > /dev/null 2>&amp;1
```

6. Save the file.

What just happened?

You just created a system user that runs the Cacti poller, and scheduled the poller to run every one-minute. Cacti, by default, is still configured for a five-minute-based polling interval, but it can be changed to one minute if needed. The poller itself can run at different intervals. You are going to configure a one minute polling interval in a later chapter.

Installing the Spine poller

By default, Cacti comes with a poller written in PHP. For small to medium installations this poller does its job just fine, but for large installations an alternative poller needs to be used, and Spine is it. It's written in C and is much faster than the original poller because it uses the multi-tasking capabilities of modern operating systems and hardware.

Time for action - installing Spine

Here we will take a deep dive into installing and configuring the Spine poller:

1. As with the Cacti main files, go to http://www.cacti.net and click on **Spine** under the **Download** section. Make a note of the latest stable version.

2. If not already done, create the CACTIVERSION variable and set it to the current Cacti version:

   ```
   export CACTIVERSION=1.1.28
   ```

3. Change directories to /tmp/ and issue the following command:

   ```
   cd /tmp
   wget
   https://www.cacti.net/downloads/spine/cacti-spine-$CACTIVERSION.tar
   .gz
   ```

4. Extract the file:

   ```
   tar -xzvf cacti-spine-$CACTIVERSION.tar.gz
   ```

5. Change to the newly created directory:

   ```
   cd cacti-spine-$CACTIVERSION
   ```

6. Prepare the directory for compilation. Please note that this step may not work on other distributions, and additional steps may be needed:

   ```
   ./bootstrap
   ```

7. Configure the compiling environment:

   ```
   ./configure
   ```

8. Compile Spine:

   ```
   make
   ```

9. Once the make command finishes, install Spine:

   ```
   make install
   ```

10. Now change the owner of the spine binary to root and set the sticky bit so you can use ICMP pings:

```
chown root:root /usr/local/spine/bin/spine
chmod +s /usr/local/spine/bin/spine
```

11. You now have Spine installed, but it needs to be configured. Therefore, copy the sample configuration file to a location where Spine will find it:

```
cp /usr/local/spine/etc/spine.conf.dist /etc/spine.conf
```

12. Edit the file in `vi`:

```
vi /etc/spine.conf
```

13. Change the database configuration to match the settings from earlier:

```
DB_Host              localhost
DB_Database          cacti
DB_User              cactiuser
DB_Pass              MyV3ryStr0ngPassword
DB_Port              3306
```

14. Create a symbolic link in `/sbin` to the `spine` binary:

```
ln -s /usr/local/spine/bin/spine /sbin/spine
```

What just happened?

You just set up a basic development environment for compiling Spine, compiled it, and then installed it. You also configured Spine to use the correct database information.

Compiling Spine on other Linux distributions:

When compiling Spine on other Linux distributions, such as Ubuntu, you will have to go through some additional steps. For more information, refer to http://docs.cacti.net/manual:100:1_installation.1_install_unix .6_install_and_configure_spine.

Differences between source and APT/yum installations

The main difference between installing Cacti from source and using apt/yum-based installations is the location of the configuration files and availability of patches. Cacti, by default, does not follow the **Filesystem Hierarchy Standard (FHS)** defined for Linux operating systems. The FHS defines directories where applications should add their configuration or log files. The apt/yum-based installations usually follow this standard. Due to this, add-ons such as the plugin architecture may not be available on all platforms using apt/yum.

The main advantage of using apt/yum based installations is the ease of installation, but as we've just seen, installing Cacti isn't very difficult.

However, the disadvantage of using apt or yum is the availability of newer Cacti versions. Source-based Cacti installations can be upgraded to the latest version as soon as they are available on the Cacti website, while apt/yum-based installs might need to wait until the package maintainers update their repositories.

Have a go hero - remote server for database hosting

Here is a little challenge for you. It's not difficult, but it will allow you to alter the installation to suit your needs. What if you want to use a remote database server? Maybe you want to use an existing, dedicated MySQL server instead of hosting the database on the same system as Cacti, or you want to separate the roles to allow more growth. Can you figure out what to change?

Solution: Create the MySQL database on the remote system using the same command as if installed locally but this time use the -h <hostname> option to specify the remote server. When creating the user and granting it permissions, use the following command, assuming the Cacti server has the IP, 192.168.0.10:

```
GRANT ALL ON cacti.* TO cactiuser@'192.168.0.10' IDENTIFIED BY
'MyV3ryStr0ngPassword';
flush privileges;
exit
```

This will allow the Cacti user access to the database from the Cacti server. Now change $database_hostname in config.php and DB_Host in spine.conf on the Cacti server to point to your remote database server. On the database server, you will also have to allow traffic to the 3306 database port using the following firewall commands:

```
firewall-cmd --permanent --zone=public --add-port=3306/tcp
firewall-cmd --reload
```

Installing Cacti on a Windows system

The installation of Cacti on a Windows system is quite different from Linux. Most of the prerequisites that are already available on a Linux platform need to be installed on a Windows system. The MySQL database is an example of such a prerequisite. Here you can find more information about the Windows installation and how you can overcome most of the manual installation procedures by making use of the community-built Windows installer.

The community-built Windows installer

Instead of installing every prerequisite by hand, the community-built Windows installer provides a convenient way of installing them together with Cacti. It was built by a long-term Cacti user and forum member BSOD2600. The installer contains all the software and is also compatible with running Cacti on an IIS web server.

For Cacti 1.x, there will not always be an up-to-date Windows installer available. Nevertheless, the main goal of the installer is to provide you with a convenient way of installing all required software with a single installer. Afterwards, you can download the latest Cacti version from the Cacti website and manually update.

Time for action - starting the Windows setup

Let's have a closer look at installing Cacti on a Windows system:

1. Download the Windows installer to the system on which you want to install Cacti. To retrieve the latest version, go to http://forums.cacti.net/viewtopic.php?t=14946 and click the download link at the end of the first post. Save the installer to your desktop.

2. Double-click on the setup file. The installer will check what has already been installed and give you a report. Click **Next >** after you have read the information:

3. The next screen shows the GPL license. Accept it and click **Next >**:

4. Then you must select a web server. If you have IIS installed you can select it here, otherwise Apache will be installed:

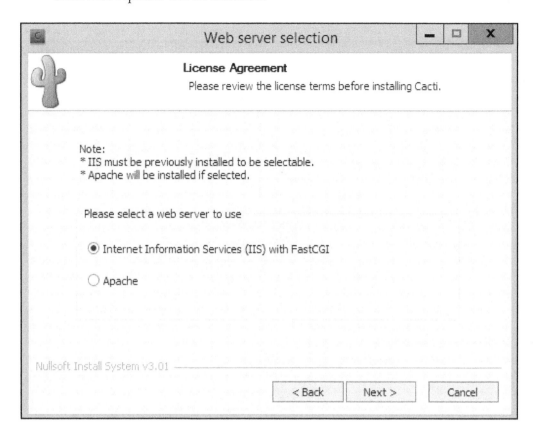

5. In the next step you can choose the components to install. Select all available options. The **Plugins** section is empty as most plugins have been added to Cacti 1.x. Now click **Next >**:

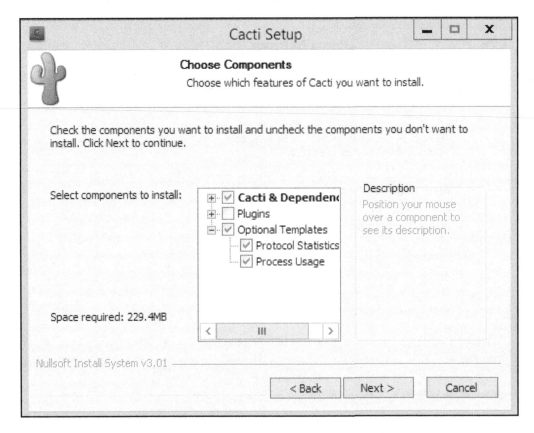

6. Keep the defaults for the installation locations and click **Next >**:

7. The final step provides an overview of the paths to be created. Click **Install** to start the installation process:

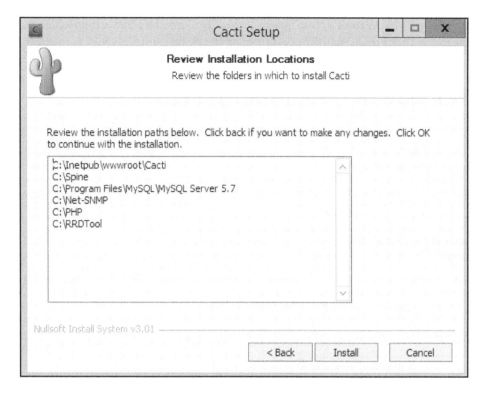

8. Please note the default Cacti admin and MySQL root passwords.
9. Open the Post-Install instructions and follow the tasks.

What just happened?

You installed Cacti on Windows, along with all the prerequisites.

Installing the Spine poller under Windows

Unlike Linux, where compilation from source is the preferred method, the community-based installer already comes with pre-compiled binaries for Windows. This greatly eases the installation part of Cacti on a Windows system, so you can concentrate on the actual configuration of Cacti.

Upgrading Cacti

Upgrading Cacti involves several steps, one of which is backing up the database. Since you created a symbolic link to the Cacti directory, you don't need to backup any files but instead we copy or move them from the old version over to the new one.

Time for action - upgrading Cacti

1. Create a backup of the database. The following command will back up the Cacti database to a file called cacti_backup.sql. You will be asked for the MySQL root password:

   ```
   mysqldump -u root -p --lock-tables --add-drop-table cacti >
   /root/cacti_backup.sql
   ```

2. Change to the /var/www/html directory. From http://www.cacti.net, download the source for the version you want to upgrade to.

3. Create the CACTIVERSION variable and set it to the current Cacti version:

   ```
   export NEWCACTIVERSION=1.1.28
   ```

4. Extract the file. This will create a new directory named cacti-1.1.28:

   ```
   cd /var/www/html
   wget https://www.cacti.net/downloads/spine/cacti-
   spine-$NEWCACTIVERSION.tar.gz
   tar -xzvf cacti-spine-$NEWCACTIVERSION.tar.gz
   ```

5. Change to the newly-created directory and edit include/config.php. Change the database entries in there to match your installation.

6. Before copying any files, you should stop the poller using the web interface. Go to **Configuration** | **Settings** and change to the **Poller** tab. Disable the poller by unchecking it:

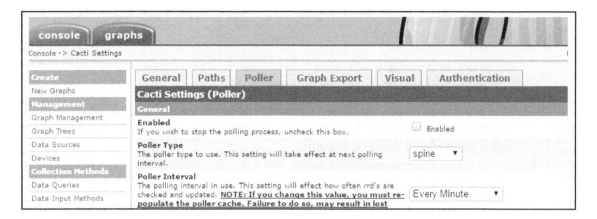

7. Copy some files from your existing installation to the new one:

```
cp /var/www/html/cacti/rra/* /var/www/html/cacti-
$NEWCACTIVERSION/rra/
cp -u /var/www/html/cacti/scripts/* /var/www/html/cacti-
$NEWCACTIVERSION/scripts/
cp -u -R /var/www/html/cacti/resource/* /var/www/html/cacti-
$NEWCACTIVERSION /resource/
```

8. Set the permissions on the `log` and `rra` folders:

```
cd /var/www/html/cacti-$NEWCACTIVERSION/
chown -R cactiuser.apache /var/www/html/cacti-$NEWCACTIVERSION/
chmod -R 775 rra/ log/ resource/ scripts/ cache/
setfacl -d -m group:apache:rw /var/www/html/cacti/rra
setfacl -d -m group:apache:rw /var/www/html/cacti/log
```

9. Change the symbolic link to point to the new directory:

```
cd /var/www/html/
ln -fs cacti-$NEWCACTIVERSION cacti
```

10. As Cacti 1.x requires the `timezone` data to be present in the MySQL/MariaDB database, you will have to import it here as well when upgrading from the 0.8.8 version of Cacti:

```
mysql_tzinfo_to_sql /usr/share/zoneinfo > /tmp/mysql_timezone.sql
mysql -u root -p mysql < /tmp/mysql_timezone.sql
```

11. You will also have to grant access to the `timezone` tables using the following SQL statement:

```
GRANT SELECT ON mysql.time_zone_name TO cactiuser@localhost
IDENTIFIED BY 'MyV3ryStr0ngPassword';
```

12. The final upgrade process is done using the web interface. Point your browser to `http://<yourserver>/cacti/install` and follow the steps. Make sure you select **Upgrade** on the second page.

13. If you are upgrading from 0.8.8 to 1.x, the upgrade process will take some time to complete depending on your Cacti installation size.

14. You can now enable the poller again using the Cacti web interface.

15. Once you have checked that everything is working fine, you can remove or archive the original Cacti directory.

What just happened?

You upgraded Cacti to a newer version. As a safety net, you created a backup of the database so you can revert back to the old version in case of an error. You copied the RRD files and other resources to the new installation and switched over by changing the symbolic link to point to the new location. You finished the upgrade process by going to the install URL, which provides the final web-based upgrade process.

Using Cacti for the first time

After the installation of the database and files, there are still several additional configuration tasks left. For these tasks, you are going to use the web interface provided by Cacti to guide you through the final part of the setup. The following steps are almost identical for Windows and Linux.

Time for action - configuring Cacti

1. Go to the installation URL: `http://<yourserver>/cacti/install`. Read the license agreement and click **Next**:

Cacti Installation Wizard

License Agreement

Thanks for taking the time to download and install Cacti, the complete graphing solution for your network. Before you can start making cool graphs, there are a few pieces of data that Cacti needs to know.

Make sure you have read and followed the required steps needed to install Cacti before continuing. Install information can be found for Unix and Win32-based operating systems.

Also, if this is an upgrade, be sure to reading the Upgrade information file.

Cacti is licensed under the GNU General Public License, you must agree to its provisions before continuing:

This program is free software; you can redistribute it and/or modify it under the terms of the GNU General Public License as published by the Free Software Foundation; either version 2 of the License, or (at your option) any later version.

This program is distributed in the hope that it will be useful, but WITHOUT ANY WARRANTY; without even the implied warranty of MERCHANTABILITY or FITNESS FOR A PARTICULAR PURPOSE. See the GNU General Public License for more details.

☑ Accept GPL License Agreement

Next

---

2. The next page provides an overview of the different installed modules and database parameters. As you have installed all prerequisites and configured the database server according to these recommendations, you can **Accept the GPL License Agreement** and click **Next** here.

3. The next page asks if you are·installing a new system, a new remote poller, or upgrading an existing one. Choose **New Primary Server** then click **Next**:

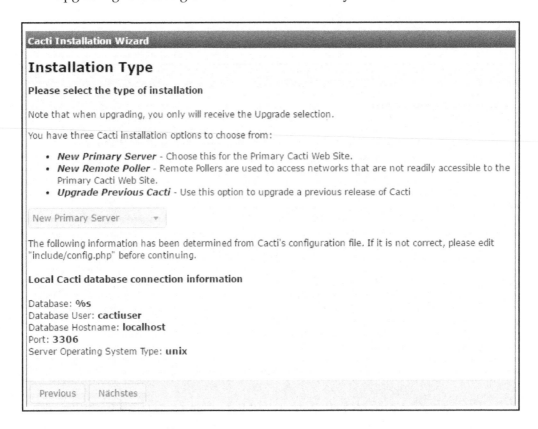

4. The next page provides an overview of all required binaries and paths. If you have followed the installation steps closely, all fields should be green. Make sure to set the theme to **Classic**:

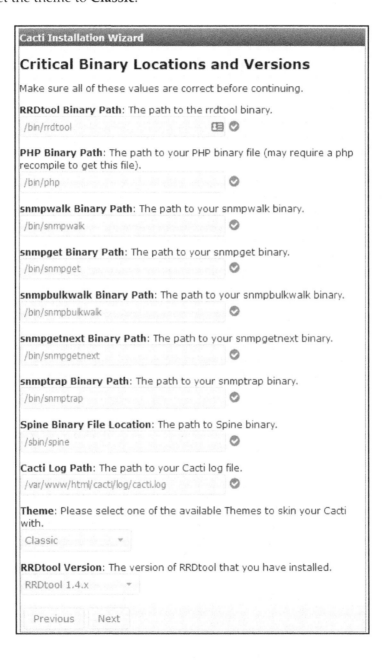

5. The following page will check for the correct files and folder permissions. If you have followed the installation guide, everything shows up green here. Click on **Next** to continue the installation:

Cacti Installation Wizard

Directory Permission Checks

Please ensure the directory permissions below are correct before proceeding. During the install, these directories need to be owned by the Web Server user. These permission changes are required to allow the Installer to install Device Template packages which include XML and script files that will be placed in these directories. If you choose not to install the packages, there is an 'install_package.php' cli script that can be used from the command line after the install is complete.

After the install is complete, you can make some of these directories read only to increase security.

Required Writable at Install Time Only

/var/www/html/cacti-1.0.2/resource/snmp_queries is Writable

/var/www/html/cacti-1.0.2/resource/script_server is Writable

/var/www/html/cacti-1.0.2/resource/script_queries is Writable

/var/www/html/cacti-1.0.2/scripts is Writable

Required Writable after Install Complete

/var/www/html/cacti-1.0.2/log is Writable

/var/www/html/cacti-1.0.2/cache/boost is Writable

/var/www/html/cacti-1.0.2/cache/mibcache is Writable

/var/www/html/cacti-1.0.2/cache/realtime is Writable

/var/www/html/cacti-1.0.2/cache/spikekill is Writable

All folders are writable

NOTE: If you are installing packages, once the packages are installed, you should change the scripts directory back to read only as this presents some exposure to the web site.

Previous   Next

6. The final step allows you to import some pre-defined templates. Select all of the templates and click **Finish** to complete the installation:

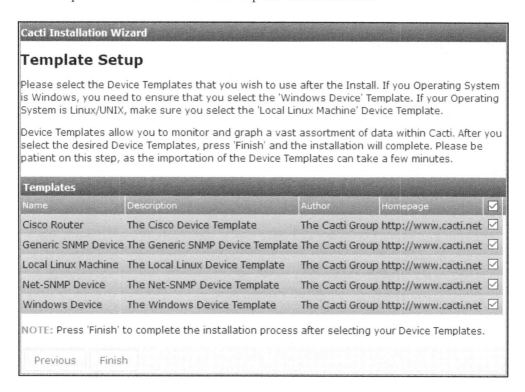

What just happened?

You finalized your Cacti installation by running the included web-based installer. If you have been following the instructions, you will have a working Cacti installation.

The installation will leave you with the default cmd.php poller. If you want to use Spine, you will now have to log on to the Cacti web interface and set the Spine poller file path in the **Paths** section of the **Settings** page. You also have to change the poller type to Spine in the **Poller** section.

The Cacti web interface explained

The first time you log in, use the username admin and password admin (for Linux). You will be forced to change the admin password, but after doing so you will be presented with the Cacti web interface:

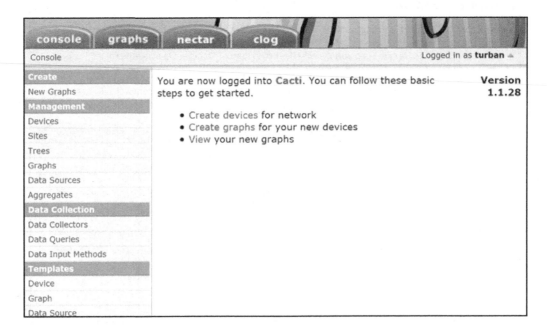

The initial page is called the **Console** and only administrators and users with special access rights are able to see it. From here you can fully administer Cacti.

The Console tab

The **Console** tab is where you manage your Cacti installation. From here you can add devices and users or create graphs and assign them to a tree. We're going to explain each of the menu sections here:

Create section

The **Create** section provides an easy access for new graph creations for specific devices. It's a shortcut to the create graphs link within each device.

Management section

The **Management** section, as its name says, allows the management of graphs, devices, data sources, graph trees, and the new Sites items as well as aggregate graphs. Sites is a new feature of Cacti and allows you to assign devices to a site. As with the old Cacti versions, within this section you can still add/edit or delete devices, delete graphs, add devices to trees, and much more.

Data Collection section

The **Data Collection** section describes the different ways that Cacti retrieves data from devices or systems. Here you can manage data queries such as SNMP retrieve methods, or manage the different input methods, which are used by external scripts called from the poller. With version 1.x, the new Data Collectors item has been added. Cacti 1.x allows you to have multiple remote pollers, and in this section you can add and manage these pollers. More to come in a later chapter.

Templates section

The **Templates** section provides an easy way of combining data templates into a graph (graph templates), graphs and data queries for a specific type of host (host templates), or different data source items (data templates). Many graph, data, and host templates are available on the Cacti forums.

Automation section

The **Automation** section is new in Cacti 1.x. It allows you to plan for automated network discovery as well as define rules for the automation of device and graph creation for auto-discovered devices. This section is based on the Discovery and Autom8 plugin which was already available for the 0.8.8 version of Cacti and has now been integrated into the main Cacti distribution.

Presets section

The **Presets** section allows you to configure the new VDEF rules as well as the old CDEF and GPRINT settings. The **Data Profiles** item is a new concept in Cacti 1.x. It defines the poller interval being used for the different data templates. This is where you will start the creation of a new one minute-based polling interval.

Import/Export section

The Import/Export section allows the import and export of templates. This is especially useful for providing templates of exotic devices to the Cacti community, or to import them from one of the many provided on the Cacti forum.

Cacti doesn't yet provide a method for importing or exporting other data (for example, device lists) from within the web interface.

Configuration section

Within the **Configuration** section we can change the settings of Cacti. These settings include:

- General settings (for example, logging levels)
- Path settings (similar to the paths page from the installer)
- Device default settings (SNMP version, timeouts)
- Poller settings (number of threads, poller type to use)
- Data storage settings (set remote or local RRD file storage)
- Visual settings (size of the graphs, font size to use, theme to use)
- Authentication settings (local authentication, LDAP or HTTP basic, password settings)
- Data source statistics settings (enable/disable data source statistics collection)
- Performance settings (enable/disable on-demand RRD file updates and image caching)
- Spikes settings (enable/disable automated spike data removal)
- Mail/reporting/DNS settings (set email options, configure nectar/reporting and DNS settings)

Utilities section

The **Utilities** section provides access to some basic system tools such as log or poller cache management, and hosts the user management interface.

The graphs tab

The **graphs** tab is the main screen for end users. Here they can view the graphs for their devices and systems, and also change some personal settings:

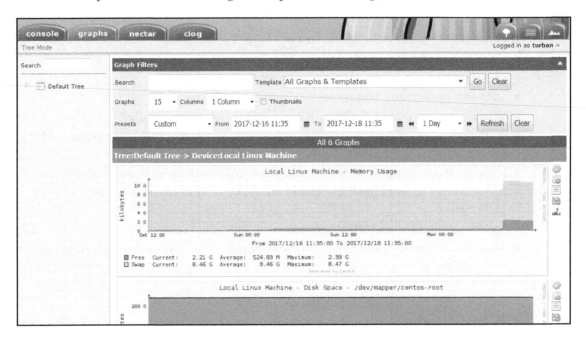

The **graph** tab contains a hierarchical tree to the left containing all devices a user is allowed to view. The main part of the page contains the graphs, and a filtering system for customizing the timeframe and graphs displayed based on a number of methods.

The nectar tab

The **nectar** tab provides you with some basic reporting functionality for Cacti. It is based on the Nectar plugin and has been integrated into Cacti 1.x:

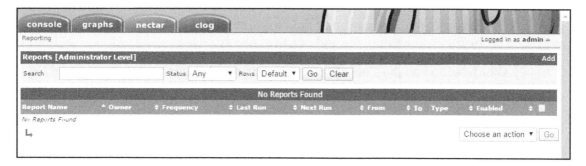

The clog tab

The **clog** tab provides the common log viewer for Cacti. From here you can view the Cacti log entries currently logging with basic reporting functionality. It is based on the Nectar plugin and has been integrated into Cacti 1.x:

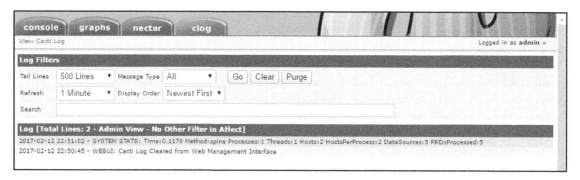

Before we continue

You now have a rough overview of the Cacti web interface and how it interacts with the database. You're going to dive a bit deeper into the details in the next few chapters, so it is not important at this stage to know where everything is or how it works in detail.

Pop quiz - a few questions about Chapter 1

1. If you are using a remote database server, which configuration files do you need to change?

    a) The `config.php` file and `spine.conf`
    b) The `global.php` file and `config.php`

2. Which section on the **Console** tab allows you to change the path to the Cacti log file?

    a) The **System Utilities** section
    b) The **Path** tab within the **Configuration Section**
    c) The **General** tab within the **Configuration Section**

3. On a CentOS 7 system, how can you configure the MySQL server to start automatically during system startup?

    a) You can use the `enableservice` command
    b) The `setstartup` command allows you to do so
    c) The `systemctl` command will do this

Summary

In this chapter, you have learned a lot of new information. You have learned how to download and install Cacti and how to set up the directory structure and permissions. You have covered how to create a database and fill it with the base Cacti data and time zone information, and learned how to configure Cacti to find its database. There have been topics about creating the Cacti system user and setting up the poller's cron entry for doing the actual monitoring work. You have also covered the installation of the Spine poller and looked into the process of upgrading an existing Cacti installation. Finally, you had a brief look at the different sections and parts of the web interface.

You're now ready to create your first few devices and graphs in the next chapter. So let's move on then!

2
Using Graphs to Monitor Networks and Devices

After having installed and configured Cacti, you are now able to add your first devices and graphs to the system. This chapter will show you how to add new devices and how to add some performance measurement graphs to them. You will also learn how to group devices using the Cacti tree.

This chapter is going to cover the following topics:

- Introduction to graph creation with RRDtool
- Adding devices to Cacti
- Adding graphs to a device
- Assigning host templates to a device
- Adding a device to the Cacti tree

So let's get started...

An introduction to Cacti graphs and RRDtool

In the preface, we talked about how RRDtool stores data. Now, you'll be looking into the actual graph creation process and what features Cacti supports.

Creating graphs with RRDtool

As you have seen in the preface, Cacti uses RRDtool to store the polled data. In addition to just storing the data, RRDtool is also used to create the actual performance graphs.

If you now expect to see a full-featured charting application, you will be disappointed. RRDtool graph functionality only offers a very limited range of chart types. They can either be line charts, area charts, or a combination of both. There is no 3D option available or any other type of chart, such as pie or scatter charts. This may be a disadvantage for some at first, but concentrating on only a few basic chart types makes it a fast, specialized rendering engine for these types. This is the main focus of the RRDtool graphing engine: quickly displaying the raw RRD data while keeping a predefined storage size.

There are several graphing features available for plotting the data, the most commonly used types are:

- **LINE**: The data is drawn as a line, which can be formatted in width and type (for example, dashed line).
- **VRULE**: A fixed vertical line is drawn at a defined value.
- **HRULE**: A fixed horizontal line is drawn at a predefined value (for example, threshold limits).
- **AREA**: A solid filled area chart is drawn. Several area charts can be stacked together.

Each of these graph types can be combined together to build the final chart image.

Let us dive into the graph creation process here to get a better understanding of the RRDtool graphing capabilities.

You need to have the RRDtool in your path for the following commands to work.

Basic RRDtool graph creation

Let us begin with the RRD example from the preface and use that RRD file as the basis for our graphs.

A note to Windows users:

The following examples also work for Windows. Simply replace the `rrdtool` command with the full path to the RRDtool binary. For example, use `C:\rrdtool\rrdtool.exe` instead of `rrdtool`.

You will also have to copy the DejaVu font from the `rrdtool` directory to your Windows `Fonts` directory.

The supplied code examples that came with this book contain some Perl scripts, which will help in the creation of the RRD file and automatically update it with random data. In order to create the test RRD file, use the following command:

```
perl create_rrdfile_linux.pl test.rrd
```

If you have installed the RRDtool to `C:\rrdtool` you can use the following command for Windows:

```
perl create_rrdfile_windows.pl test.rrd
```

Having created the test data, you can now start to generate our first RRDtool-based graph. It is going to be a very simple graph displaying only the pure data.

Execute the following code at the **command line interface (CLI)** to create your first 500-pixel-wide graph:

```
rrdtool graph -w 500 data_image.png \
--start 1488153600 \
--end 1488218400 \
DEF:intspeed=test.rrd:data:AVERAGE \
LINE2:intspeed#FF0000
```

This will create the following graph:

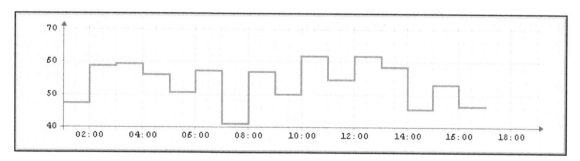

So what does this command actually do? Using the command, you defined a start and end time in the Unix time format, and defined the RRD file and dataset you want to plot. You also told RRDtool to draw a two-pixel line (LINE2) using this dataset and store the resulting graph as data_image.png. The RRDtool automatically creates the *x* axis and *y* axis for you, and also inserts the time and value description. This is the most basic way of creating a RRDtool-based graph.

Advanced RRDtool graph creation

Although this basic graph image already has a lot of information in it, it is still missing some important information. It neither describes what is being graphed, nor does it provide additional information, such as threshold breaches or max/min values. So, let us go back to this basic graph and look at how you can enhance it, step-by-step, using some of the advanced RRDtool features.

Adding a label and title to the graph

The first enhancement to our graph will be a label and a graph title so someone looking at the graph gets some additional information. For this you can use the --vertical-label and --title parameters:

```
rrdtool graph -w 500 data_image.png \
--start 1488153600 \
--end 1488218400 \
--vertical-label bps \
--title "Interface Speed" \
DEF:intspeed=test.rrd:data:AVERAGE \
LINE2:intspeed#FF0000
```

The resulting graph now has a title at the top and a description to the left as can be seen here:

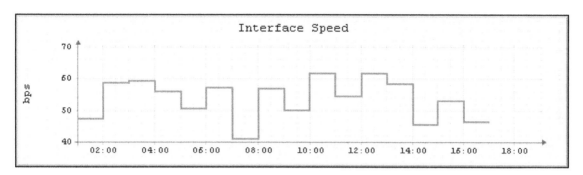

As you can see, the RRDtool command added a rotated description to the Y-Axis and also added the title at the top of the graphs. The graph is now bigger in dimensions than the first one. The RRDtool uses the width and height information to set the actual chart size only. Everything else will be added to the graph. You can see this behavior throughout the next few examples.

Adding a legend to the graph

Now that you have added some description to the graph, you can go on and also add a legend to it. For this, you are going to use the LAST, AVERAGE, and MAX poller values. The function of the GRPINT item is to add additional graph information to the legend. You are also going to add a description field to the LINE2 item. Adding a description to the LINE or AREA items will automatically create a legend entry for you.

The LAST, AVERAGE, and MAX values are always calculated using the data limited by the start and end time. Therefore, they directly relate to the chart being displayed.

Let us look at the following command:

```
rrdtool graph -w 500 data_image.png --start 1488153600 --end
1488218400 \
--vertical-label bps --title "Interface Speed" \
DEF:intspeed=test.rrd:data:AVERAGE \
LINE2:intspeed#FF0000:"Interface eth0" \
GPRINT:intspeed:LAST:"Current\:%8.0lf" \
GPRINT:intspeed:AVERAGE:"Average\:%8.0lf" \
GPRINT:intspeed:MAX:"Maximum\:%8.0lf\n"
```

The resulting image now also contains a small legend at the bottom:

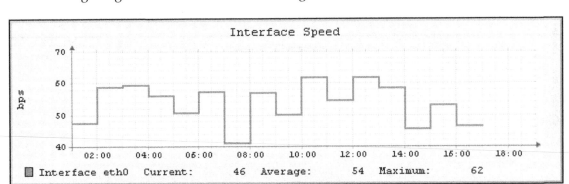

As you can see, the legend was added to the bottom of the graph, expanding its height. By adding a description to the LINE2 line (**Interface eth0**) the description was automatically placed at the bottom along with the color being used to draw that line. The GPRINT text and values have then been added right after the description. If you want to add some more text to the next line, you need to make sure that the last GRPINT value contains a \n (newline) string at the end.

Although the height is automatically adjusted, RRDtool does not do the same for the width. In case your legend is larger than the graph image, you will have to manually increase the width yourself. This can be achieved using the -width parameter.

Adding a threshold line to the graph

Now, let us also set a threshold and display a line marking the threshold on the graph. This can be achieved by using the HRULE item. You are going to set a threshold at 50 and use a light-gray color to display it on the graph. The following command creates this line and also adds an additional entry to the legend. In addition, you are also going to change the LINE2 item to an AREA item, so the data being displayed is shown as a filled area:

```
rrdtool graph -w 500 data_image.png --start 1488153600 --end
1488218400 \
--vertical-label bps --title "Interface Speed" \
DEF:intspeed=test.rrd:data:AVERAGE \
HRULE:50#C0C0C0FF:"Threshold ( 50 )\n"   \
AREA:intspeed#FF0000:"Interface eth0" \
GPRINT:intspeed:LAST:"Current\:%8.01f" \
GPRINT:intspeed:AVERAGE:"Average\:%8.01f" \
GPRINT:intspeed:MAX:"Maximum\:%8.01f\n"
```

You can see the light-gray line being printed horizontally on the image, providing a good overview of the time that the data exceeded the threshold:

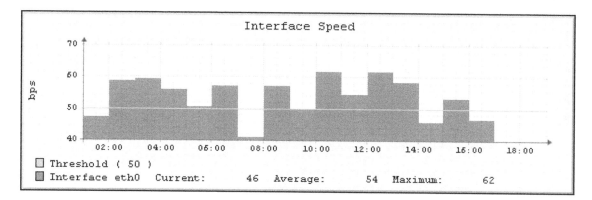

Using the newline character \n in the description string for the HRULE item allows you to add manual line breaks to the legend section. As you can see in the graph, the following text items are added to the next line.

Adding threshold breaches to the graph

You have now seen how you can add a threshold line to the graph, but you probably also want to change the color of the data every time the threshold is breached. Let us assume that you want to have the color go red at, or above, the threshold, and go green once it is below. This can be achieved by using a **Computed DEFinition (CDEF)** and the LIMIT statement.

You define a CDEF named isGreen which returns a number as long as the value of intspeed is between 0 and 50, otherwise no value is returned. You are going to use this CDEF to change the color of the displayed area.

Instead of using the intspeed value, you assign this new CDEF, isGreen, to the AREA item and change the color of the AREA to green (RGB: 00FF00). You also create a new AREA entry, which you now assign the intspeed value, set the color to red and give it a description Over Threshold\n. For this to work correctly, you need to place this new AREA above the old AREA statement.

Why are there two AREA statements? In fact, changing the color of one AREA as it is displayed is not possible, so you need to do a little trick here. The first AREA statement will graph all values in red, as well as the ones which are below the threshold, like you can see in the previous example. With the second AREA statement, a green area will be drawn at all data values that are below the threshold. As the color is not transparent, the red area will disappear. You can see the total red area when you remove the second AREA statement.

The complete code now looks like this:

```
rrdtool graph -w 500 data_image.png --start 1488153600 --end
1488218400 \
--vertical-label bps --title "Interface Speed" \
DEF:intspeed=test.rrd:data:AVERAGE \
CDEF:isGreen=intspeed,0,50,LIMIT \
HRULE:50#C0C0C0FF:"Threshold ( 50 )\n" \
AREA:intspeed#FF0000:"Over Threshold\n" \
AREA:isGreen#00FF00:"Interface eth0" \
GPRINT:intspeed:LAST:"Current\:%8.01f" \
GPRINT:intspeed:AVERAGE:"Average\:%8.01f" \
GPRINT:intspeed:MAX:"Maximum\:%8.01f\n"
```

Run this code from the command line and you will see the resulting graph:

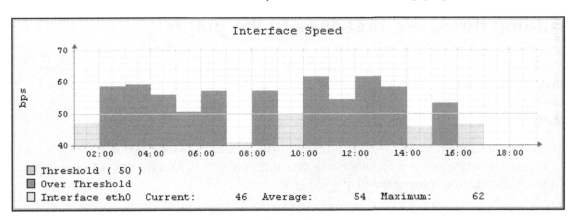

All of the graphs you have just created can be created in Cacti using the Cacti web interface. This section does provide a small and very limited overview of the capabilities of the RRDtool graphing functions, but should give you enough ideas to start playing around with it to create your own graphs.

Variable definition (VDEF)

In contrast to CDEF definitions, which only work for each data point in a graph, a VDEF definition works over the entire dataset. This allows you to calculate different values for the data being displayed and then re-use this value within the different graph items. You are now going to use this function to draw a HRULE element, which displays the current maximum of the data being displayed.

The complete code now looks like this:

```
rrdtool graph -w 500 data_image.png --start 1488153600 --end
1488218400 \
--vertical-label bps --title "Interface Speed" \
DEF:intspeed=test.rrd:data:AVERAGE \
VDEF:maximum=intspeed,MAXIMUM \
CDEF:isGreen=intspeed,0,50,LIMIT \
HRULE:50#C0C0C0FF:"Threshold ( 50 )\n"  \
HRULE:maximum#202020FF:"Maximum of this period\n" \
AREA:intspeed#FF0000:"Over Threshold\n" \
AREA:isGreen#00FF00:"Interface eth0" \
GPRINT:intspeed:LAST:"Current\:%8.01f" \
GPRINT:intspeed:AVERAGE:"Average\:%8.01f" \
GPRINT:intspeed:MAX:"Maximum\:%8.01f\n"
```

Running this code from the command line will create the following graph:

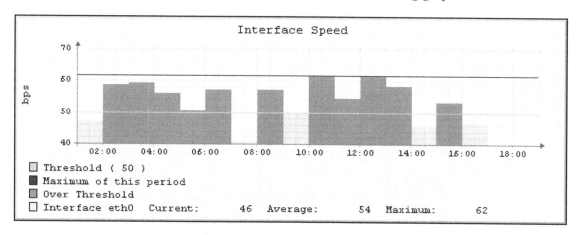

You can see a new dark blue line appearing right at the 62-bps mark, showing the **Maximum of this period**. You calculated this line using the VDEF definition for maximum and using the entire dataset, then you have used the HRULE element to display the maximum variable on the graph. You can use this new feature in Cacti 1.0 to easily calculate different types of data, such as 95th percentile or simple maximum lines as shown previously.

Further reading

The RRDtool webpage does provide some very good documentation on the RRDtool and the graphing functions. The features you have seen here are only a small set of what is possible with the RRDtool. Unfortunately, providing information on all of the features is beyond the scope of this book, but it is recommended to especially look at the gallery at http://oss.oetiker.ch/rrdtool/ for some ideas for the graphs. There's also an excellent website available from *Alex van den Bogaerdt*, which explains the functionality of RRDtool in greater detail. You can visit his page at http://rrdtool.vandenbogaerdt.nl/.

Please remember that, although Cacti does provide many of the functions of the RRDtool, there are some which may not yet be available.

Have a go hero - create your own visual warnings

Let's assume the green and red areas are not granular enough, you also want to have a yellow area, where you can immediately see that the threshold is about to be breached. This yellow warning area should be displayed between the values 45 and 50.

Have a look at the following image:

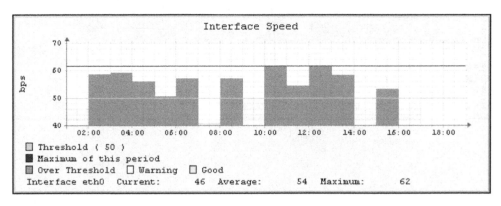

What would you need to change in the above RRDtool command line to get this image?

Solution: You need to add one additional CDEF and another AREA for this to work. You also need to change the isGreen CDEF. The following command line will create and display the yellow warning area and the appropriate legend:

```
rrdtool graph -w 500 data_image.png --start 1488153600 --end
1488218400 \
--vertical-label bps --title "Interface Speed" \
DEF:intspeed=test.rrd:data:AVERAGE \
VDEF:maximum=intspeed,MAXIMUM \
CDEF:isGreen=intspeed,0,44,LIMIT \
CDEF:isYellow=intspeed,45,50,LIMIT \
HRULE:50#C0C0C0FF:"Threshold ( 50 )\n"  \
HRULE:maximum#202020FF:"Maximum of this period\n" \
AREA:intspeed#FF0000:"Over Threshold" \
AREA:isYellow#FFFF00:"Warning" \
AREA:isGreen#00FF00:"Good\n" \
COMMENT:"Interface eth0" \
GPRINT:intspeed:LAST:"Current\:%8.01f" \
GPRINT:intspeed:AVERAGE:"Average\:%8.01f" \
GPRINT:intspeed:MAX:"Maximum\:%8.01f\n"
```

 Note that we use a COMMENT item to add the Interface eth0 text at the beginning of the graph legend.

Adding devices to Cacti

A device in Cacti can be anything that can be monitored remotely or locally. This can be a storage device, Windows or Unix servers, and of course network devices. For Cacti to be able to monitor a device it needs to be reachable by ping or SNMP, but the actual data retrieval can also be done using scripts and commands, or a set of SNMP queries. With Cacti 1.0, a new management item has been introduced called Site. The site item allows you to group devices by site and also store site-specific information, such as address, time zone, and GPS coordinates. Before you add a new device, you will therefore first create a site to which you will be assigning the device later.

Creating a new site

Site creation is a new menu item in the management section of the Cacti web interface. Sites do not have sub-items, so you will not be able to create a site and have different districts belong to it. For now, sites do not provide a lot of additional functionality to the core Cacti but can be used by other plugins like Manage to group alerts by this site item.

Time for action - creating a new site in Cacti

Let's look into the different steps involved for creating a new site:

1. Log in as an admin user to your new Cacti installation.
2. Click on the **Sites** link under the **Management** menu. This will open a table with all sites added so far. For a new Cacti installation this table will be empty.
3. In the top-right of the new page click on **Add**. This is the default position for this **Add** link:

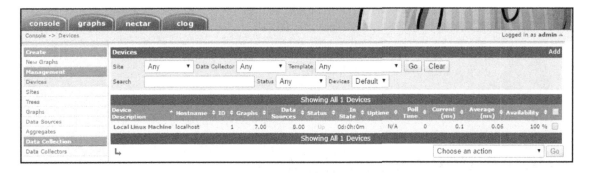

4. You will now be presented with the **Site [new]** screen. Have a look at this screen and make yourself comfortable with the different fields.
5. Now enter a **Name** for the site and select the correct **TimeZone**:

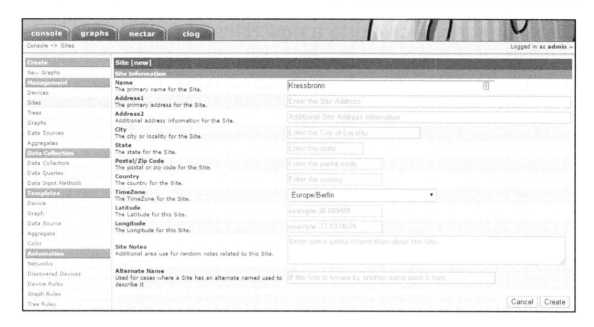

6. You can also add some notes. Click the **Create** button once you are finished.

You have just created your first site within Cacti by providing a name and the time zone the site is located in. You can now continue with adding your first device to Cacti.

Creating a device

Creating a device in Cacti can be achieved by using the Cacti web interface or the Cacti CLI. In this chapter, you will focus on using the Cacti web interface, so you are going to add your first device here. While looking at the different steps it takes to add a device, we are not going too much into detail on every field as most of the user interface is self-explanatory and provides a detailed description of each field.

Before you start: Create a naming standard

If you have not already done so, you should now think about a naming standard for your devices. Creating and keeping to a naming standard is the first step to automation. Later in this book, you will go through some device and graph creation automation, where it is assumed that you have a naming standard for your devices in place.

Time for action - creating a new device in Cacti

The following steps will show you the process of adding a new device to Cacti:

1. Click on the **Devices** link under the **Management** menu. This will open a table with all devices added so far. For a new installation there should only be the localhost device showing up.

2. In the top-right of the new page, click on the **Add** link:

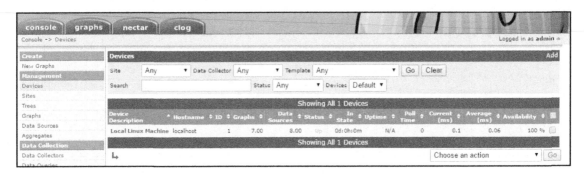

3. You will now be presented with the **Devices [new]** screen. Have a look at this screen and make yourself comfortable with the different fields.

4. Enter a **Description** and **Hostname** (or IP address).

5. If you add an SNMP-enabled device, select **Ping or SNMP Uptime** as the **Downed Device Detection** method. Otherwise select **Ping**. When selecting **Ping** you can choose the protocol type and port to use:

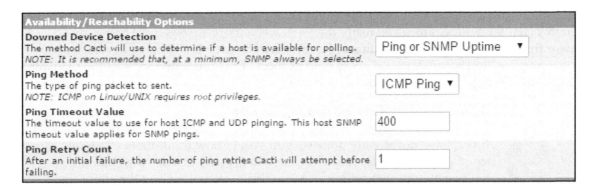

6. Enter the SNMP community and select the correct version (some additional fields will show up when you choose SNMP version 3). If the device is not SNMP capable, you can select **Not used**.

7. You can also add some notes. Click the **Create** button once you are finished:

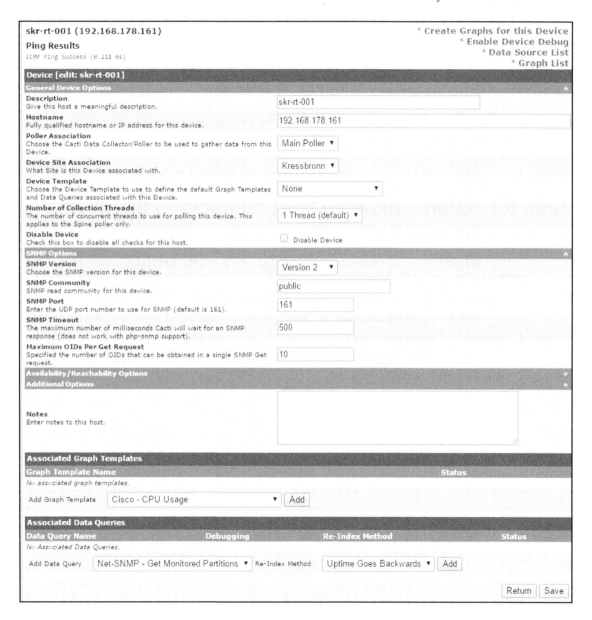

In this section, you created your first device within Cacti by providing some basic information such as an IP address and SNMP management options. With this information, Cacti is now able to poll the device. It still does not have any graphs associated with it.

Selecting host templates for the device

You may have noticed the **Host Templates** field, but what is a **Host Template**? A host template is a pre-defined package of graphs or data queries that can be assigned to a device. Using a template for complex devices reduces the administrative task for adding devices. Here you are going to assign a template to the device. Host templates can also be selected once the device has been created. Cacti does come with some very basic host templates, like Cisco Router, Windows 2000/XP Host, or Generic SNMP-enabled Host. All of these contain pre-defined graphs or data queries for these hosts.

Time for action - adding a host template to the device

Let's now add a host template to the device you just created:

1. Go back to the device overview page by clicking on the **Devices** link under the **Management** menu.
2. Click on the device (the description) you have just created.
3. In the **Host Template** drop-down box, select a template that fits your device best.
4. Click on the **Save** button.
5. Note the additional entries in the **Associated Graph Templates** and **Associated Data Queries** fields:

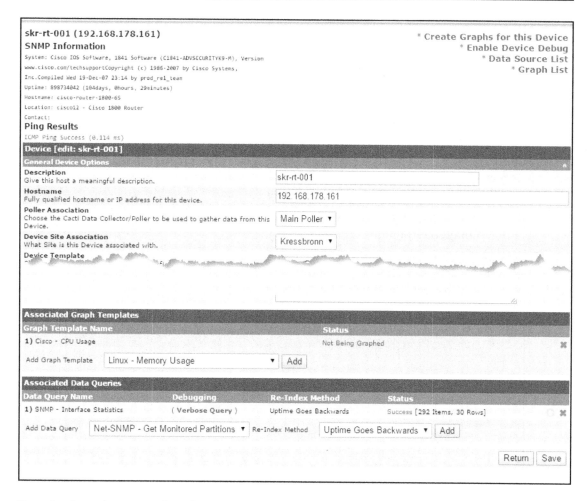

By selecting a host template for the device, you have added a pre-defined package of graph templates and data queries to the host. This is a convenient way of reducing the administrative tasks of adding these manually through the provided drop-down lists. You will come back to templates later in the book, so you do not have to fully understand the concept of templates right now.

Adding graphs to the device

Cacti displays performance data as graphs, therefore we are now going to add some basic graphs to the device we have just added. The first graph that you are going to add is a simple ping graph. Let's go ahead and add the ping template to the host and later add the associated graph to the device.

Time for action - adding graphs to the device

Let's look at the steps required for adding new graphs to your device:

1. Go back to the device overview page by clicking on the **Devices** link under the **Management** menu.
2. Click on the device you have just created.
3. In the **Associated Graph Templates** section, select the **Unix - Ping Latency** from the drop-down list and click the **Add** button:

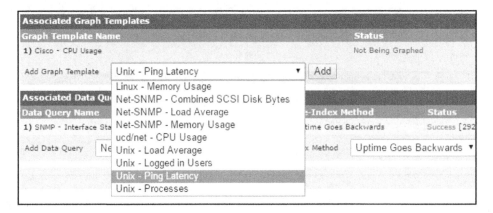

4. Click on the **Save** button at the bottom of the page.
5. Go to the top of the page and click on the link **Create Graphs for this Host**.

6. Select **Unix - Ping Latency**:

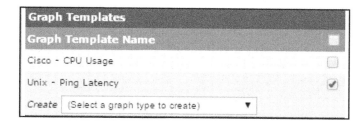

7. Click the **Create** button.
8. A new screen will show up, where you can choose a legend color and text, but for now just click **Create**.
9. You will be redirected back to the graphs selection screen with the entry we selected being grayed out:

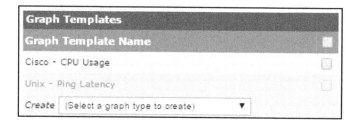

You just added your first graph to a Cacti device by adding a graph template to the device and selecting it during the graph creation screen. Cacti will now start to poll the data for this graph and generate the associate RRD file for it.

The Unix templates:

Except for the Ping Latency template, all other default Unix templates are for localhost only and will not provide any information for remote systems.

Adding interface graphs to a device

Adding interface graphs is a little different than adding a generic one, such as the ping graph. Normal network devices do have several network interfaces, all of which can be polled for performance data. Cacti provides a nice interface for selecting the different network interfaces using the web interface. In this section, you are going to look into this kind of graph selection.

Time for action - adding interface graphs to a device

The following steps will show you how to select and add graphs for different interface ports:

1. Go back to the device overview page by clicking on the **Devices** link under the **Management** menu.
2. Click on the device you have just created or create any other SNMP capable device that has network interfaces.
3. Configure the device to use SNMP and click the **Save** or **Create** button:

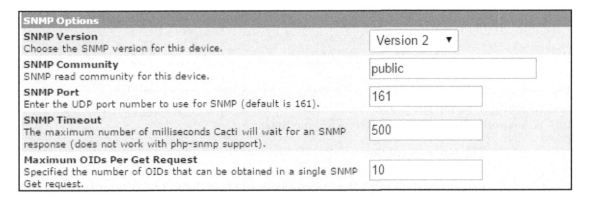

4. Make sure that, at the top of the page, something identical to the following image shows up. This will show that the device is SNMP capable:

skr-rt-001 (192.168.178.161)

SNMP Information

System: Cisco IOS Software, 1841 Software (C1841-ADVSECURITYK9-M), Version

www.cisco.com/techsupportCopyright (c) 1986-2007 by Cisco Systems,

Inc.Compiled Wed 19-Dec-07 23:14 by prod_rel_team

Uptime: 898734042 (104days, 0hours, 29minutes)

Hostname: cisco-router-1800-65

Location: cisco12 - Cisco 1800 Router

Contact:

Ping Results

ICMP Ping Success (0.125 ms)

5. In the **Associated Data Queries** section, select the **SNMP - Interface Statistics** from the drop-down list and click the **Add** button. If it is already showing up like in the screenshot, then skip this step:

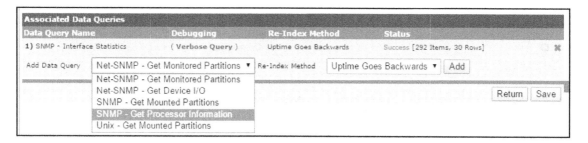

6. Click on the **Save** button at the bottom of the page.
7. Go to the top of the page and click on the link **Create Graphs for this Host**.
8. On the new page, select the interfaces you want to monitor and select a graph type from the drop-down list.

9. Click the **Create** button:

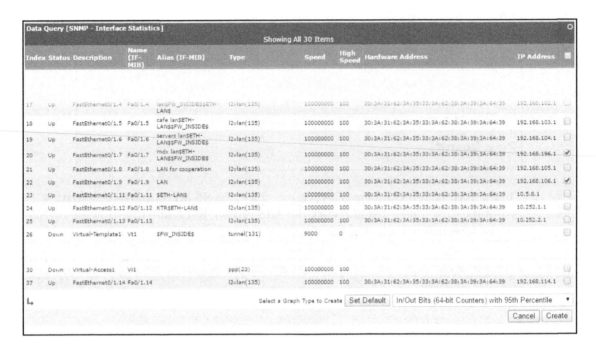

You have now successfully added the SNMP - Interface data query to the device and selected some interfaces from the interfaces list.

The SNMP - Interface data query is a special package, containing the graph definitions and a kind of blueprint for Cacti to poll information for the interfaces of a device.

Adding devices to the Cacti tree

The Cacti tree lists sub-trees, hosts, and graphs in a tree-like interface. It is the main user interface for the **Graphs** tab. There can be more than one tree, which allows for a granular definition of the tree structure. Before creating the Cacti tree, think about a good structure for it. Changing the tree later can involve quite a bit of manual work.

With the new 1.0 version of Cacti, the Cacti tree has undergone a major change from the 0.8 version. Previously, the tree management page was built using a static HTML page, which caused a large amount of work when managing large Cacti deployments. Version 1.0 introduced a dynamic JavaScript-based interface with drag-and-drop support, so the tree creation process and, especially, rearranging devices is now a lot easier.

Creating a tree

Cacti already has a default tree defined, which holds the localhost. You are going to leave this default tree empty and create your very own tree.

Time for action - creating a Cacti tree

Let's see how to create a new tree to Cacti so you can group your devices by Customer:

1. Click on **Trees** under the **Management** menu.
2. You will see the default tree. Click on the **Add** link to the top-right of that table.
3. Enter a name, for example Customer A, and make sure to enable the **Publish** checkbox.
4. Click on the **Create** button:

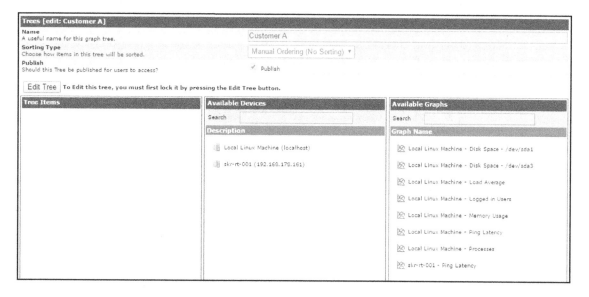

You created a new Cacti tree called Customer A, which you can now use to add all Customer A-specific entries. Using separate trees for customers or business units will enable you to better allow or deny access to these for specific users. You are going to see the interaction between a tree and the user later in the book.

Sub-tree items

A sub-tree item enables the creation of sub-entries to the Cacti tree. These can be entries such as a country, site, or business unit. Creating sub-tree items allows end-users to easily find their devices on the Cacti tree.

Time for action - adding a sub-tree

Creating a sub-tree allows you to group devices. Let's look at the steps involved for creating such a sub-tree:

1. First you will need to enable tree editing. Click **Edit Tree** on the left.
2. Click **Add Root Branch** to add a new sub-tree or root branch.
3. Enter Country A as the title.
4. Click **Add Root Branch** again to add another root branch.
5. Enter Site A as the title.
6. Move (drag-and-drop) the new item to the Country A branch you created.
7. Click the **Save** button:

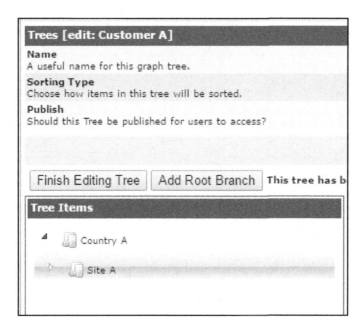

You can right-click on an item in order to rename, delete, and do some other tasks on that selected branch or item.

You created your first site for `Customer A`. You can now use this tree to add all countries, sites, and buildings into a nice manageable tree structure. Your end-users will immediately recognize the structure and be able to quickly find the needed information.

Adding the device to the tree

Now that you have created a tree and its sub-tree items, you can move on and add a device to the tree.

Time for action - adding a device to the Cacti tree

The final task is adding devices to your newly created tree and sub-trees. The following steps will show you how to do this:

1. Drag-and-drop the device you have created earlier from the **Available Devices** box to the **Site A** branch. There should also be a localhost listed. This is the Cacti server.
2. You can repeat this with any device you like, or even add specific graphs to a specific branch.
3. Click on the **Save** button.

4. If you do not want to add any more items, click the **Finish Editing Tree** button:

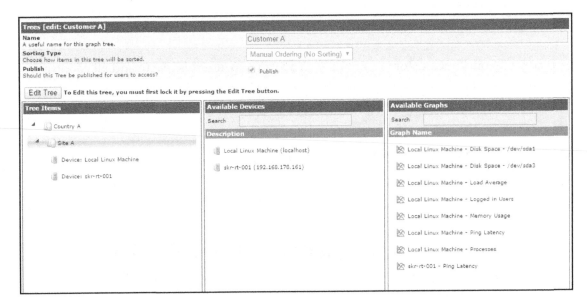

By adding your first device to your newly-created Cacti tree, you have completed all of the basic tree management tasks. As you may have noticed, adding devices or graphs to specific tree branches involves less steps than the Cacti 0.8 version.

Before we continue

You now have a basic knowledge of the RRDtool graph functionality, and also have your first device added to Cacti.

Pop quiz - a few questions about Chapter 2

1. If you want to add an additional threshold line, what do you need to add?
    - A LINE2 item
    - A THRESHOLD item
    - AN HRULE item

2. What information will be displayed when you create an SNMP-enabled device?
   - The hardware configuration of the device
   - A message of the day
   - The contact information and hostname of the device

3. Where do you add the Cisco - CPU Usage graph?
   - On the Cacti tree
   - On the RRDtool command prompt
   - On the device screen

Summary

In this chapter, you have learned quite a bit about the RRDtool graph generation features.

Specifically, we have covered how to create some basic graphs using the RRDtool as well as adding advanced features such as threshold lines and color changes based on the threshold. You have briefly covered the concept of adding a device to Cacti and assigning graphs and interface graphs to it. Finally, you have created a new Cacti tree containing sub-tree items and the previously added device.

You now have a running Cacti server, polling and graphing at least one device.

In the next chapter, you will learn how to create your own Cacti templates, where you can directly apply everything you have learned here.

3
Creating and Using Templates

Cacti provides a facility to create templates for data, graphs, and hosts. This chapter is going to explain how to create these templates and apply them to the devices.

This chapter is going to cover the following topics:

- An introduction to templates
- Defining a data template
- Defining a graph template
- Defining a host template
- Assigning a host template to a device
- Importing/exporting templates
- References to the template repository

So let's get started...

An introduction to templates

To ease the manual creation and administration of graphs and assigning those to specific types of hosts, Cacti provides the concept of templates. There are three different types of templates that are important for creating graphs: Graph, Device, and Data Source. With Cacti 1.0, two additional templates have been introduced, the Aggregate and Color templates. Both originate from the Aggregate plugin that has been integrated into Cacti 1.0. Due to Aggregate templates being a more complex topic, we're not going to deal with these special templates in this book.

If you still want to look into the Aggregate template, you can have a look at the aggregate plugin page, which contains a downloadable how-to with examples. Although the guide is for the Cacti 0.8 versions, the functionality is still the same, see `https://docs.cacti.net/ plugin:aggregate`.

Data Source templates

Data Source templates describe the data that Cacti is going to store in the RRD files. This basically comes down to the RRDtool `create` command. Having a template for this ensures that RRD files for a specific set of data sources are always created in a common way. It is within the data source templates where you decide to poll every five minutes or in a more frequent polling interval.

Please note that once a data template is being used to create an RRD file, changes to the data template will not be reflected on that RRD file.

Data Source templates are either based on data queries or data input methods. So, let's look what these are.

Data input methods

Data input methods describe different methods for Cacti to retrieve data to be inserted into the data sources. There are several methods available to retrieve data. The most common ones are through executing external scripts or using SNMP.

Data queries

We just heard about "Data Queries," but what are they? A data query is a special way of retrieving indexed data such as a list of network interfaces or running processes on a Linux server. It consists of an XML file defining the location of the data to be retrieved and the actual method for retrieving it. In addition to the XML file, a data query also needs to be defined in Cacti in order for Cacti to map the data to an associated graph template.

Graph templates

Graph templates define the look and feel of a graph. Graph templates provide the skeleton to the RRDtool graph function, defining the data sources to use and the graph items to display. Changes to a graph template get propagated to all graphs based on that template. Cacti 1.0 introduced new settings for the graph generation to better fit your graphing requirements, including new options for the Axis labels, more granular settings for the Grid and the ability to manipulate the Legend position and design.

Device templates

Device templates have been renamed from the old Host template of Cacti 0.8 to better visualize that Cacti is able to monitor not only hosts, but a wide range of devices. Host templates are like shopping baskets for graph templates and data queries. Let's assume a specific device type should contain several different graphs. Instead of adding each single graph template and data query to each single device, you can simply define these within a device template and assign that device template to the device.

With Cacti 1.0, you can now sync the devices with these device templates so changes to the template are being propagated to the device.

Defining a data source template

You are now going to define a data source template for the host `MIBhrSystemProcesses`. Although a data template already exists for this, it provides a good example of how to create SNMP-based data templates. For this to work, let's assume that your CentOS-based Cacti server is already configured with an SNMP daemon. You can check your box with the following command:

```
[root@localhost ~]# snmpwalk -On -c public -v 2c localhost HOST-
RESOURCES-MIB::hrSystemProcesses.0
.1.3.6.1.2.1.25.1.6.0 = Gauge32: 432
```

Time for action - defining a data source template

The `hrSystemProcesses` MIB provides information on the current number of running processes on a system supporting the host resource MIB. This MIB is a collection of system-specific data such as logged in users, disk space, installed software packages, and other valuable information that can be retrieved using SNMP:

1. Log on to your Cacti system and go to **Templates | Data Source**.
2. Click the **Add** link at the top-right corner of the list. This will open a new page where you can define your data source template.
3. Enter `Host-Resource-Mib: Running Processes` in the **Name** field.
4. Enter `|host_description|- Running Processes` as the **Name** for the **Data Source**. The **|host_description|** text is a special Cacti variable that will be replaced with the actual host description of the device where this data template will be added. You can find a list of these Cacti variables in the Appendix.
5. Select **Get SNMP Data** as the **Data Input Method**.
6. Select **System Default** as the **Data Source Profile**, we will look into the **High Collection Rate** at a later time:

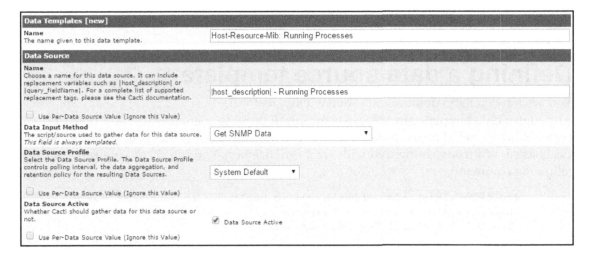

7. Enter `runProcesses` as the **Internal Data Source Name** of the **Data Source Item**.
8. The **Data Source Type** should be **Gauge**, as this is what the preceding `snmpwalk` example returns.
9. Enter `1000` as the **Maximum Value ("U" for No Minimum)**. This will tell Cacti to check the data against this value.

10. Keep everything else to the default values and click **Create**:

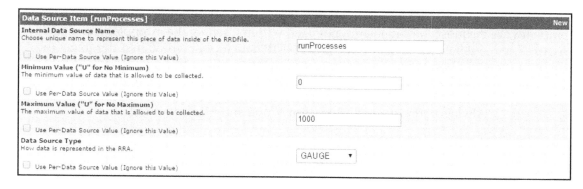

11. You're not done yet. Clicking the **Create** button should have added some additional fields to the end of the page. Here you can add the SNMP-specific **Custom Data**.

12. As you are going to retrieve the active processes, enter `.1.3.6.1.2.1.25.1.6.0` as the **OID**. You can leave the SNMP settings as their default values:

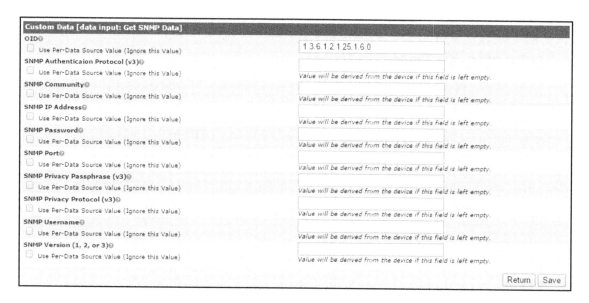

13. Click the **Save** button and you're done.

What just happened?

You just created your first SNMP-based data source template. SNMP-based data source templates are the most common templates used within Cacti. In the example, you used the `hrSystemProcessesMIB` to template a **Get SNMP data** input method in order to get the actual running processes on a system. You also set a **Maximum Value** so Cacti is able to check the data against this value. Any data above this value will be ignored by Cacti.

Always define a good **Maximum Value** and **Minimum Value**:

If the value is defined at **0**, the SNMP poller will always fail with an error message of **WARNING: Result from SNMP not valid. Partial Result**: U so make sure to set a good max or min value. If you do not know the maximum value, then you can set this to U so Cacti will not check the value against a maximum or minimum value.

This basic example can be adapted to create a data template for any kind of SNMP. A good webpage to find SNMP OIDs/MIBs to poll is www.mibdepot.com. This site provides free information on almost any SNMP data that can be queried.

Have a go hero - create your own TCP connections template

Let's assume that you have a server with performance issues. Maybe users are unable to connect to it at a specific time of the day. Wouldn't it be good to have some data on the server that will provide you with some valuable information for further troubleshooting or even lets you identify a problem before the users are aware of it? In this special case, we want to know the number of currently-established TCP connections on a system to identify a possible build up of connections to a point where no more connections can be created. What does the data template for this look like? A small hint: Look for the **TCP-MIB**.

Here is the step-by-step solution to creating a TCP connections template:

1. Take the data source template example and duplicate it.
2. Go to **Templates | Data Source** and select it.
3. From the drop-down box at the bottom, select **Duplicate** and then **Go**.
4. In the following page, enter `TCP-MIB: Established TCP Connections` as the title then click **Continue**.
5. Edit the template again and change the name fields to fit the new data.

6. Enter `tcpCurrEstab` as the **Internal Data Source Name** and use
   `.1.3.6.1.2.1.6.9.0` as the **OID**.

7. Change the **Maximum Value** to U, click **Save**, and you're done.

Defining a graph template

Remember the *Have a go hero* challenge from `Chapter 2`, *Using Graphs to Monitor Networks and Devices*? The graph did show a yellow area reaching a defined threshold and a red one once the threshold was breached. Now you're going to define the same type of graph template for a Running Processes graph template.

CDEF definition

As a prerequisite, you're first going to create your two CDEFs, one for the green area and one for the yellow area. The threshold is set at 435 for the yellow and 470 for the red threshold, but you can change this to fit your needs. Let's have a look at the two CDEFs you're going to create shortly:

```
CDEF:isGreen=intspeed,0,434,LIMIT
CDEF:isYellow=intspeed,435,470,LIMIT
```

Cacti does not use named variables such as `intspeed`, but defines them according to the alphabet from *a* to *z*, so your definition from a Cacti view actually looks like:

```
CDEF:cdefa=a,0,434,LIMIT
CDEF:cdefb=a,435,470,LIMIT
```

`isGreen` and `isYellow` also have been changed. Don't worry, Cacti takes care of this automatically. Just remember that your green area will go from 0 to 434, the yellow area will show up once the number of processes is between 435 and 470, and it will show red above 470.

Time for action - defining a CDEF in Cacti

Let's look at how you can create these CDEF definitions within Cacti:

1. Go to **Presets** and click the **CDEFs** menu item.

2. On the usual screen, click the **Add** link to the top right.

3. Now you can give the new CDEF a useful name. Enter isGreen_0-434 and click **Create**.

4. Another table will show up. Click the **Add** link there.

5. For **CDEF Item Type**, select **Custom String** from the drop-down box.

6. Enter a, 0, 434, LIMIT into the **CDEF Item Value** field and click **Create**. The first CDEF is created and you will see your CDEF definition together with **Save Successful.** at the top:

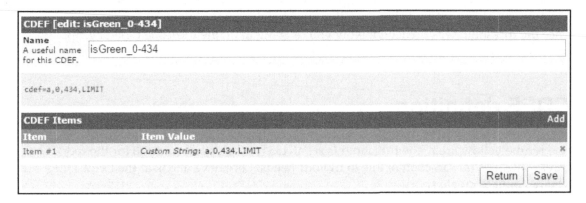

7. Repeat the steps and create a new CDEF called isYellow_435-470 and the **Item Value** of a, 435, 470, LIMIT.

8. Now, as you have defined your two CDEF items, you can proceed with the graph template creation.

You have now created the two CDEF items which you are going to use to change the appearance of your running processes graph, to go yellow or red when reaching a threshold, and stay green when it is way below the threshold.

Defining the graph template

Now that you have created your CDEFs, you can create your special graph template. The graph will have the green, yellow, and red areas defined, as well as the HRULE item showing the threshold. The threshold is set at 470.

Time for action - defining the graph template

All graphs within Cacti are based on graph templates. Let's walk through the process of creating one for the **Running Processes** graph.

1. Go to **Templates** | **Graph** and click the **Add** link in the upper-right corner of the page.
2. Enter Host - Running Processes as the name of the graph.
3. Enter |host_description| - Running Processes as the **Title (--title)** of the graph template.
4. Enter processes as the **Vertical Label (--vertical-label)**.
5. Leave everything else as the default and click the **Create** button. This will create the base graph template to work with. As you can see in the following screenshot, some additional fields have been added:

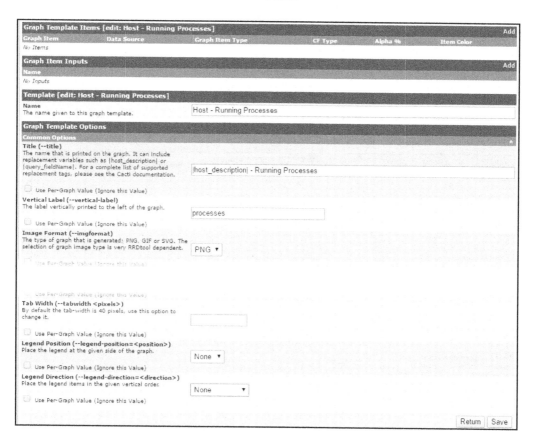

With the last step, you have created your first graph template. There will be two new sections showing up now, **Graph Template Items** and **Graph Item Inputs**.

Adding the threshold line

The threshold line will immediately show viewers what the threshold is set to and whether the graph is breaching it somewhere. Let's add this line to it.

Time for action - Adding new graph template items

The graph template items represent the actual data being displayed. As you have created the basic graph template itself, you can now start adding the actual items to it.

1. At the **Graph Template Items** section, click the **Add** link.
2. Set the **Graph Item Type** to **HRULE** and enter 470 as the **Value**.
3. Select **None** as the **Data Source.**
4. Select a light-gray color (for example, **Platinum (E5E4E2)**).
5. Enter Threshold (470) as the **Text Format** and check the **Insert Hard Return** box.
6. Click **Create**:

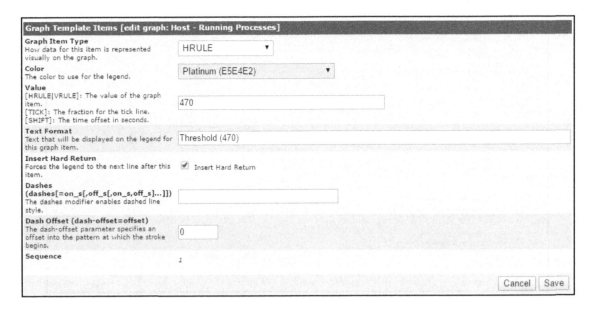

You just added your first item, a HRULE graph item, to your graph representing your threshold line. HRLUE items are based on a fixed value, therefore you did not choose any data source, but instead input your threshold value into the value field. Now all of your graphs based on this template will show a light-gray line at the 50 value.

Adding the green, yellow, and red areas

You are now going to add your green, yellow, and red areas by making use of your newly-created CDEF items.

Time for action - adding the color areas

This time you are not going to add just one item, but all three areas:

1. Add another item.
2. Select **AREA** as the **Graph Item Type** and put Over Threshold into the **Text Format** field.
3. Select **Host-Resource-Mib: Running Processes** as the data source.
4. Select a **Red** color.
5. Click **Create**.
6. For the yellow area, you need to add yet another item.
7. Select **AREA** as the **Graph Item Type**, choose a yellow color, and put Near Threshold into the **Text Format** field.
8. Select **isYellow_435-470** as the CDEF function to use.
9. Click **Create**.
10. The last one will be the green area, so click **Add** again.
11. Select **AREA** as the **Graph Item Type**, choose a green color, and put Under Threshold into the **Text Format** field.
12. Select **isGreen_0-434** as the CDEF function and check the **Insert Hard Return** box.

13. Click **Create**. Your graph definition should now look like the following screenshot. Verify that you have defined all of the items in the same way:

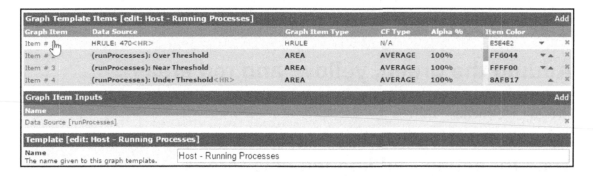

As you can see in the last screenshot, you have now added your three colored areas to the graph. Using the same principle as for the RRDtool graph command, you based the values of the single areas on a CDEF value. This will make sure that only the relevant area shows up on the graph, depending on the data value.

By selecting a data source, you can also see that this data source is automatically added to the **Graph Item Inputs** list.

Adding a legend to the graph

Your graph is now nearly complete, but is missing some basic statistics, called a "Legend." So, let's add this one now to finish your graph template.

Time for action - adding a legend

By default, the Cacti graphs only show the data items on the graph without any explanation or description. In order to distinguish between the different items easily, you will have to add a Legend to the graph, which also allows you to add some general statistics for the MAX, Average, and Current values:

1. The graph is still missing the Legend, so click the **Add** link of the **Graph Template Items** again.
2. Select **COMMENT** as the **Graph Item Type**.
3. Enter Running Processes into the **Text Format** field.
4. Click the **Create** button.
5. Let's add some more statistical information to your Legend. Click the **Add** link.
6. Select **LEGEND** as the **Graph Item Type**.
7. Click the **Create** button:

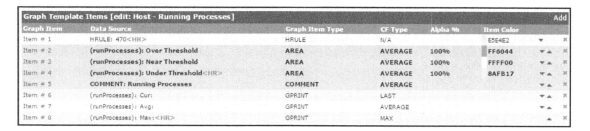

You have added a comment describing the statistical information you added. The Legend command adds three GPRINT statements to the graph. The first GPRINT statement prints the last polled value, another one the average value of the displayed graph and the last one prints the maximum value polled.

8. You can now assign this graph template to a device. After you added the graph template to a device, you need to wait for three polls to pass. The first poll actually creates the necessary RRD file. The other two polls are needed for the RRDtool as it will start graphing values only when it has at least two data values within the RRD file. Once that time has passed, go to **Graphs** within the **Management** section and look for the graph there:

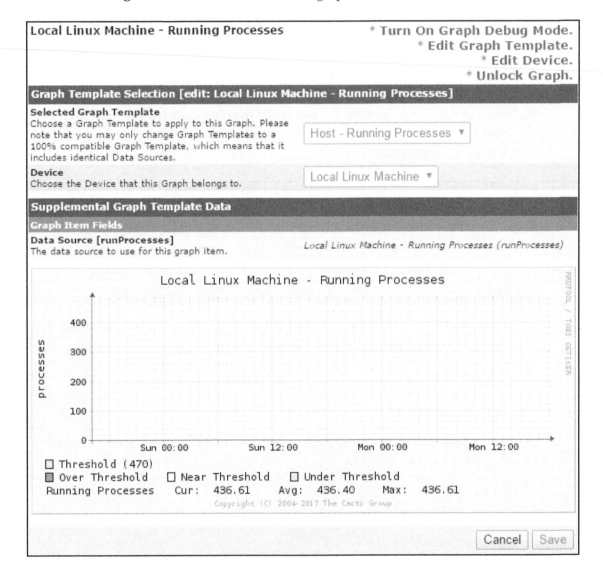

Turn on graph debugging:

After turning on the graph debugging option, the graph management page will display the RRDtool graph command used to create the graph. Any errors, such as a missing RRD file, will be displayed here. This debugging information is useful for troubleshooting the graph generation.

Back to the basics - rrdtool graph command

Let's look at the `rrdtool` graph command that Cacti uses to create this graph:

```
/bin/rrdtool graph -
--imgformat=PNG
--start='-180000'
--end='-300'
--pango-markup
--title='Local Linux Machine - Running Processes'
--vertical-label='processes'
--slope-mode
--base=1000
--height=150
--width=500
--alt-autoscale-max
--lower-limit='0'
--border 1 --slope-mode
--watermark 'Copyright (C) 2004-2017 The Cacti Group'
DEF:a='/var/www/html/cacti/rra/local_linux_machine_runprocesses_21.rrd'
:'runProcesses':AVERAGE
CDEF:cdefc='a,435,470,LIMIT'
CDEF:cdefd='a,0,434,LIMIT'
HRULE:470#E5E4E2FF:'Threshold (470) n'
AREA:a#FF6044FF:'Over Threshold '
AREA:cdefc#FFFF00FF:'Near Threshold '
AREA:cdefd#8AFB17FF:'Under Thresholdn'
COMMENT:'Running Processes '
GPRINT:a:LAST:'Cur:%8.21f %s'
GPRINT:a:AVERAGE:'Avg:%8.21f %s'
GPRINT:a:MAX:'Max:%8.21f %sn'
```

Doesn't this one look familiar? It's almost the same command that you hopefully came up with in the *Have a go hero* challenge of `Chapter 2`, *Using Graphs to Monitor Networks and Devices*. Here you can see the tight integration of the `rrdtool` with the web interface of Cacti.

Defining a device template

As you have already learned, a device template is a collection of graph templates and data queries. Let's create a device template for an SNMP-enabled CentOS server now.

Time for action - defining a host template

Cacti comes with a very small number of host templates for general use only. To reduce some manual work, you want to create your own host template. Let's look at how to create one for the CentOS system:

1. Go to **Templates** | **Device** and click the **Add** link.
2. Enter SNMP Enabled Cent OS Server as the **Name** for this host template.
3. Click **Create**.
4. Two additional sections will show up. At the **Associated Graph Templates** section, select your **Host - Running Processes** template and click **Add**.
5. At the **Associated Data Queries**, add **SNMP - Get Mounted Partitions**, **SNMP - Get Processor Information**, and the **SNMP - Interface Statistics** data query.
6. Click the **Save** button:

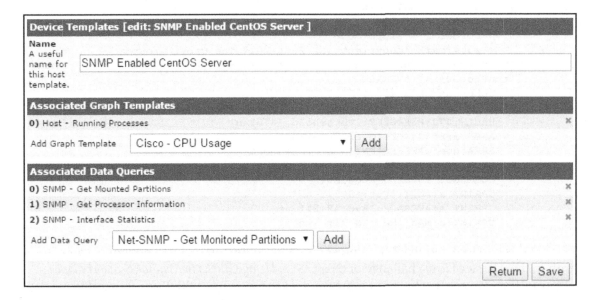

You created your first device template containing your newly-created graph template and three SNMP-based data queries. Once you assign this device template to a device, all four items will be automatically added to that device.

Create device templates for standard devices in your network:

Creating a device template will reduce the time for creating a device within Cacti, especially if there are many devices in a network that share the same graphs.

Assigning a host template to a device

You already assigned a device template to a device in `Chapter 2`, *Using Graphs to Monitor Networks and Devices*, so now let's briefly talk about what is happening when a device template gets assigned to a device.

As you know, device templates are a collection of graphs and data queries. In contrast to Cacti 0.8, the new Cacti 1.0 version stores the link between a device template and its associated devices. This allows you to sync any changes you have made to a device template to its associated devices, reducing the administrative effort significantly when dealing with a lot of devices.

Importing/exporting templates

As graph, host, and data templates become very complex and are usually crafted to fit a specific device type, Cacti offers the ability to export and share these templates with the community as well as import already existing templates.

This really eases the administrative tasks for creating these templates! So, let's see how you can import and export these templates.

Importing templates

As Cacti does come with a limited set of templates, importing templates will probably be the first action you will take when trying to graph some special data of a device.

Templates on Cacti.net:

A majority of Cacti templates can now be found at the documentation section of the Cacti website. You can find them on the following page: `http://docs.cacti.net/templates`

As your Cacti installation probably is running on an Apache web server, you want to get and graph some additional information on it. Let's look at how to import such a template.

Time for action - importing a template

Instead of creating you own graph templates and data sources, you can also import existing templates from the Cacti website and forum:

1. Start your web browser and go to `https://docs.cacti.net/ usertemplate:graph:apache`.
2. Download the `cacti_host_template_webserver_apache.zip` file and extract the `cacti_host_template_webserver_-_apache.xml` file from the archive to your desktop.
3. Log on to your cacti server.
4. Go to your cacti installation and navigate to the scripts directory. On CentOS, the command is:

   ```
   cd /var/www/html/cacti/scripts
   ```

5. Download the third file to that directory:

   ```
   wget
   'https://docs.cacti.net/_media/usertemplate:graph:ws_apachestats.zi
   p' -O ws_apachestats.zip
   ```

6. Unzip the file:

   ```
   unzip ws_apachestats.zip
   ```

7. Now log on to your Cacti installation.

8. Go to **Import/Export | Import Template**:

Import Templates

Import Template from Local File
If the XML file containing template data is located on your local machine, select it here.

Datei auswählen cacti_ho...ache.xml

Import Template from Text
If you have the XML file containing template data as text, you can paste it into this box to import it.

Preview Import Only
If checked, Cacti will not import the template, but rather compare the imported Template to the existing Template data. If you are acceptable of the change, you can them import.

☐ Preview Import Only

Remove Orphaned Graph Items
If checked, Cacti will delete any Graph Items from both the Graph Template and associated Graphs that are not included in the imported Graph Template.

☐ Remove Orphaned Graph Items

Data Source Profile
Select the Data Source Profile. The Data Source Profile controls polling interval, the data aggregation, and retention policy for the resulting Data Sources.

System Default ▼

Import

9. Select the XML file from your desktop and click the **Import** button. You will see some status information as well as the templates, data input methods, and other items that have been imported to your Cacti system:

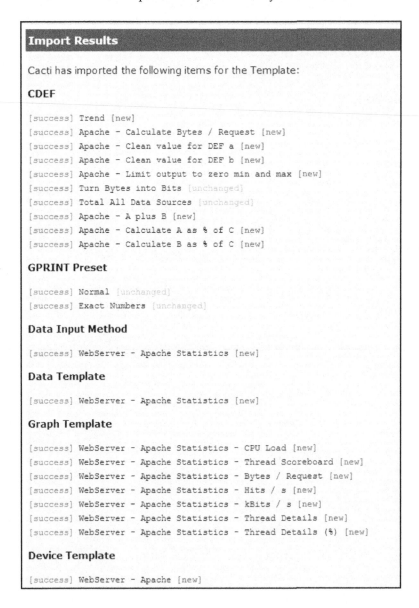

Import Results

Cacti has imported the following items for the Template:

CDEF

[success] Trend [new]
[success] Apache - Calculate Bytes / Request [new]
[success] Apache - Clean value for DEF a [new]
[success] Apache - Clean value for DEF b [new]
[success] Apache - Limit output to zero min and max [new]
[success] Turn Bytes into Bits [unchanged]
[success] Total All Data Sources [unchanged]
[success] Apache - A plus B [new]
[success] Apache - Calculate A as % of C [new]
[success] Apache - Calculate B as % of C [new]

GPRINT Preset

[success] Normal [unchanged]
[success] Exact Numbers [unchanged]

Data Input Method

[success] WebServer - Apache Statistics [new]

Data Template

[success] WebServer - Apache Statistics [new]

Graph Template

[success] WebServer - Apache Statistics - CPU Load [new]
[success] WebServer - Apache Statistics - Thread Scoreboard [new]
[success] WebServer - Apache Statistics - Bytes / Request [new]
[success] WebServer - Apache Statistics - Hits / s [new]
[success] WebServer - Apache Statistics - kBits / s [new]
[success] WebServer - Apache Statistics - Thread Details [new]
[success] WebServer - Apache Statistics - Thread Details (%) [new]

Device Template

[success] WebServer - Apache [new]

As in the preceding example, a template may not always consist of XML files, but may also have an associated script that needs to be added to the Cacti installation. The template you just imported did contain such a script. You have downloaded, renamed, and extracted it into the scripts directory. This directory contains all the scripts being used within data input methods.

You then imported the XML file for the **WebServer - Apache** device template. The XML file contained all definitions for the necessary graph templates and input methods needed for Cacti to graph the data.

The imported device template can now be used and assigned to the devices. As with all external files, make sure you read and follow the corresponding readme files or install instructions.

10. If you have done everything correctly, you should see the following graph after a few polling cycles:

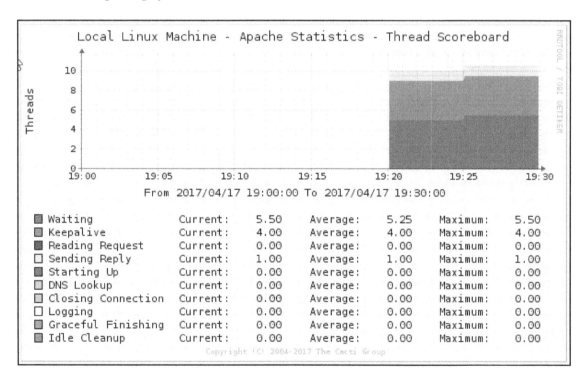

Exporting templates

Exporting a template allows users to share their hard work in creating these templates with the Cacti community. The export mechanism only exports the graph, device, or data template definitions, but not the scripts that are necessary for some of the data input methods. SNMP-based templates do not need scripts, so these are complete.

Time for action - exporting a template

As you may have noticed, there are many users that contributed to Cacti by providing their templates. By exporting them you can not only store them for your own re-use, but also make them public to the community as well. Let's look at the export process in more detail:

1. Go to **Import/Export** and click the **Export Templates** link.
2. Select **Device Template** as the template type that you want to export.
3. Select your device template, **SNMP Enabled CentOS Server**, as the **Device Template to Export.**
4. Leave the rest as their default values.
5. Click **Export**. You can now save the XML file to your desktop:

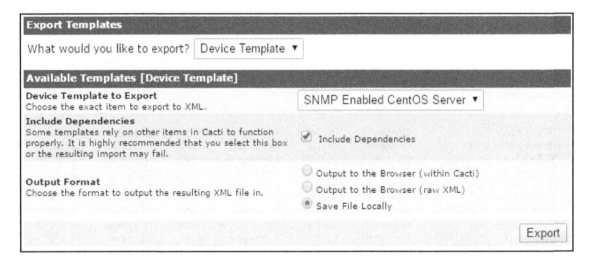

You have exported your first host template. The XML file contains all the necessary information for the device template. This includes:

- The device template itself
- All graph templates
- All data source templates
- All CDEFs needed (`isYellow_435-470` and `isGreen_0-434`)
- Everything else needed for the device template to work, but excluding scripts or other additional files you've created.

When re-importing this XML file, Cacti will only create items that do not already exist.

The template repository

As you have seen, you can export your templates and make them available to other users. A lot of Cacti administrators have used this feature to provide quite a few templates to the community. Until some time ago, finding these templates was a wearisome task as they were hidden in the *Scripts and Templates* section of the Cacti forum, at `https://forums.cacti.net`.

For a while now, the Cacti developers have created a page containing most of these templates. This template repository provides an overview of the existing templates, as well as some detailed information on how to add these to Cacti. Go and have a look, at `http://docs.cacti.net/templates`.

Before we continue

This chapter completes the basic administration of Cacti. You have installed Cacti, created a first host, and also designed your own enhanced graph templates. The following chapters will dive into more advanced topics, such as Windows systems monitoring with WMI, enhancing Cacti with plugins, or enterprise reporting capabilities.

Pop quiz - a few questions about Chapter 3

1. Where can you change the width and height of graphs?

    a) At the general Cacti settings screen
    b) At the data source template
    c) At the Graph template

2. If an SNMP data template you defined does not produce any data, what may be wrong?

    a) The Maximum value field is set to 0
    b) The Maximum value field is not set
    c) The Minimum value field is not set

3. If you want to change the threshold of the processes graph, which items do you need to change?

    a) You need to define a new CDEFS
    b) You need to add a new HRULE
    c) All of the above

Summary

You went through some more advanced topics of Cacti, creating graphs, as well as device and data templates. Specifically, you have covered the creation of basic templates for data sources, graphs, and devices. With data source templates, you can monitor simple SNMP and script-based data, allowing you to immediately start monitoring specific items on your devices. By creating a graph template, you are now able to visualize the data and also create special graphical items to display thresholds and thresholds breached within your graphs. Finally, the creation of a device template allows you to group relevant graphs, for simple selection, for a specific device group such as CentOS servers.

During this chapter, you have also learned how a data query works and how to re-build the interface data query. This will allow you to build more complex queries for a set of items from a device.

You have now learnt the basic Cacti administration tasks for devices, graphs, and templates, so let's move on to the next chapter which deals with Cacti user management and permissions!

4
User Management

We now have a working Cacti installation, which also has some nice graphs to show. So, let us now add some users to our Cacti installation.

In this chapter, we are going to:

- Add new users and groups
- Set up Realms and Graph Permissions for a user
- Integrate LDAP/Active Directory authentication
- Manage users with the Cacti CLI

So, let's get started...

An introduction to Cacti user management

Cacti integrates a granular user management, which lets administrators define access and permissions to trees, hosts, or single graphs, as well as some additional administrational functionality. This section will provide you with some detailed information about user management.

Users

Users within Cacti can be divided into three different groups:

- Guest/anonymous users
- Normal users
- Administrators

The difference between those users is the way they authenticate against the system and what access rights they have. No special groups exist for these different types of users.

Guest accounts would be used for a public Cacti server, offering the viewing of graphs to any interested person. This can be an internal server or one that monitors your own home network.

Normal user accounts need to authenticate against the server and can then access different parts of the system. Normal users can be restricted to viewing just a single Cacti tree, therefore making them the first choice for sharing a Cacti installation between different customers (for example, within a hosting environment).

Administrator accounts can administer Cacti by using the Cacti console. They cannot be restricted to, for example, administer just a small group of users, but different tasks within Cacti can be allowed or denied to an administrator. These include permissions to access global settings as well as updating hosts or graph templates.

Groups

With Cacti 1.0, the concept of groups has been introduced, so the administration of users for different customers is now a lot easier to handle.

Permissions

As mentioned earlier, permissions in Cacti can be set as granular as giving access to one specific graph only. Permissions within Cacti are divided into Realm Permissions and Graph Permissions. Realm permissions define the access rights of the Console, whereas Graph Permissions define access to the tree and graphs.

Creating a user

Let's get started with creating our first Cacti users!

Time for action - creating the first Cacti user

Creating users along with the correct permissions is essential to provide access to the correct information for your customers. The following steps will allow you to create a new user within Cacti:

1. Log on to your Cacti system as the admin user.
2. Go to **Configuration** | **Users**. You will be presented with a list of already existing users. For a newly installed Cacti system, there will only be **admin** and **guest** listed, as shown in the following screenshot:

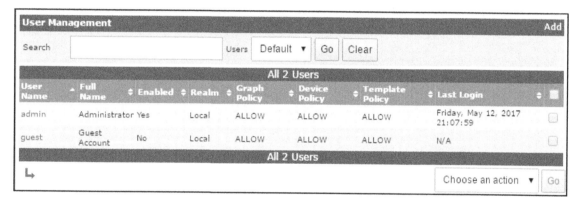

3. Click on the **Add** link. You will be redirected to the **User Management [new]** screen.

4. Fill in the fields **User Name**, **Full Name**, **Email Address**, and **Password**, check the **Enabled** box, and hit the **Create** button.

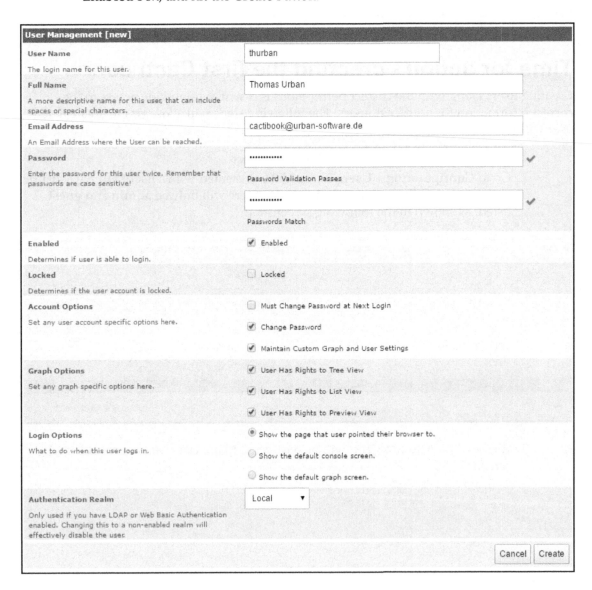

You just created your first Cacti user. If you try to log on to your Cacti system with this new user, you will see that this is working, but you will also see that there will be nothing displayed.

Why is that so? Although you added the View Graphs permission for your user, the user does not have any permission to actually view any trees or graphs defined. You are going to do this in the next step, but first let's look at the different options available.

General User Settings

There are a few general settings which can be checked for each user. These settings include the Authentication Realm or access to the different Graph Options.

Graph Options

Graph Options are not related to any options for the actual graphs, but describe the type of view on the graphs that the user has access to. There are three different options available:

- User Has Rights to Tree View
- User Has Rights to List View
- User Has Rights to Preview View

These views relate to the small tabs on the upper right of the Cacti screen when you are using the **graphs** tab:

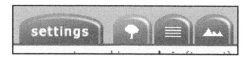

Login Options

Login Options allow you to predefine the entry page of the user. Most of the time, you can leave this setting to the default option show the page that the user pointed their browser to, so external links sent by email will send them right to the graph or page for that link.

Authentication Realm

The Authentication Realm defines the type of access authentication used when a user logs in to Cacti. There are three different options available:

- Local
- LDAP
- Web-Basic

The Local Realm uses the built-in authentication from Cacti. LDAP Authentication can authenticate users against any LDAP server, including Active Directory servers. Web-Basic authentication is handled by the web server itself (for example, using `.htaccess` files).

Permissions tabs

By default, new Cacti users will not have any permission to view graphs or administer the system. The access rights for these functions are set in the different tabs available once you have created the user. Let's look at these different tabs and what you can do with them.

Permissions

There are several generic permissions that can be set for a user. They are grouped by functionality:

- **Normal User**
- **Template Editor**
- **General Administration**
- **System Administration**
- **External Link Permissions**
- **Plugin Permissions**

Normal User permissions

Normal User permissions include the ability to view graphs and logs and to create reports and view external links:

Template Editor

The **Template Editor** enables everything required for creating, importing, and exporting Data or Graph templates. This section is required if you want to allow a user to define new templates for your devices or change existing templates:

General Administration

General Administration enables a user to create devices or sites, define new trees, or change the automation settings. These permissions are required if you want to allow a user to monitor the different devices in your network.

System Administration

As the name already describes, these permissions enable a user to create new users, create or delete reports, and change the Cacti settings or manage plugins.

External Link Permissions

In this section, you enable the display of the different external links that you may have created. This section will be empty on a freshly installed Cacti system.

Plugin Permissions

The last section will contain any special permissions related to external plugins. As with the External Link Permissions, this section will be empty.

Group Membership

Group Membership is a new feature of Cacti 1.x. It allows you to assign the user to a User Group. As you have not yet created any groups, this list will be empty for now:

Graph Permissions

In this section, you will be able to assign graphs to the user.

Device Permissions

The **Device Permissions** page allows you to allow a user to view all graphs from a specific device, or prevent them from doing so. The default policy will define what access the user has. This can either be **Allow** to view all devices, or **Deny** to stop the user from being able to view any devices. By default, no devices will be listed in the table unless you uncheck the **Show Exceptions** checkbox. The wording is a bit misleading as it actually hides the default permissions and only shows the permissions explicitly set by you:

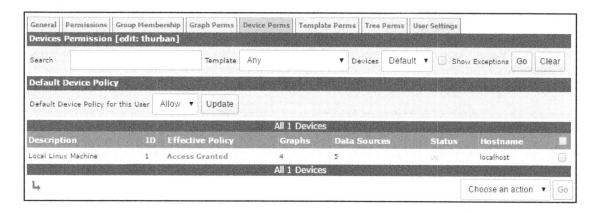

Template Permissions

Template Permissions enable you to allow a user to view all graphs based on a specific template, or prevent them from doing so. This will help you to give specific users responsible for a specific device group access to all graphs for that device group. If, for example, you have a template that monitors the performance of a specific application and the application group wants to monitor these, you can assign these templates to all users of the application group:

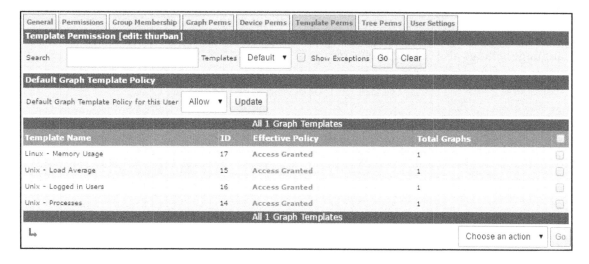

Tree Permissions

In the **Tree Permissions** tab, you can allow or deny access to a complete tree to a user. This is especially useful if you are monitoring different customers with a single Cacti instance and want to provide each customer access to their devices:

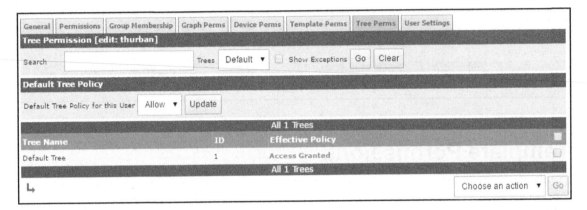

User Settings

User Settings are user-specific preferences of the graph presentation. Preferences can be set for nearly every aspect of the graph frontend. Settings such as the thumbnail dimensions or number of graphs displayed on the tree view panel can be set, but the **Theme** and **User Language** settings also belong to this part:

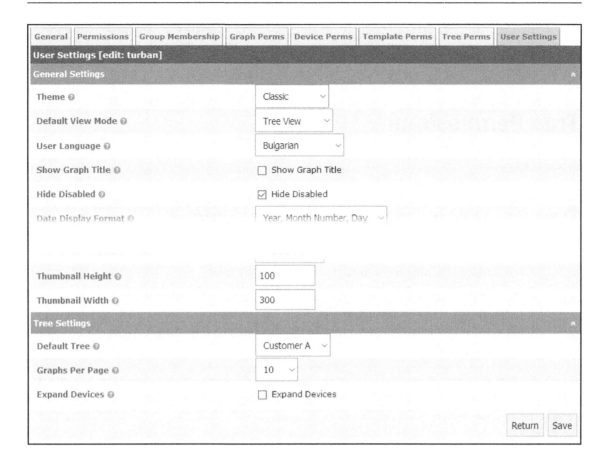

Time for action - setting general permissions

It's time for you to add some permission to your newly created user. So, let's move on and give him access to managing devices, collection methods, graphs, and templates.

1. Go to **Configuration** | **User** and select your previously created user.
2. Click on the permissions tab and select all fields from the **Normal User**, **Template Editor**, and **General Administration** sections, then click the **Save** button.

You just added all permissions to your user to manage devices and all that is required to create graphs. By default on a Cacti 1.x system, a newly created user will be able to view all graphs and devices.

Tree Permissions

Let's change the Tree Permissions of the user, so you can actually limit the access of the user to a specific tree.

Time for action - setting Tree Permissions

You will now remove permission to view the default tree from your user:

1. Go to **Configuration** | **Users** and click on your user.
2. Click on the **Tree Perms** tab and uncheck the **Show Exceptions** checkbox.
3. Change the **Default Policy** for the Tree Permissions to **Deny.**
4. Select the **Default Tree** item and select **Revoke Access** from the drop-down box.
5. Click on the **Go** button:

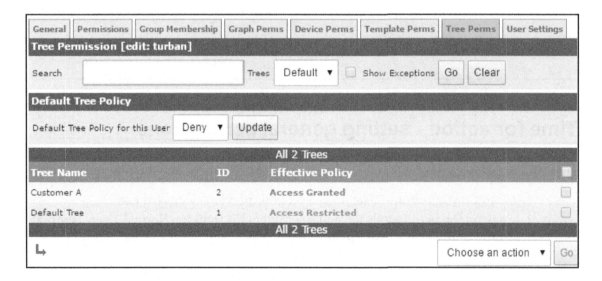

You just allowed your user to view all the graphs that have been added to the **Customer A** tree. The default policy defines the default access granted for a user. By revoking access to the **Default Tree**, you effectively denied access to that tree for the users. By setting the default policy to **Deny**, any newly created tree will be automatically denied to that user. If you change the default policy to **Allow**, your user will have access to all trees except the **Customer A** tree, which will be reflected by the **Effective Policy** column.

Denying or allowing access to a tree does not automatically deny or allow access to the graphs configured under the tree. Although you denied access to the **Default Tree** tree, your user will still be able to access the graphs from **Default Tree**, as the default policy for the graphs is set to **Allow**. To prevent this behavior, you will need to change the default policy for the **Graph Perms**, **Device Perms,** and **Template Perms** to **Deny** and grant access to all the devices belonging to **Customer A** in the **Device Perms** list, so that your user is only able to access the graphs for these devices.

User Groups

As described earlier, User Groups have now been integrated into Cacti 1.x, which greatly simplifies the management of users by being able to set the graph, device, and Tree Permissions once within the group, and any changes made are then automatically propagated to the group members.

Time for action - creating a User Group for Customer A

Let's create a User Group for **Customer A** containing the same permissions as the recently created user:

1. Go to **Configuration** | **User Groups** and you will see an empty list:

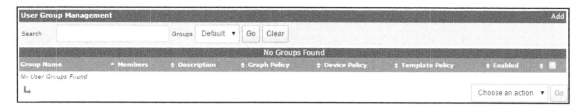

2. Click on the **Add** link. You will be redirected to the **User Group Management [new]** screen.

    Enter a **Group Name** and **Group Description**; check the **Enabled** box and select **Restrict Access** for the **Tree Rights**, **Graph List Rights,** and **Graph Preview Rights**; then hit the **Create** button:

User Group Management [edit: Customer A Group]	
Group Name @	Customer A Group
Group Description @	A user group for the Customer A tree
Enabled @	☑ Enabled
General Group Options @	☐ Allow Users of this Group to keep custom User Settings
Tree Rights @	○ Defer to the Users Setting ○ Grant Access ◉ Restrict Access
Graph List Rights @	○ Defer to the Users Setting ○ Grant Access ◉ Restrict Access
Graph Preview Rights @	○ Defer to the Users Setting ○ Grant Access ◉ Restrict Access
Login Options @	○ Defer to the Users Setting ◉ Show the Page that the User pointed their browser to ○ Show the Console ○ Show the default Graph Screen
	Return Save

3. Set the **Default Policy** for the **Graph Perms, Template Perms, Tree Perms,** and **Device Perms** to **Deny** and **Grant Access** to the same devices and trees as you did with the previously created user.
4. Now, click the **Save** button.

You just added a new group and set the group permissions to only allow members of this group to view the devices and graphs of the **Customer A** tree. To add a user to this group, you can either use the **Members** tab of the group or go to the user and add the group using the **Group Membership** tab there.

The template user

A template user can be any user and is not specifically marked as a template user. With the introduction of User Groups, the template user is now only required for the Web-Basic and LDAP Authentication to set up the basic settings for each user.

In a multi-customer environment, the template user should follow an easy to understand naming standard and should always be disabled.

Use a naming standard for template users:
An example for such a naming standard would be _customername_user.

Time for action - installing the missing packages

Let us create a template user for our **Customer A**:

1. Go to **Configuration | Users** and add a new user.
2. Add CustomerA_user as the **User Name.**
3. Add Template User for Customer A as the **Full Name.**

4. Make sure the **Enabled** checkbox is not checked as seen in the following screenshot:

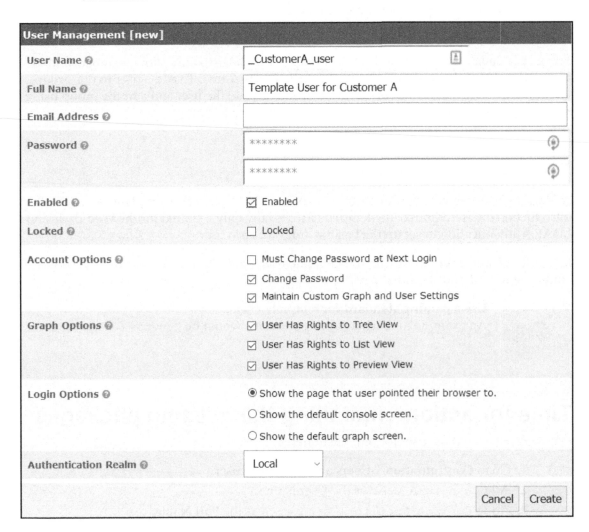

5. Click on the **Create** button.

6. Switch to the **Group Membership** tab and assign the user to the **Customer A** group:

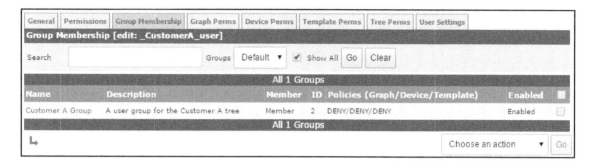

You just created your first template user. You can now use this template user to create new users or use it as a template for new LDAP and Web-Basic authenticated users.

Copying permissions - the Batch Copy mode

In the user management section, a function called Batch Copy exists. This function allows the copying of permissions from one user (such as your template user) to one or more other users. It does not change any user-specific information, such as usernames or passwords, but only transfers the permissions.

Time for action - Batch Copy

As a preparation, you will need to create a new user. Just fill in the User Name and Password fields and hit save. You do not need to worry about the permissions:

1. Go to **Configuration | Users.**

2. Select the user you just created.

3. Choose **Batch Copy** from the drop-down box and hit **Go.**

4. A confirmation box will show up where you can select the template user from a drop-down box, as shown in the following screenshot:

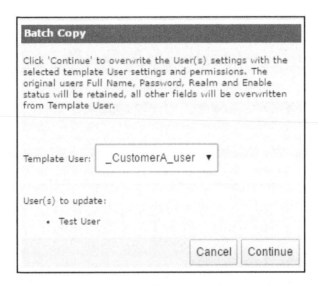

5. Select **_CustomerA_user** as the template user and hit the **Continue** button.

You just copied all permissions, as well as some default User Settings, to your newly created user. You can select more than one user for the Batch Copy function. By using this functionality, you can quickly change users in case you are not working with a User Group.

Integrate LDAP/Active Directory authentication

Cacti not only has its own built-in user authentication mechanism, but can also be configured to use one or more LDAP or even Active Directory servers for authentication. As the authorization (access rights and permissions) are not stored on the external server, the user has still to be created within Cacti. So, how does Cacti know if a user is going to authenticate against the external server or is using the built-in method? Cacti uses the concept of an Authentication Realm for this. An Authentication Realm is basically the authentication method an end user uses to log on to Cacti. A user can only belong to one realm. When using LDAP Authentication, local users can still log on by choosing the Local Realm from the login dialog:

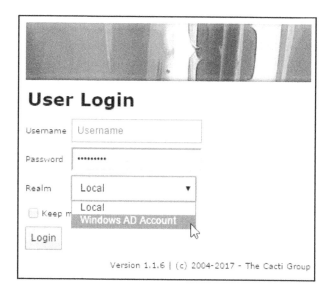

The Web-Basic authentication does not allow this, as it always expects to get a user ID from the browser and displays an error message if it does not get a user ID.

External User management

You are now going to set up LDAP/Active Directory authentication. Most companies either have an LDAP system running or use the Active Directory equivalent. This section will deal with setting up Active Directory authentication.

Time for action - setting up Active Directory authentication

Let us enable LDAP/Active Directory integration.

1. Log on to your Cacti web interface as an admin user.
2. Glick on the **Settings** link under the **Configuration** section.
3. On the new page that shows up, click on the **Authentication** tab to bring up the settings for authentication.
4. Select **LDAP Authentication** from the **Authentication Method** drop-down box.
5. Select **No User** as the **Guest User**.
6. Select **_CustomerA_user** as the **User Template**.

7. Enter the IP address of your domain controller into the **Server** field.

8. As the **Distinguished Name (DN)**, enter `<username>@MYDOMAIN.local` and replace `MYDOMAIN.local` with your domain name.

9. Hit the **Save** button:

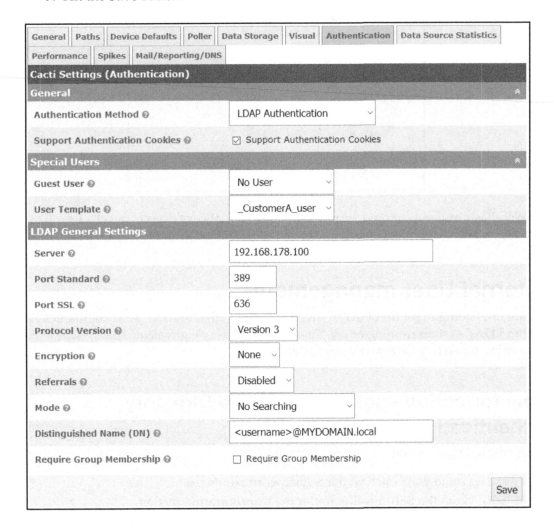

You just enabled your Cacti server to authenticate users against an LDAP/Active Directory server. Users can now log on to your Cacti system without you needing to have them created first. Although this is good for internal only servers, for Cacti servers hosting graphs for multiple customers, the permissions for these users still need to be changed.

Cacti 1.x also allows you to have multiple LDAP/AD servers enabled. This is especially useful if you want to authenticate different customer to different LDAP/AD groups. Each of these servers also has their own template users, which allows you to set up a multi-customer environment far more easily.

Managing users with the Cacti CLI

Users can not only be managed using the web interface, but can also be created using Cacti CLI scripts. In Cacti version 1.x, the only script that exists is one which copies an existing user in order to create a new one out of it. An equivalent to the Batch Copy functionality is not available for the command line interface.

Let's assume that you need to add a large amount of users to your Cacti system. You have two options for doing so:

- Use the web-based user management page to create each user
- Use the copy functionality to copy an existing user as a new user

Both options involve quite a few manual steps.

Importing a list of users

To reduce the manual work needed to create a large group of users within Cacti, you are going to create a small PHP-based script that takes a list of users as input and creates the users based on a template user within Cacti.

First, create a file called `users_list.txt` with the following content:

```
user1;User Name1
user2;User Name2
user3;User Name3
user4;User Name4
```

This will be the basis for the import. The first part is the actual user name of the new user, and the last part in the file is going to be the full name for that user.

Time for action - importing users from the CLI

Now that you have created the import file, let's import it:

1. Log on to the command line of your Cacti server.
2. Go to the `cli` sub-directory under the Cacti directory:

   cd /var/www/html/cacti/cli

3. Place the `import_user.php` script in this directory.
4. Put the `users_list.txt` file in the `/tmp` directory.
5. Run the following command to add the users to the Local Realm with `_CustomerA_user` as the template user:

   php import_user.php /tmp/users_list.txt _CustomerA_user 0

```
[root@localhost cli]# php import_user.php /tmp/users_list.txt _CustomerA_user 0

It is highly recommended that you use the web interface to copy users as this sc
ript will only copy Local Cacti users.

Cacti User Copy Utility
Template User: _CustomerA_user
Realm: Local

Copying/Creating User...
New User: user1
New User: user2
New User: user3
New User: user4
User copied...
[root@localhost cli]#
```

You just imported all users from the import file to your Cacti installation. The users now have the same permissions as the template user. Go to the user management of Cacti and you will see the users listed there:

user1	User Name1	No	Local	ALLOW
user2	User Name2	No	Local	ALLOW
user3	User Name3	No	Local	ALLOW
user4	User Name4	No	Local	ALLOW
_CustomerA_user	Template User for Customer A	No	Local	ALLOW

Let us have a closer look at the CLI script `import_user.php`. Besides reading the command line options and several print statements, it consists of three major parts. The first part deals with input validation for the `realm id`, the second part reads in the import file, and the last part actually copies the user and changes the full name and `realm id` of the user.

Input validation

As a quick run of the script without any parameters reveals, the CLI takes three input parameters:

```
Syntax:
 php import_user.php <import file> <template user> <realm id>
```

The import file is the text file with the user IDs you created earlier. The template user will be your _CustomerA_user. The `realm id` references the ID of the Authentication Realm and can be a number between 0 and 2:

- Realm id 0 - Local Authentication
- Realm id 1 - LDAP Authentication
- Realm id 2 - Web Authentication

The following code checks the entered `realm id` for its valid range and sets it to Local Authentication (0) if it has not been set correctly:

```
// Realm Id can be: 0 - Local, 1 - LDAP, 2 - Web Auth
if ( ( $realm_id < 0 ) || ( $realm_id > 2  ) ) {
    // The realm id will be local unless a valid id was given
    $realm_id = 0;
}
```

Checking the existence of the template user

The next code section checks the Cacti database to see whether the template user exists. If it does not exist, the program immediately stops with an error message:

```
/* Check that user exists */
$user_auth = db_fetch_row("SELECT * FROM user_auth WHERE username = '" .
$template_user . "' AND realm = 0");
if (! isset($user_auth)) {
        die("Error: Template user does not exist!\n\n");
}
```

Reading in the import file

Now that the script has checked the template user and the `realm id`, it starts reading in the actual import file. The `file` command reads the file and provides the content of the file as an array of the lines. The script then cycles through each line, stripping off the newline character with the `rtrim` command. The remaining lines will be split at the semi-colon, resulting in an array holding the `username` and `fullname`:

```
if ( file_exists( $import_file ) ) {
    // read in the import file
    $lines = file( $import_file );
    foreach ($lines as $line)
    {
        // cycle through the file

        // remove the new line character from the line
        $line = rtrim ($line);

        // split the line data at the ";"
        $data = preg_split ("/;/",$line);

        $new_user_username = $data[0];
        $new_user_fullname = $data[1];
```

Now the script has all the necessary information to create the new user by copying the template user. The following code does this part of the job:

```
user_copy($template_user, $new_user_username)
```

Copying the template users would leave you with a list of users created, with all of them having the same full name and authentication set to local. The script then goes on and changes the full name and `realm id` of the newly created user by executing two database SQL UPDATE statements:

```
db_execute("UPDATE user_auth SET full_name = '".$new_user_fullname."' WHERE
username='".$new_user_username."'");

db_execute("UPDATE user_auth SET realm=".$realm_id." WHERE
username='".$new_user_username."'");
```

The first SQL statement updates the **full_name** field of the new user; the second statement updates the **realm** field to match your selection from the command line parameter.

This import script is useful for environments where you do not automatically want to create all users based on the same template user, but have different users be assigned different user profiles.

Before we continue

As you have learned quite a bit of new information about user management and the provided CLI interface, let's look at a few questions to check your knowledge.

Pop quiz - a few questions about Chapter 4

1. What would you use the guest account for?

   To allow guest users to log on to the system

   To view the number of guest users within the company

   To allow guests to use the internal network

   To allow public viewing of graphs

2. What permissions do you need to give a user to add new devices to Cacti?

   Console Access and Sites/Devices/Data Sources/Data Collectors

   Device Management permissions

   Console Access and Graph Management permissions

3. What permissions do you need to use the CLI command line scripts from Cacti?

   Console Access permissions

   CLI Management permissions

   Update Data Sources permissions

   No special permissions are required

Summary

You learned a lot about user management with Cacti in this chapter. You have now created your first user and applied some basic settings to the user.

By using the new concept of groups, you have created a common set of settings and permissions which will be applied to your users, helping you to reduce the overall effort of user management significantly.

During user and group creation, you have also learned how to allow or deny permissions for specific Cacti items and defined the required permissions to only allow your user a specific set of devices.

You have also learned how to create a template user and how to use the Batch Copy method to apply permissions from a template user to other users.

Using built-in LDAP Authentication, you have also integrated Cacti into an existing LDAP or Active Directory environment for even easier user management.

Finally, by using the provided scripts, you have learned how to import users into the Cacti system using the CLI interface.

Now that you have users on your system, it's time to give them more than just the standard Cacti graphs. In the next chapter, you will learn how to create your own data input methods and data queries and how to retrieve data using remote SSH commands.

5
Data Management

Retrieving data for graphing with Cacti is more than just pulling SNMP data. Cacti allows several different methods for data retrieval. Besides SNMP, Cacti can retrieve data using remotely executed scripts, pulling data from databases, or building data by utilizing the **Windows Management Interface (WMI)**.

In this chapter, we are going to:

- Provide a short overview of Cacti's data management
- Explain how to build a data input method
- Build a data query
- Develop a complete remote SSH data input method

Let's start!

An introduction to Cacti data management

Cacti provides different methods for remote data query. You already learned about the data input methods for retrieving a single SNMP value, but this method is not limited to SNMP. You can use several other methods, such as scripts or the WMI, for retrieving and graphing data.

Data input methods

Data input methods are commonly used when it comes to basic data retrieval. They can be external scripts, simple SNMP queries, or anything that does not involve indexed data.

Data queries

Data queries are being used when it comes to indexed data. A good example for indexed data is retrieving interface statistics for switches where each data entry (for example, the interface inOctets data) is linked to the interface using an index. Therefore, for complex data, you will need to create a data query.

Creating data input methods

We have already seen how to create a data input method for simple SNMP queries. Let's look into creating a script-based data input method for retrieving some information out of the secure log file. The secure log file contains information about failed and successful logins. Please note that the following example will only work on a Linux system.

The book comes with an exported version of the data input method as well as the data template. The file cacti_data_template_unix_-_secure_log_input.xml can be imported into Cacti and is provided as a reference for you. The file does not contain the graph template, which you will have to create yourself.

You should still try and follow this chapter so that you get familiar with the different steps involved in creating your own data input methods and data templates.

Preparation - creating the script

For a script/command data input method, you will need a script for gathering the required data and providing it to Cacti. Look at the unix_secure_log.pl file. This Perl script will collect the necessary data for you.

Differences between CentOS and other Linux versions

As you may have noticed, the book mainly focuses on the CentOS/RHEL based Linux system. Some of the settings and paths in the following scripts may not be the same on your Linux version. An example is the /var/log/secure file, which contains failed login and authentication failures in CentOS. For Debian based systems this is actually /var/log/auth.log. Please make sure to check your file paths in case you run into any issues with the scripts.

Let's have a look at the commands used in the script. Within the first line of interest, you configure the path and filename to look for the data:

```
# Where do we find the secure log file ?
# Debian/Ubuntu: /var/log/auth.log
# CentOS/RHEL   : /var/log/secure
my $secure_log = '/var/log/secure';
```

Gathering the data

The following important lines within the script retrieve the relevant Cacti data by executing a sequence of operating system commands:

```
# Retrieve the number of lines containing a "authentication failure" or
"Invalid user" string
$data{'invalid_users'} = `egrep " authentication failure|Invalid user"
$secure_log  | wc -l`;

# Retrieve the number of lines containing a "New session" or "Accepted
password" string
$data{'valid_logons'} = `egrep " New session|Accepted password" $secure_log
| wc -l`;
```

The first line looks for the string Invalid user within the secure log file by using the grep command. This command will print all lines containing this string. By using the special pipe character, |, we redirect the output from this command to the wc (abbreviation for word count) command. By using the -1 switch, the wc command will count the number of lines. The output of this command is then stored within the $data{'invalid_users'} variable.

Preparing the data for output

The variables `$data{'invalid_users'}` and `$data{'valid_logons'}`now contain the number of lines containing the `Invalid user` and `Accepted password` strings, but they also have a line ending character. For Cacti to use this data, you will need to remove this line ending character. This can be achieved by using the `chomp` function:

```
# Remove the line ending character from the string:
chomp( $data{'invalid_users'} );
chomp( $data{'valid_logons'} );
```

You can now use these variables to print the data as a Cacti compliant string:

```
# Print the data as "Name1:Var1Name2:Var2". Do not put a line ending to the
string !
print
"InvalidUsers:".$data{'invalid_users'}."ValidLogons:".$data{'valid_logons'}
;
```

As the comment already describes, the data needs to be printed as a `Name:Variable` pair separated by a space. This is the last step of the script. An example output of this script can be seen here:

```
# perlunix_secure_log.pl
InvalidUsers:0ValidLogons:3
#
```

Installation of the script

All scripts need to be placed into the scripts subdirectory of your Cacti installation. After you have copied the script to this location, you can use it to create the data input method within Cacti.

Modifying the secure log permissions

In order for the Cacti polling user to read the `secure` log file, you will have to add read permissions to it for the Cacti user. The following code will add this permission to the file:

```
setfacl-m user:cacti:r /var/log/secure
```

Time for action - creating a data input method - step 1

Log on to your Cacti installation as an admin user and change to the **Console** tab:

1. Go to **Data Collection|DataInputMethods**.
2. Click on the **Add** link to the top right.
3. Enter **Unix-SecureLogInput** as the **Name**.
4. Select **Script/Command** as the **InputType**.
5. Enter `perl<path_cacti>/scripts/unix_secure_log.pl` as the **InputString**.
6. Click on the **Create** button:

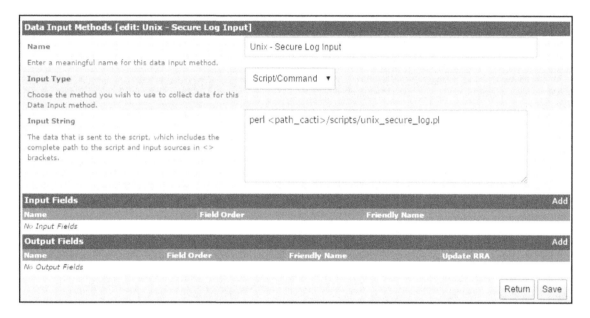

You just created a basic Script/Command-based data input method. You also told Cacti how to execute the script by defining the **InputString**. Selecting the **Script/Command** as **InputType** made Cacti automatically add fields for data input and data output after clicking on the **Save** button.

Time for action - creating a data input method - step 2

Now that you have created the input method, you will have to define the output of the script so Cacti knows what data it can expect:

1. Click on the **Add** link at the **OutputFields** table. This will open a new form.
2. Enter **InvalidUsers** as the **Field[Output Field]**.
3. Enter **InvalidUsers** as the **FriendlyName**.
4. Click on the **Create** button.
5. Click on the **Add** link of the **OutputFields** table again.
6. Enter **ValidLogons** as the **Field[Output Field]**.
7. Enter **ValidLogons** as the **FriendlyName**.
8. Click on the **Create** button:

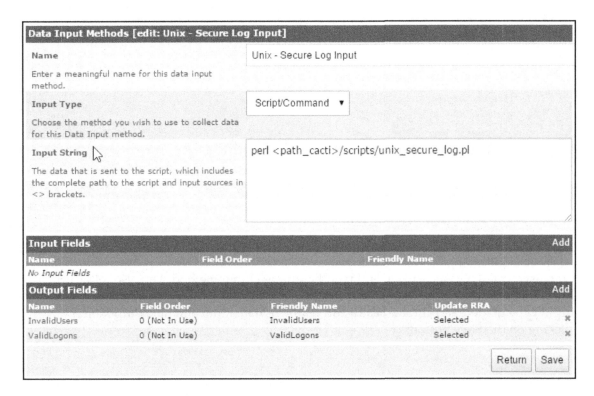

You just added the two output fields from the script to this data input method. Cacti is now able to use this information and fill the RRD files with the data retrieved from the script.

The data template

As you've already learned in `Chapter 3`, *Creating and Using Templates* you will need to create a data template for this data input method to be used within a graph. You can now either import the template that comes with this book, or better still, try to create the data template yourself. The following picture shows the final data template:

Creating data queries

Data queries are more complex than simple data input methods. As already mentioned, they do involve indexes. For you to get an easy start with data queries, you will now rebuild the SNMP-based data query for network interfaces.

Building the XML data file

Building a script or SNMP query always starts with an XML file providing the relationship between input, output, and the index. Look at the `interface_book.xml` file that comes with this book for an example of such a XML file.

The interface_book.xml file:

This XML file contains the complete data file for the interface SNMP query. The following section provides an overview of the different parts of this XML file. Although the file contains multiple input and output fields, as a minimum these XML files can contain one input and one output field.

Have a look at the file first and then read the next few headings to better understand the different parts of the file.

XML header

The XML header sets some generic information for Cacti. A generic description, as well as the SNMP OID index, can be set here:

```
<name>Get SNMP Interfaces</name>
<description>Queries a host for a list of monitorable
interfaces</description>
<oid_index>.1.3.6.1.2.1.2.2.1.1</oid_index>
<oid_num_indexes>.1.3.6.1.2.1.2.1.0</oid_num_indexes>
<index_order>ifDescr:ifName:ifHwAddr:ifIndex</index_order>
<index_order_type>numeric</index_order_type>
<index_title_format>|chosen_order_field|</index_title_format>
```

Let us look at the SNMP output of the `oid_index` and `oid_num_index` for the CentOS box:

```
# snmpwalk -c public -v 2c localhost .1.3.6.1.2.1.2.2.1.1
IF-MIB::ifIndex.1 = INTEGER: 1
IF-MIB::ifIndex.2 = INTEGER: 2
IF-MIB::ifIndex.3 = INTEGER: 3
IF-MIB::ifIndex.4 = INTEGER: 4
# snmpwalk -c public -v 2c localhost .1.3.6.1.2.1.2.1.0
IF-MIB::ifNumber.0 = INTEGER: 4
```

If you are instead seeing an error message of `Timeout: No Response from localhost` or `No Such Object available on this agent at this OID` then your SNMP daemon is not running or the access to the SNMP daemon is not allowed. In that case, quickly head over to `Chapter 7`, *Network and Server Monitoring* where you will learn how to enable the SNMP daemon and allow access to the required OIDs.

This CentOS system has four interfaces: a loopback (`127.0.0.1`), one Ethernet interface (`eno16777736`), and something called `virbr0` and `virbr0-nic`, which are only used when Centos is providing virtualization functionality. The `oid_num_indexes` provides us with the number of interfaces available in the system, which is four. The `oid_index` provides a table of indexes available. The index is important to match an interface with its corresponding data value (for example, `inOctets`).

The `index_order` list defines a unique index, on which Cacti can order and index the data. The `index_order_type` defines the default sort order of the `index_order`.

XML input

Input fields describe the fields taken as input for the data query. Basically, the fields will be shown on the data query table when creating new graphs for a host. All input fields will be shown there.

Let's look at the very first input field, the `ifIndex` definition:

```xml
<ifIndex>
<name>Index</name>
<method>walk</method>
<source>value</source>
<direction>input</direction>
<oid>.1.3.6.1.2.1.2.2.1.1</oid>
</ifIndex>
```

Input as well as output fields always contain at least the following five fields:

- name: A name that is being displayed on the data query table.
- method: The SNMP method to retrieve the data. This can be get or walk.
- source: The source for the field, its value returns the plain data; there is also OID/REGEXP and VALUE/REGEXP. They both use regular expression to either get part of the OID as the value, or part of the retrieved plain data as the value.
- direction: Can be input or output, depending on the field type.
- oid: The oid to use for the get or walk method.
- output_format (optional): Can be hex, ascii, or left empty to let Cacti guess what the value will be. In our case, we don't add the output_format field, which will let Cacti guess the format.

The example will walk the ifIndexoid and simply return the values (1,2,3, and 4) as input data. If you later look at the data query table, you will see those values again.

XML output

The output fields are used by Cacti to actually gather the data for the RRD files. Let's look at the interface inOctets definition:

```
<ifInOctets>
<name>Bytes In</name>
<method>walk</method>
<source>value</source>
<direction>output</direction>
<oid>.1.3.6.1.2.1.2.2.1.10</oid>
</ifInOctets>
```

As you can see, it is defined similarly to the input fields, except that the direction is now output. If you take the oid and use the snmpwalk command to retrieve the data from the CentOS system, you can see the importance of the index:

```
# snmpwalk -On -c public -v 2c localhost .1.3.6.1.2.1.2.2.1.10
.1.3.6.1.2.1.2.2.1.10.1 = Counter32: 17170591
.1.3.6.1.2.1.2.2.1.10.2 = Counter32: 2937246893
.1.3.6.1.2.1.2.2.1.10.3 = Counter32: 0
.1.3.6.1.2.1.2.2.1.10.4 = Counter32: 0
```

Each interface has its own inOctets number. The oid for it can be defined as oid + index. In order to retrieve the inOctets for the interface with index 1 (eno16777736), you will need to retrieve the oid.1.3.6.1.2.1.2.2.1.10.1.

Installing the XML file

The final XML file needs to be put to the `resource/snmp_queries` subdirectory of Cacti. For script queries, the directory will be `resource/script_queries`.

Creating the data query within Cacti

Now that you have created the base XML file for the data query, let's move on and finally create it within Cacti.

Time for action - creating a data query - step 1

Your first step will be the actual creation of a data query. This contains the basic steps involved and will be required to add the graph templates later:

1. Go to **Data Collection | DataQueries** and click on the **Add** link which is to the top right.
2. Enter **SNMP-InterfaceStatisticsSimple** as the **Name**.
3. Enter **Simple (In/OutOctets) InterfaceStatistics** as the **Description**.
4. Enter `<path_cacti>/resource/snmp_queries/interface_book.xml` as the **XMLPath**.
5. Select **GetSNMPData (Indexed)** as the **DataInputMethod**.
6. Click on the **Create** button:

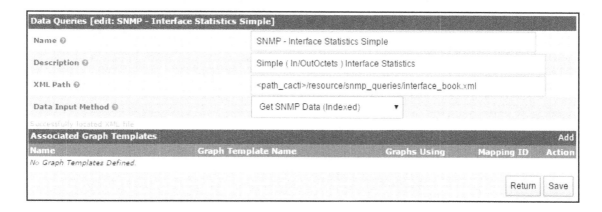

You just told Cacti where to find the XML file you created earlier and what data input method to use for retrieving the data. You can now add one or more graph templates to this query.

During the next step, you're going to add a graph and a data template to this data query. This step is needed, as a data query can provide different views on the data. Interface traffic, for example, can consist of 32-bit or 64-bit values, or you may want to have the total bandwidth used displayed as calculated on some graphs. As all of this data, as well as the graphs, are based on the same data query for interface traffic, you need to add the **AssociatedGraphTemplates** for these during the next step.

Time for action - creating a data query - step 2

Now, you're going to add one **Associated Graph Template** to this data query:

1. Click on the **Add** link of the **Associated Graph Templates** table.
2. Enter **In/OutBits** as the **Name**.
3. Select **Interface - Traffic (bits/sec)** as the **Graph Template**. If you do not find the graph template you need, you will need to create one first.
4. Click on the **Create** button. There will be several new tables showing up now:

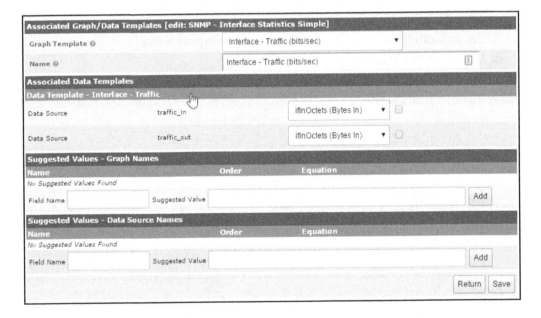

5. Select **ifOutOctets (Bytes Out)** for the **traffic_out** data source.

6. Check both checkboxes from the **AssociatedDataTemplates** table.

7. Now enter |**host_description**|- Traffic - |**query_ifName**| in the **Suggested Value** field of the **Suggested Values - Graph Names** section.

8. Enter **title** as the **FieldName** and click on the **Add** button:

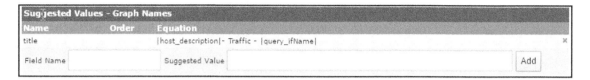

9. Enter |**host_description**|- Traffic - |**query_ifName**| in the **Suggested Value** field of the **Suggested Values - Data Source Names** section.

10. Enter **name** as the **Field Name** and click the **Add** button next to it.

11. Enter |query_ifSpeed| in the **Suggested Value** field of the **Suggested Values - Data Source Names** section:

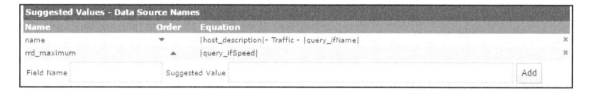

12. Enter **rrd_maximum** as the **FieldName** and click on the **Add** button again. You will now have two entries in the first table:

13. Click on the **Save** button:

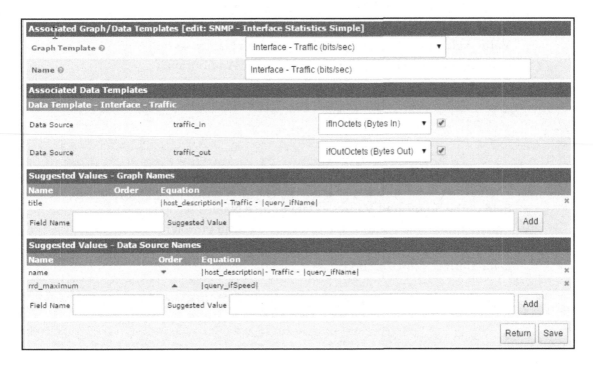

You have finished creating your first data query. You have defined the default names for the automatically created data templates and the maximum value the RRD file for this data template can store by setting the **rrd_maximum** variable to the interface speed. You have also defined the default title for the graphs by defining the `title` variable.

You can now add this data query to your device.

Creating a remote SSH data input method

Besides SNMP queries, remote data retrieval is an important part for creating Cacti performance graphs. You may get into a situation where SNMP data retrieval is not possible and you only have SSH access to a device. Let's assume that you want to graph the I/O performance of some server drives using the `iostat` utility. You will now learn the different steps it takes to create such a remote SSH data input method.

Please note that the book comes with an exported version of the data input method, the data template as well as the graph template. The file `cacti_graph_template_unix_-_remote_iostats_command_graph.xml` can be imported into Cacti and is provided as a reference for you.

You should still try to follow the steps provided here in order to see the different tasks involved to setup your own SSH-based data and graph.

Preparation

As a preparation for the data input method, you will need to create two different scripts and set up public key authentication.

The remote script

The remote script will execute local commands and prepare the data on the remote system. The data will be returned to the local script. If you have not already installed the `iostat` utility on the remote system, you can call the following command to do so on a CentOS system:

```
yum install sysstat
```

This will install the `iostat` utility on the system.

Let's call this utility and look at the output:

```
# iostat
Linux 2.6.32-642.11.1.el6.x86_64 (localhost.localdomain)        05/28/2017
_x86_64_  (8 CPU)

avg-cpu:  %user   %nice %system %iowait  %steal   %idle
           0.02    0.00    0.02    0.00    0.00   99.96

Device:           tpsBlk_read/s   Blk_wrtn/s   Blk_readBlk_wrtn
sda               0.74      13.73        15.92   15072838   17472276
```

In this example, we can see that this utility provides statistics for all partitions in the system. We are going to look at the `sda` partition which, in this case, holds the root partition. The following command for retrieving extended status data just for the `sda` device will be used:

```
iostat -dxk sda
```

The command prints some statistics about the selected device, as you can see in the following screenshot:

```
Linux 2.6.32-642.11.1.el6.x86_64 (localhost.localdomain)       05/28/2017      _x86_64_      (8 CPU)

Device:         rrqm/s   wrqm/s     r/s     w/s    rkB/s    wkB/s avgrq-sz avgqu-sz   await r_await w_await  svctm  %util
sda               0.09     1.53    0.23    0.51     6.86     7.96    40.14     0.00    3.40    0.69    4.62   0.86   0.06
```

The `-dk` option will make sure that only the `sda2` device is shown and that we see the KB read and writes to the disk. The `-x` option will provide extended status information, such as the IO utilization `%util`. One important notice about `iostat` utility is the fact that the very first status report will always be the combined data since system start. To get a more accurate snapshot of the actual data, the command needs to be told how often and how long it should gather IO status data.

The remote script looks like the following:

```
#!/bin/bash
iostat -dxk $1 5 6 | grep $1
```

The parameters tell `iostat` to poll IO data every five seconds for a total of six polls. The `$1` will be provided by the local calling script and is the first parameter to the remote script. The `grep $1` command will make sure that only the line with the device information will be returned. Of course, the drawback of this is that it will definitely increase the poller runtime as it needs to wait for the remote script to finish, but it will still finish before the default five minute polling interval ends.

The local script

The local script deals with connectivity to the remote system using SSH and executing the remote script. It also provides the returned data to Cacti. Let's look at the different sections of the local script.

Input variables

The local script takes several input variables:

```
# Get the command line arguments (input fields from Cacti)
my $host = $ARGV[0];
my $user = $ARGV[1];
my $diskDevice = $ARGV[2]; # e.g. sda

# take care for tcp:hostname or TCP:ip@
$host =~ s/tcp:/$1/gis;
my $sshHost = $user.'@'.$host;
```

The $host variable takes the Cacti host information. The $user defines the remote userID under which the iostat command will run. Finally, the $diskDevice variable takes the partition to check. From these input values we also define the $sshHost variables which you will need for the SSH command.

The SSH command execution

Using the input values you can now create the SSH command for the remote command execution:

```
my $returnValue = `/usr/bin/ssh $sshHost'/root/getIoStats.sh $diskDevice'`;
```

This command assumes that the remote script getIoStats.sh is stored in the root directory. It connects to the remote system ($sshHost) using the default locally stored private key, which we will create shortly, and calls the remote command with the $diskDevice as parameter. The data being returned by the remote script is stored in the variable $returnValue.

Preparing the data

The returned data is made out of a bunch of lines containing the relevant data. You first need to separate each line into a separate data item. This can be achieved using the split function, splitting the returned data at the line ending character \n:

```
# Separate the returned data at the line ending character
# and store each line as an element of the returnData array
my @returnData = split/\n/,$returnValue;
```

Now that you have each line stored as an item of the `returnData` array, you can move on and initialize the Cacti data to be returned. You are going to use a Perl hash variable to store the data. Hashes in Perl have the advantage. The advantage is that the key for the hash can be a string value. Therefore, it is more readable than using arrays, which only accept numbers as keys:

```
# Initialize the Cacti return data
my %cactiData;
$cactiData{'device'} = $diskDevice;
$cactiData{'Reads'} = 0;
$cactiData{'Writes'} = 0;
$cactiData{'kbReads'} = 0;
$cactiData{'kbWrites'} = 0;
$cactiData{'ioUtil'} = 0;
```

You also need to know how many lines you actually got back from the remote script. This can be achieved with the following command, returning the number of items within the `returnData` **array**:

```
my $allDataChecks = $#returnData;
```

Now that you have initialized the data, it is time to actually retrieve the data and to store the retrieved values into the corresponding hash value. As you have previously learned, you need to skip the first line, so the `for` loop starts from the second line. Please note that the very first item of a Perl array starts at 0:

```
# Cycle through each line and skip the very first one ( line = 0 )
for ( my $line = 1; $line < $allDataChecks; $line++ ) {
        my @lineData = split/\s+/,$returnData[$line];
        $cactiData{'Reads'} = $cactiData{'Reads'} + $lineData[3];
        $cactiData{'Writes'} = $cactiData{'Writes'} + $lineData[4];
        $cactiData{'kbReads'} = $cactiData{'kbReads'} + $lineData[5];
        $cactiData{'kbWrites'} = $cactiData{'kbWrites'} + $lineData[6];
        $cactiData{'ioUtil'} = $cactiData{'ioUtil'} + $lineData[13];
}
```

Within the preceding `for` loop, each line is split at the space character, \s, treating several adjacent spaces as one by using the special + character. If you take the sentence you are reading now as an example, `$lineData[0]` would store `If,$ lineData[1]you,` `$lineData[2]take,` and so on.

As the remote script returned several lines with data, the `for` loop will sum up each line of data. Therefore, your next step will be dividing the data by the number lines being returned. Again, you will need to reduce the number by one:

```
# Average the data
$cactiData{'Reads'} = $cactiData{'Reads'}  / ($allDataChecks - 1);
$cactiData{'Writes'} = $cactiData{'Writes'} / ($allDataChecks - 1);
$cactiData{'kbReads'} = $cactiData{'kbReads'} / ($allDataChecks - 1);
$cactiData{'kbWrites'} = $cactiData{'kbWrites'} / ($allDataChecks - 1);
$cactiData{'ioUtil'} = $cactiData{'ioUtil'} / ($allDataChecks - 1);
```

The final step will be to print out the retrieved, averaged data in a Cacti compliant way:

```
print "Reads:".$cactiData{'Reads'}."".
"Writes:".$cactiData{'Writes'}."".
"ReadsKb:".$cactiData{'kbReads'}."".
"WritesKb:".$cactiData{'kbWrites'}."".
"ioUtil:".$cactiData{'ioUtil'};
```

Now you're ready for the next step.

SSH public key authentication

SSH public key authentication is the recommended way of executing commands on a remote system. You'll need to create a public key for the remote system and a private key for the local system. For simplicity, let's assume that you will connect to the remote system using the root user account.

Let's start by creating the keys using the ssh-keygen tool.

Time for action - create SSH keys with ssh-keygen tool

The ssh-keygen tool provides an easy way of creating a SSH public key and easily distribute it to other systems:

1. Log on to your Cacti system with the root account.
2. Become the Cacti user:

   su - cactiuser

3. Execute the ssh-keygen tool:

   ssh-keygen

4. Use the default filename **id_rsa** by pressing the return key.

5. Leave the passphrase empty:

```
Generating public/private rsa key pair.
Enter file in which to save the key (/home/cactiuser/.ssh/id_rsa):
Created directory '/home/cactiuser/.ssh'.
Enter passphrase (empty for no passphrase):
Enter same passphrase again:
Your identification has been saved in /home/cactiuser/.ssh/id_rsa.
Your public key has been saved in /home/cactiuser/.ssh/id_rsa.pub.
The key fingerprint is:
20:21:41:48:94:35:3f:f8:7b:ff:5f:05:fd:a0:b9:b4 cactiuser@localhost.localdomain
The key's randomart image is:
+--[ RSA 2048]----+
|o=*+.            |
|.. .+.         . |
|  ..o.        o .|
|  ....       o o.|
|   . S    +   o|
|    .    . o  .|
|    . .   E  . |
|     . .     . |
|        .....   |
+-----------------+
```

6. Now copy the new key to the remote host:

   ssh-copy-id root@remotehost

7. You should see the following output for this command:

```
$ ssh-copy-id  root@remotehost
The authenticity of host 'remotehost (192.168.178.43)' can't be established.
RSA key fingerprint is fb:96:30:ad:40:ce:42:fe:2c:d7:d6:d5:26:9b:08:ba.
Are you sure you want to continue connecting (yes/no)? yes
/bin/ssh-copy-id: INFO: attempting to log in with the new key(s), to filter out any that are already installed
/bin/ssh-copy-id: INFO: 1 key(s) remain to be installed -- if you are prompted now it is to install the new keys
root@remotehost's password:

Number of key(s) added: 1

Now try logging into the machine, with:   "ssh 'root@remotehost'"
and check to make sure that only the key(s) you wanted were added.
```

8. Execute the following ssh command in order to test the remote access:

   ssh root@remotesystem '/root/getIoStats.sh sda'

You just created a public and private SSH key which can be used to automatically log in to a remote system without any user interaction. You've allowed the Cacti system (`cactiuser`) to use this SSH key to execute the `getIoStats.sh` script on the remote system.

Creating the data input method

The data input method for this script involves some advanced steps, as it does contain input variables.

Time for action - creating the data input method

The data input method for the IO stats data also contains input strings. Let's look at how to create and make use of these:

1. Create a data input method.
2. Enter **Unix - Remote IOStats Command** as the **Name**.
3. Select **Script/Command** as **InputType**.
4. Enter `perl <path_cacti>/scripts/diskIo.pl <host> <user> <diskDevice>` as the **InputString**.
5. Click on the **Create** button.
6. Click on the **Add** link at the **InputFields** section.
7. Select **host** as the **Field[input Field]**.
8. Enter **Hostname** as the **FriendlyName**.
9. Enter **hostname** as the **SpecialTypeCode**.
10. Click on the **Create** button.
11. Add the remaining input fields for **user** and **diskDevice** by following steps 6 to 10 and only adding a **FriendlyName**.

12. Add the output fields for Reads, Writes, ReadsKb, WritesKb, and ioUtil:

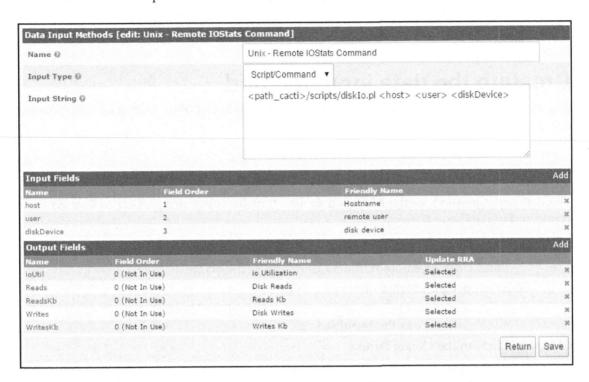

You've just created the data input method for retrieving the output from the iostats command of a remote system. You've defined the input fields like the remote username to use for logging in to the. The data retrieved from this command will be stored in the output fields you've defined.

Creating the data template

The data template can be built as outlined in the secure log input example described right at the beginning of this chapter. There will be a slight difference to it, as the data template will have a table called **CustomData**, this table defines the input data. The following screenshot shows this table and the entries you'll need to make:

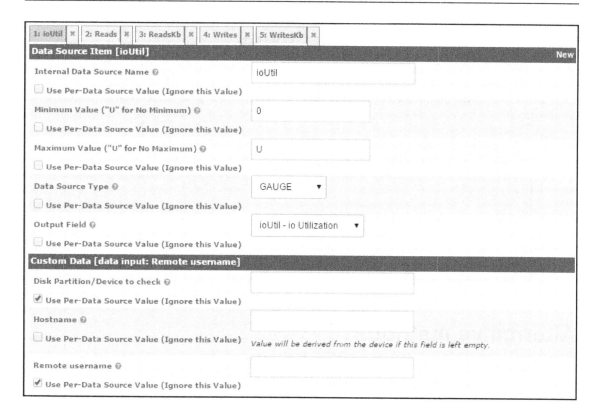

Creating the graph template

The data input method contains three different types of data: number of average reads, average KB reads, and a percentage value for the IO utilization. For each of these, you'll need to create a graph template. As you've already learned how to create graph templates, this is a perfect opportunity for you to check your knowledge and create these.

Adding the graph to the device

Once you've created the graph templates, you can go on adding the graph template to the device for which you want to gather the data. You're asked to enter the custom data for the disk partition/device and the remote username during the process, as seen in the following screenshot:

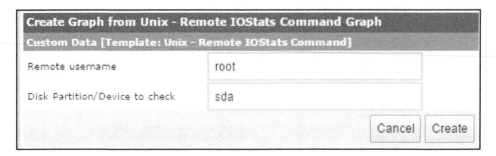

Alternative methods

If the system you want to retrieve data from is able to provide data using SNMP, you can also use the special `exec` command within the remote SNMP server configuration to provide the data via the SNMP interface. There exist, many ways for retrieving data, from parsing command line output, to retrieving webpages to be parsed, as well as using webservices.

Have a go hero - remote command execution using SNMP

Let's assume that your remote system does already run an SNMP daemon. What do you need to do in order to retrieve the secure log data from a remote system utilizing the SNMP interface?

Solution: You need to create a script called `/root/getSecureLogonsData.sh` with the following lines of code:

```
#!/bin/bash
# CentOS/RHEL:    /var/log/secure
# Debian/Ubuntu: /var/log/auth.log
egrep " authentication failure|Invalid user" $secure_log  | wc -l
egrep " New session|Accepted password" $secure_log  | wc -l
```

You also need to add the following line to the `/etc/snmp/snmpd.conf` file:

```
extendinvalidLogons /bin/bash /root/getSecureLogonsData.sh
```

After restarting the `snmpd` daemon, you can check the output of the `oid`:

```
# snmpwalk -c public -v 2c localhost 'NET-SNMP-EXTEND-
MIB::nsExtendOutLine."invalidLogons"'
NET-SNMP-EXTEND-MIB::nsExtendOutLine."invalidLogons".1 = STRING: 0
NET-SNMP-EXTEND-MIB::nsExtendOutLine."invalidLogons".2 = STRING: 2
```

The values for `oids` ending with 1 and 2 are the numbers returned by the `Invaliduser` and `Acceptedpassword` line of the script. You can then create a data input method using these **oids**. If you want to know the exact numeroid, you can use the `snmptranslate` command.

```
snmptranslate -On 'NET-SNMP-EXTEND-MIB::nsExtendOutLine."invalidLogons"'
```

Before we continue

Creating data input methods using scripts or queries involves quite some programming and network knowledge. This chapter built up the complexity by going from a simple local data input method to a more complex data query and building a remote executed input method. If you feel lost in one of these exercises, you should try to focus on one of them before moving on to the next step. If you want to learn more about data queries, you should visit the How To sections on the Cacti website as well as the relevant section on the Cacti online manual.

- How To: `http://docs.cacti.net/howto:data_query_templates`.
- Manual: `http://docs.cacti.net/manual:100:3a_advanced_topics.3d_script_data_query_walkthrough`.

Pop quiz - a few questions about Chapter 5

1. Where will you define the remote username to be used to connect to the remote host?
   - In the `config.php` file of Cacti
   - In the Cacti settings page
   - When adding the special graph template to a device
   - When adding or editing a device

2. What do you need an indexed SNMP query for?
   - In order to easily retrieve special values from a SNMP tree
   - In order to link SNMP data to the relevant device
   - Indexed queries are required for data which is provided as a table with indexes
   - In order to retrieve multiple SNMP values at once

3. Which command will you need to use to create a ssh key file?
   - The Putty KeyGen tool
   - The sshd-keygen tool
   - The ssh-keygen tool

Summary

You should now be able to create your own data input methods and create custom scripts to gather remote data.

This chapter covered the creation of a new data input method which gathers data from the local Cacti system using a local script. You've also learned how to create more complex data queries and understand the underlying XML file required for gathering indexed data. Finally, you have set up a remote SSH data input method and looked at how to retrieve and display data from a remote system using the SSH public key authentication method.

Having covered the data management chapter, you should now be able to comfortably manage a Cacti system. In the next chapter, you're going to have a closer look into maintaining Cacti by scheduling backup jobs, maintaining log files and more.

6
Cacti Maintenance

We have looked into installing and running a Cacti instance, but what about its maintenance and upkeep? This chapter will show you how to create backups and restores of your Cacti installation, as well as providing you with information on how to keep your Cacti instance clean of dead hosts and unneeded files.

In this chapter we are going to:

- Provide a short overview of maintaining Cacti
- Explain the directory structure of Cacti
- Describe backup and restore procedures
- Look into log file management with Cacti's new logrotate feature
- Clean up unused RRD files
- Provide a short overview of the Cacti CLI functionality

Let's begin!

An introduction to Cacti maintenance

Cacti maintenance defines the standard procedures needed for backing up the database and managing the RRD files. As you've learned, the RRD files contain the polled performance data, whereas the database only holds configuration data. Let's take a look at both from a data management point of view.

Database

As you've seen in previous chapters, the MySQL/MariaDB is the main configuration repository for any Cacti installation, and all your defined hosts, templates, and graph definitions are stored there.

RRD files

The RRD files contain all your performance data, but without the database you will be unable to link these files to their original devices and data sources. Cacti offers two different ways of storing these files. One method stores all RRD files within a single directory. The other method creates sub-directories based on the host and local graph ID.

The Cacti directory structure

Let's look at the default directory structure of Cacti and some of the important sub directories:

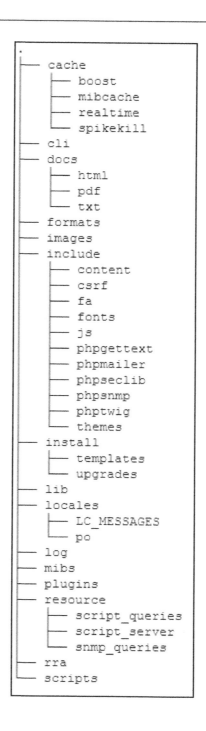

The cache directory

The `cache` directory contains all files and directories which are created on a temporary basis. With the inclusion of boost, real time, and other plugins, this directory now provides a common place for these files.

The cli directory

The `cli` directory contains all cli scripts used to manage Cacti from the command line. The scripts within this directory will help you to fix database issues or simply add new devices or users by utilizing the cli scripts.

The docs directory

The `docs` directory contains the full Cacti manual in different formats. The manual can be used as a quick reference for the various Cacti topics and also provides information on how to debug some of the more common issues you'll face.

The Cacti manual can be viewed within your browser by going to the following URL (replacing `<server>` with your Cacti server):

```
http://<server>/<cacti dir>/docs/html/index.html
```

The include directory

The `include` directory contains files like the `config.php` and `global.php` file. As you know, the `config.php` file contains the database and Cacti URL settings. With Cacti 1.x, several sub directories have been created which contain additional libraries for managing the email communication, cross-site request forgery preventions, and other functionality. The `themes` directory within this `include` directory contains the new Cacti themes.

The install directory

The `install` directory contains the installation files, as well those needed to upgrade a Cacti installation. Once you have setup Cacti, you can safely delete this directory.

The lib directory

The lib directory provides the common functionality of Cacti which is being used by the different user interfaces or plugins.

The locales directory

The locales directory contains the translations of Cacti.

The log directory

The log directory contains all of the Cacti log files. This is where the cacti.log file resides. In a default Cacti installation, there will be no log file management on these files.

The mibs directory

Within this directory you can find the definitions for the special Cacti MIB, which is being used by the new included Cacti SNMP agent.

The plugin directory

This directory holds any additional plugins for Cacti. It should be empty after a fresh install.

The resource directory

The resource directory holds all the XML files for Cacti's data queries. There are also some files used by the PHP script server stored in this directory.

The rra directory

This is probably the most important directory. The rra directory contains all the RRD files that hold your performance data.

The scripts directory

The `scripts` directory contains the scripts which are referenced in your data input methods.

Backup and restore procedures

As with any other application or data, you should always have well planned and properly documented backup and restore procedures in place in order to keep your data secure. Backing up the Cacti data assures you that you're not going to lose weeks or even years of valuable performance data. Although the following steps show you how to backup Cacti to the local system, you should save the backup files to a remote system. Off-site backups are also a good idea.

The MySQL/MariaDB database

MySQL/MariaDB comes with a basic backup application called `mysqldump` which dumps the content of one or more databases to a plain text file. You will be using this program to create your database backup file, but we'll further enhance its functionality by wrapping it in a shell script to automate the filename and compressions tasks.

Time for action - backup your Cacti database

Let's go through the different steps of creating your first database backup:

1. Logon to your Cacti system and become the root user.
2. Execute the following command to create a `backup` directory:

   ```
   mkdir /backup
   ```

3. Execute the following command and replace `<password>` with your MySQL database password (all in one line):

   ```
   mysqldump --user=root --password=<password> --add-drop-table --
   databases cacti > /backup/cacti_database_backup.sql
   ```

4. Verify that the backup file was created by issuing the following command:

   ```
   ls -l /backup
   ```

5. Look at the file with the `more` command:

> `more /backup/cacti_database_backup.sql`

6. The following screenshot shows the first few lines of the command. If you press the space bar a few times, you will see that it contains the different SQL commands required to create the database, rebuild the tables and fill them with the actual data:

```
root@localhost:/var/www/html/cacti                          —    □    ×
-- MySQL dump 10.16   Distrib 10.1.21-MariaDB, for Linux (x86_64)
--
-- Host: localhost    Database: localhost
-- ------------------------------------------------------
-- Server version        10.1.21-MariaDB

/*!40101 SET @OLD_CHARACTER_SET_CLIENT=@@CHARACTER_SET_CLIENT */;
/*!40101 SET @OLD_CHARACTER_SET_RESULTS=@@CHARACTER_SET_RESULTS */;
/*!40101 SET @OLD_COLLATION_CONNECTION=@@COLLATION_CONNECTION */;
/*!40101 SET NAMES utf8 */;
/*!40103 SET @OLD_TIME_ZONE=@@TIME_ZONE */;
/*!40103 SET TIME_ZONE='+00:00' */;
/*!40014 SET @OLD_UNIQUE_CHECKS=@@UNIQUE_CHECKS, UNIQUE_CHECKS=0 */;
/*!40014 SET @OLD_FOREIGN_KEY_CHECKS=@@FOREIGN_KEY_CHECKS, FOREIGN_KEY_CHECKS=0
*/;
/*!40101 SET @OLD_SQL_MODE=@@SQL_MODE, SQL_MODE='NO_AUTO_VALUE_ON_ZERO' */;
/*!40111 SET @OLD_SQL_NOTES=@@SQL_NOTES, SQL_NOTES=0 */;


--
-- Current Database: `cacti`
--

CREATE DATABASE /*!32312 IF NOT EXISTS*/ `cacti` /*!40100 DEFAULT CHARACTER SET
latin1 */;
--More--(0%)
```

What just happened?

You just created a backup of your Cacti database, which includes everything that is stored in your Cacti database, from user IDs to graph templates and all the hosts added to your instance.

Although you now have a backup of your database, you don't have a backup of the actual database user. You will need to remember to create a database user for Cacti when restoring it to a freshly installed system. The backup also does not contain the actual graph data.

Enhancing the database backup

Now that you've created a database backup, you should think about a way to automate this procedure. You do not want to execute that command manually every night; so, the first step is to create a script that takes care of your database backup. Later in this chapter, you will learn how to schedule this script to back up your database regularly.

Let's think about some basic requirements for a script:

- Automatically add a date/time stamp to the filename
- Compress the backup to save space
- Remove backup files older than 3 days

Automatic file naming

The `date` command can be used to create a date string in the format: yyyymmdd, for example, 20170608. This can be used to create a filename which contains the current date in it. The following command will create such a string:

```
date +%Y%m%d
20170608
```

In a bash script file, this can be used to create the file name of the backup file:

```
# Set the backup filename and directory
DATE=`date +%Y%m%d` # e.g 20170608
FILENAME="cacti_database_$DATE.sql";
```

Remove old backup files

When using dynamic filenames like the ones created with the backup script, removing old backup files is essential to avoid filling the drive with backups. The following command will find all Cacti database backup files older than three days in the backup directory and delete them:

```
find /backup/cacti_database*.sql.gz -mtime +3 -exec rm {} ;
```

The database backup

The actual database backup is performed by the `mysqldump` command, as mentioned earlier. This command is called with all the parameters defined so far:

```
# execute the database dump
mysqldump --user=$DBUSER --password=$DBPWD --add-drop-table --databases
$DBNAME > $BACKUPDIR$FILENAME
```

The `$DBUSER` and `$DBPWD` variables are the database user credentials to access you Cacti database. You should set `$DBNAME` to the name of your Cacti database.

Compress the backup

On most Linux distributions, the `gzip` utility should be pre-installed, allowing us to compress the database dump. Calling gzip with the `-f` parameter will make sure that any already existing files (such as those from a test run) will be overwritten. The following command will compress the file `cacti_database_20170608.sql` and rename it to the `cacti_database_20170608.sql.gz`:

```
gzip -f cacti_database_20170608.sql
```

The whole script

The finished database backup Bash script `backupCacti.sh` then consists of the following lines of code:

```
#!/bin/bash

# Set the backup filename and directory
DATE=`date +%Y%m%d`  # e.g 20170608
FILENAME="cacti_database_$DATE.sql";
BACKUPDIR="/backup/";

# Database Credentials
DBUSER="cactiuser";
DBPWD="MyV3ryStr0ngPassword";

# Change to the root directory
cd /

# Where is our gzip tool for compression?
# The -f parameter will make sure that gzip will
# overwrite existing files
```

```
GZIP="/bin/gzip -f";

# Delete old backups older than 3 days
find /backup/cacti_*gz -mtime +3 -exec rm {} ;

# execute the database dump
mysqldump --user=$DBUSER --password=$DBPWD --add-drop-table --databases
$DBNAME > $BACKUPDIR$FILENAME

# compress the database backup
$GZIP $BACKUPDIR$FILENAME
```

The backup could use the Cacti database user to create the dump, as this user does in fact have sufficient access rights to the database to do so. You do not need to use the root MySQL user for the database backup process.

The Cacti files

The Cacti files that you need to backup do not only consist of the files within the Cacti directory. Examples of other files that you will need to take care of are:

- The Cacti cron job file
- The MySQL database backup file
- System files such as php.ini

Let's take a look at all the files we need to backup.

Building the backup file list

Depending on the setup of your Cacti installation, there are several files you will need to consider for a backup. Assuming you've followed this book closely and are using a CentOS based Cacti installation with Spine, then you'll need to keep a backup of the following files and directories:

File/Directory	Description
/etc/cron.d/cacti	Cacti cron job
/etc/php.ini	PHP main configuration file
/etc/php.d	PHP modules configuration files
/etc/httpd/conf	Apache main configuration files

/etc/httpd/conf.d	Apache modules configuration files
/etc/spine.conf	Spine configuration
/usr/local/spine	Spine directory
/var/www/html/cacti	Symbolic link to the Cacti main directory
/var/www/html/cacti-1.1.28	The Cacti main directory

Now that you have a list of which files need to be included in the backup, you can now use the `tar` command to create a first backup file.

Time for action - backup your Cacti files

Now that you have defined the set of files we need to backup, let's look into the different steps that are involved in creating the actual backup file:

1. Log on to your Cacti system.
2. Go to the root directory:

   cd /

3. Execute the following command to create a backup of all the files defined earlier:

   tar -czvpf /backup/cacti_files_20170608.tgz ./etc/cron.d/cacti ./etc/php.ini ./etc/php.d ./etc/httpd/conf ./etc/httpd/conf.d ./etc/spine.conf ./usr/local/spine ./var/www/html/cacti ./var/www/html/cacti-1.1.28

4. Verify that the backup file exists by issuing the following command:

   ls -l /backup

5. A similar listing to the following will be displayed:

```
[root@localhost /]# ls -l /backup/
total 260
-rw-r--r-- 1 root root    692 Jun 10 13:41 backupCacti.sh
-rw-r--r-- 1 root root  82095 Jun 10 13:43 cacti_database_20170610.sql.gz
-rw-r--r-- 1 root root 173512 Jun 10 13:42 cacti_files_20170608.tgz
[root@localhost /]#
```

What just happened?

You just created your first complete backup that contains all the files and directories you defined and is also already compressed. Together with the database backup, you are now able to restore your Cacti installation.

Enhancing the database backup script

Now that you know how to back up the database and the Cacti related files, you can add the `tar` command to the backup script created earlier.

Time for action - enhancing the backup script

The manual command you have just used to create your first backup needs to be added to the backup script. Let's see how this can be done in a more general way:

1. Open the `backupCacti.sh` script and add the following line between the `FILENAME` and `BACKUPDIR` line:

   ```
   TGZFILENAME="cacti_files_$DATE.tgz";
   ```

2. Add the following two lines at the end of the script:

   ```
   # Create the Cacti files backup
   tar -czpf $BACKUPDIR$TGZFILENAME ./etc/cron.d/cacti ./etc/php.ini
   ./etc/php.d ./etc/httpd/conf ./etc/httpd/conf.d ./etc/spine.conf
   ./usr/local/spine ./var/www/html/cacti ./var/www/html/cacti-1.1.28
   ```

3. Remove any earlier backups from the `backup` directory:

   ```
   rm /backup/cacti_*
   ```

4. Start the `backup` script:

   ```
   /bin/bash /backup/backupCacti.sh
   ```

5. Verify that the database and the files backup have been created:

   ```
   ls -l /backup
   ```

What just happened?

You have enhanced the script to also create a backup of the Cacti files. Now, you can issue this single command to create a complete backup. The extra dot you have added to the paths of the tar command will allow you to extract that tar file in a sub-directory without accidently overwriting an existing Cacti installation. This is especially useful if you only want to restore a specific file instead of all files.

Adding remote transfer with SCP

Having a backup is a good starting point, but you should also make sure to transfer the backup off to a different system in case your Cacti hardware has an issue and you will not be able to access any data on it.

 You should already have a public key authentication set up with the target system. If you are unsure, go back to *Creating a remote SSH data input method*, section of `Chapter 5`, *Data Management* which describes the necessary steps.

Time for action - Adding SCP to the backup script

Let's look at how to integrate an SCP transfer to a remote system:

1. Log on to the target server where you want to put the backup. Let's assume that server has the IP address `192.168.44.134`.

2. Create the directory holding the backups from your Cacti system:

   `mkdir /cactibackup`

3. Now log on to your Cacti system.

4. Open the `backupCacti.sh` script and add the following line after the `BACKUPDIR` line. Make sure to change the IP address to match your target server:

   ```
   SCPTARGETSERVER=192.168.44.134; # Change this IP
   ```

5. Now add the following line at the end of the script:

   ```
   # Transfer the Cacti files backup to a remote system
   scp $BACKUPDIR$TGZFILENAME $SCPTARGETSERVER:/cactibackup
   ```

6. Start the `backup` script:

```
/bin/bash /backup/backupCacti.sh
```

7. Log on to the remote target system again and verify that the backup file has been transferred:

```
ls -l /cactibackup
```

What just happened?

You have added a remote transfer using the SCP command to your backup script. This will make sure that your backup is safely stored on a different hardware.

> The backup files being transferred to the remote system have a unique name. As the transfer does not take care of cleaning up any files on the remote system, you should create a cleanup script on that system.

Creating the cronjob - automating the backup

Now that you have created a single script that performs both the database and Cacti backups, you can use this script to schedule the backup on a regular basis. In Linux, a scheduled task is called a cronjob, so this is what you are now going to create.

Time for action - creating a cronjob

Having completed the final script allows you to actually schedule the backup task. The following steps will create a cron job for this:

1. Log on to your Cacti system.
2. Create a crontab file:

```
vi /etc/cron.d/cactiBackup
```

3. Enter the following lines to this file:

```
# Cacti Backup Schedule
0 2 * * * root /bin/bash /backup/backupCacti.sh > /dev/null 2>&1
```

4. Save the file and exit the editor.

What just happened?

You created a backup job which will start at 02:00 in the morning every day of the week. You now have a daily backup of your Cacti database and files.

Restoring from a backup

Now that you have a daily backup of your Cacti instance, what steps do you need to take to actually restore your backup? Let's have a look at the different tasks needed.

Restoring the Cacti database

Restoring the Cacti database involves using the standard `mysql` command.

Time for action - Restoring the Cacti database

Having created a backup of Cacti database, it's time to restore it:

1. Log on to your Cacti server.
2. Change to the `backup` directory:

   ```
   cd /backup
   ```

3. Extract the latest backup file:

   ```
   gunzip cacti_database_20170608.sql.gz
   ```

4. Restore the database. Make sure to change the username and Cacti database name to fit your installation. Please note that this command is going to overwrite your existing database:

   ```
   mysql -u cactiuser -p cacti < cacti_database_20170608.sql
   ```

What just happened?

You restored your Cacti database from a backup. Please note that any changes you have made after the backup has been created, such as adding new devices to the server, will be lost.

Restoring the Cacti files

Restoring files from a backup will involve two methods:

- Restoring all of the Cacti files
- Restoring a single file

Restoring all Cacti files

Restoring all files is only necessary in case of a full disaster recovery like a hard disk failure. Thankfully your backup should contain all necessary files to restore a Cacti installation from the ground up.

Time for action - restoring all Cacti files

Having the latest backup file, you can easily restore your Cacti files using the extract operator from the `tar` command. You can use this approach when you do want to completely overwrite an existing Cacti system:

1. Log on to you Cacti server.
2. For this example, let's assume you have it copied into the `/backup` directory.
3. Change to the `root` directory:

   cd /

4. Extract the contents of the `backup`:

   tar -xzvpf /backup/cacti_files_20170608.tgz

5. You will see the content of the archive being displayed on the screen during the extraction process:

```
./var/www/html/cacti-1.1.28/cache/mibcache/
./var/www/html/cacti-1.1.28/cache/mibcache/index.php
./var/www/html/cacti-1.1.28/cache/mibcache/.htaccess
./var/www/html/cacti-1.1.28/cache/index.php
./var/www/html/cacti-1.1.28/cache/boost/
./var/www/html/cacti-1.1.28/cache/boost/index.php
./var/www/html/cacti-1.1.28/cache/boost/.htaccess
./var/www/html/cacti-1.1.28/boost_rrdupdate.php
./var/www/html/cacti-1.1.28/automation_tree_rules.php
./var/www/html/cacti-1.1.28/automation_templates.php
./var/www/html/cacti-1.1.28/automation_snmp.php
./var/www/html/cacti-1.1.28/automation_networks.php
./var/www/html/cacti-1.1.28/automation_graph_rules.php
./var/www/html/cacti-1.1.28/automation_devices.php
./var/www/html/cacti-1.1.28/auth_profile.php
./var/www/html/cacti-1.1.28/auth_login.php
./var/www/html/cacti-1.1.28/auth_changepassword.php
./var/www/html/cacti-1.1.28/aggregate_templates.php
./var/www/html/cacti-1.1.28/aggregate_items.php
./var/www/html/cacti-1.1.28/aggregate_graphs.php
./var/www/html/cacti-1.1.28/about.php
./var/www/html/cacti-1.1.28/README.md
./var/www/html/cacti-1.1.28/LICENSE
[root@localhost /]#
```

What just happened?

You extracted the files from your backup. The $-p$ option tells tar to maintain the permissions as they were at the time of backup. By using the $-v$ (verbose) option, the name of each file currently being extracted is displayed to the screen, allowing you to monitor its progress. You will need to restart all relevant services afterwards, or reboot the system to make all the changes of the configuration files active.

Restoring the Cacti files to separate system:

If you intend to restore the backup archive to another Linux distribution or just want to restore a single file, simply change to a sub directory of your choice and run the restore tar command. All files within the archive will then be restored to the sub directory without overwriting any existing files.

Restoring a single file from the backup

Sometimes, it happens that just a single file gets corrupted and needs to be restored. By using the dot character at the beginning of each file and directory during the backup creation, you can actually extract the backup file to any directory you want. Let's have a look at this.

Time for action - restoring the Cacti config.php file

Since you've a backup of the Cacti database, you can also restore a single file using the following steps.

1. Log on to your system.
2. Change to the /tmp directory:

   ```
   cd /tmp
   ```

3. Create a directory named cactirestore and change to that directory:

   ```
   mkdir cactirestore
   cd cactirestore
   ```

4. Extract the backup file to the cactirestore directory:

   ```
   tar -xzvpf /backup/cacti_files_20170608.tgz
   ```

5. Check the tmp directory for the existence of the etc, var and usr directories:

   ```
   ls -l
   ```

6. The following screenshot displays the existence and permissions on these directories:

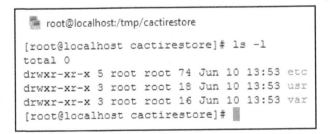

7. Change to the Cacti directory under `var`:

```
cd var/www/html/cacti/
```

8. Use the `pwd` command to check if you are in the correct directory:

```
[root@localhost cacti]# pwd
/tmp/cactirestore/var/www/html/cacti
```

9. Copy the `config.php` file from the `include` directory to you existing Cacti installation:

```
cp include/config.php /var/www/html/cacti/include
```

10. The following screenshot shows you the process including the confirmation request before overwriting the `config.php` file:

```
root@localhost:/tmp/cactirestore/var/www/html/cacti              —   □   ✕

[root@localhost cactirestore]# cd var/www/html/cacti/
[root@localhost cacti]# pwd
/tmp/cactirestore/var/www/html/cacti
[root@localhost cacti]# cp include/config.php /var/www/html/cacti/include
cp: overwrite â/var/www/html/cacti/include/config.phpâ? y
[root@localhost cacti]#
```

11. Change to the root directory and delete the temporary restore location:

```
cd /
rm -rf /tmp/cactirestore
```

What just happened?

You just restored your `config.php` file from a backup. You can use this method to restore any file from your backup archive, such as corrupted RRD files or data queries you may have accidentally deleted.

Log file management

Cacti is able to create a log file with information on what it is doing but depending on the log settings, this log file can become huge and can stop Cacti from working properly. Therefore, you will need to introduce some log file management.

Fortunately, Cacti now comes with an included logrotate functionality. This feature is able to manage the log file on the system but is not enabled by default. Let's look at how you can configure it to manage your Cacti logs.

Time for action - configuring logrotate

The following steps will show you how to configure the new logrotate functionality within Cacti:

1. Log on to the Cacti web interface using an admin account.
2. Go to the **Configuration** section and click on the **Settings** link.
3. Click on the **Paths** tab to the top and look at the **Logging** section:

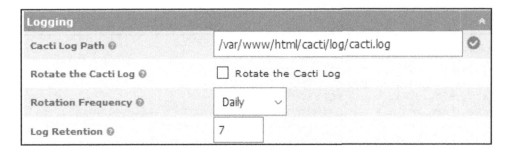

4. To enable the log rotation, hit the checkbox next to **Rotate the Cacti Log** and select **Daily** from the drop-down.
5. Keep all other setting to their default values and hit the **Save** button at the bottom of the screen.

What just happened?

You just enabled the automated log file rotation. Cacti will now rotate the log file daily and keep the last seven log files. This will make sure that your log file is not exceeding any file size limits or filling up your file system.

Cacti maintenance

You have now learned how to perform some general maintenance tasks for making backups and managing the Cacti log file. Let's look into some more specific Cacti maintenance tasks.

List RRD files with no associated host

After running a Cacti installation for some time, data items and files may get orphaned as you delete and re-create graphs. Let's check for the common issue of left-over RRD files. Cacti 1.x does provide some help with managing these orphaned files through the web-interface.

Time for action - finding orphaned RRD files

The following steps shows you how to enable the automatic RRD files cleanup:

1. Log on to the Cacti web interface using an admin account.
2. Go to the **Configuration** section and click on the **Settings** link.
3. Go to **Paths** and look at the **RRD Cleaner** section:

4. Enable the checkbox next the **RRDFile Auto Clean**.
5. A new drop-down will appear. Keep that to **Delete** and hit the **Save** button.
6. Next, go to the **Management** section and click on the **Data Sources** link.

7. Select **Orphaned** from the drop-down box from the **Orphaned** section:

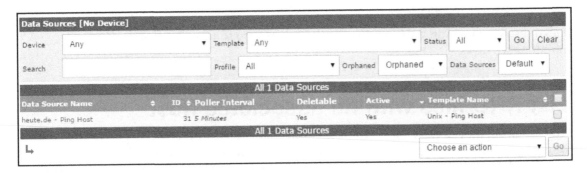

8. Select all the data sources you want to delete, then select **Delete** from the drop-down box at the bottom and hit **Go.**

9. After confirming your selection, the orphaned RRD files should be gone.

What just happened?

You have used the new user interface feature from Cacti to find unused RRD files which can be removed from the file system.

A short overview of the Cacti CLI functionality

As you've learned in previous chapters, Cacti comes with several CLI scripts suitable for some of Cacti's maintenance tasks. The CLI scripts can be found in the cli directory of base Cacti installation.

The cli directory contains two repair scripts which you may want to use in case of database corruption or template errors and you do not want to lose all the configuration data since your last backup.

Repairing templates

It may happen that some of the data or graph templates have errors. You can then try to repair these templates by using the `repair_templates.php` script. Issue the following command to check for errors. Using the `-execute` parameter will try to fix any errors shown:

```
cd /var/www/html/cacti/cli
php repair_templates.php
```

The following output will be shown on a working system:

```
cactiuser@localhost:/var/www/html/cacti/cli
[cactiuser@localhost cli]$ php repair_templates.php
NOTE: Performing Check of Templates
NOTE: Performing Check of Data Templates
NOTE: No Damaged Data Templates Found
NOTE: Performing Check of Graph Templates
NOTE: No Damaged Graph Templates Found
[cactiuser@localhost cli]$
```

Repairing the database

Cacti also provides a repair utility for checking and repairing the database structure. Using the `repair_database.php` script may save you from restoring an older database backup. In the event that you have database issues, this script should be run in order to check for any database issues. The script combines several tasks, which include calling the REPAIR TABLE statement on the tables, as well as deleting orphaned datasets when being called with the `--force` parameter:

```
cd /var/www/html/cacti/cli
php repair_database.php
```

The following output will be shown on a working system:

```
cactiuser@localhost:/var/www/html/cacti/cli
[cactiuser@localhost cli]$ php repair_database.php
Repairing All Cacti Database Tables
Repairing Table -> 'aggregate_graph_templates' Successful
Repairing Table -> 'aggregate_graph_templates_graph' Successful
Repairing Table -> 'aggregate_graph_templates_item' Successful
Repairing Table -> 'aggregate_graphs' Successful
Repairing Table -> 'aggregate_graphs_graph_item' Successful
Repairing Table -> 'aggregate_graphs_items' Successful
Repairing Table -> 'automation_devices' Successful
Repairing Table -> 'automation_graph_rule_items' Successful
Repairing Table -> 'automation_graph_rules' Successful
Repairing Table -> 'automation_ips' Successful
```

Pop quiz - a few questions about Chapter 6

1. Where do you add a new scheduled task?

   a) To the `config.php` file of Cacti
   b) The `/etc/tasks` file
   c) To a new file in the `/etc/cron.d` directory

2. What MySQL/MariaDB command will you need to run after a full restore on a newly installed system?

   a) `mysql -u cactiuser -p cacti import cacti_database_20170608.sql`
   b) `mysql -u cactiuser -p cacti restore cacti_database_20170608.sql`
   c) `mysql -u cactiuser -p cacti < cacti_database_20170608.sql`

3. What file do you need to change if you want to have the automated backup run at 22:00 each day?

   a) `/etc/tasks`
   b) `/etc/cron.d/cacti`
   c) `/etc/cron.d/cactiBackup`

Summary

You should now be able to create automated backups of your Cacti installation as well as do some basic maintenance work.

You have created an automated database and file backup and learned which files are needed to create a complete Cacti backup along with all important files. Using this backup, you have performed a restore of the database as well as single files. As the Cacti logs grow constantly, you have configured the integrated log file rotation feature of Cacti to create daily log files. You've also looked at the process of checking for orphaned RRD files and how to delete these. Finally, by using the Cacti repair utilities, you have seen how to utilize these CLI scripts for repairing templates and the database.

You should now be able to perform some basic Cacti maintenance tasks. In the next chapter, you're going to learn how to retrieve performance data from network devices and servers using various methods.

Network and Server Monitoring

Let's now look at how you set up the different devices to be monitored by Cacti. In this chapter, you'll learn how to set up some Cisco devices and prepare Windows systems to be monitored using WMI.

In this chapter we are going to:

- Provide a short overview of device monitoring
- Describe the setup of Cisco network devices
- Configure a VMware ESX server
- Prepare a Windows system for WMI monitoring

Let's start!

An introduction to network and server monitoring

The main task of Cacti is to measure the performance of network devices and SNMP capable servers. With some add-ons, Cacti is also able to monitor WMI enabled Windows hosts. So, let's first look at the different options you have in more detail.

Network devices

Most business-class network devices are SNMP capable and therefore can be monitored by Cacti. For security reasons, SNMP access should be limited to the network management stations only using an access list. The most common performance values measured on a network device are inbound and outbound traffic of network ports and the CPU utilization of the device itself. There are many more performance items available, depending on specific capabilities of the network device.

VMware ESX

During the past years, more and more physical servers have been converted to virtual machines, using one of the available virtualization platforms available. VMware's main hypervisor offering is ESXi, and it can be configured to allow SNMP-based performance measurement of the host and guest systems. In general, it is always better to do performance measurements of the guest systems directly, because you get platform specific numbers and features which are not available through a plain SNMP monitoring of the ESXi system.

Linux server

By default, most Linux servers come with a SNMP daemon for performance monitoring. This daemon can be configured to not only provide the basic network statistics, but also provide information by executing external programs.

Windows WMI monitoring

Performance measurement of Windows systems can be achieved by either enabling the SNMP service or by using WMI. WMI provides a common method for applications to provide performance statistics, so this is what you will use.

Monitoring a network device

Let's look at the configuration of a Cisco Switch and PIX firewall device. You will learn how to secure the SNMP communication to the Cisco devices by using access lists and specifically defining the Cacti server as a trusted communication partner. The configuration will only deal with SNMPv2.

Configuring SNMP access on Cisco Switch

In order to configure and secure SNMP communication between the network device and your Cacti server, you will need to know its IP address or network range. For the following examples, let's assume that your Cacti server has the IP address `10.40.0.161` and the network range of your network management systems is `10.40.0.0/255.255.255.0`. Look at the following access list and SNMP commands:

```
access-list 80 remark /*****************************************
access-list 80 remark SNMP RO authorized servers
access-list 80 remark *****************************************/
access-list 80 permit 10.40.0.161
access-list 80 permit 10.40.0.0 0.0.0.255
access-list 80 deny   any
access-list 83 remark /*****************************************
access-list 83 remark SNMP RW authorized servers
access-list 83 remark *****************************************/
access-list 83 permit 10.40.0.161
access-list 83 permit 10.40.0.0 0.0.0.255
access-list 83 deny   any
!
snmp-server community public RO 80
snmp-server community private RW 83
snmp-server location EMEA/GERMANY/Kressbronn/BA/+1/
snmp-server contact +49 0123 456789/IT-Group
```

The commands define two access lists, one for accessing the read-only community and one for the read-write community of the device. The `remark` statements define some comments which will be displayed when looking at the device configuration.

The `snmp-server` commands assign the previously defined access lists to the different SNMP community strings. They also define some basic information like the location string and contact information for the device. The location and contact information string will be shown in Cacti when adding the device.

Time for action - setup SNMP on Cisco devices

Let's now look at how to add the above configuration to the device.

1. Log on to your network device.
2. Go into enable mode using following command:

   ```
   enable
   ```

3. Go into configure mode:

   ```
   configure terminal
   ```

4. Copy and paste or manually enter the previously listed.
5. Press *Ctrl + Z*.
6. Save the configuration:

   ```
   write mem
   ```

7. View the current configuration:

   ```
   sh run
   ```

What just happened?

You just configured a Cisco network device to allow SNMP polls from your Cacti server. You also setup access lists to limit the hosts that are allowed to poll the device using SNMP.

Adding Cisco Switch to Cacti

Now that you have configured the SNMP agent of the device, you can now add it to Cacti.

Time for action - adding a Cisco Switch to Cacti

You can take the following steps to add the Cisco Switch to Cacti.

1. Go to **Management** and click on **Devices**.
2. Click the **Add** link in the top-right corner.
3. Enter the hostname and **Description** of your Cisco device.

4. Select **Cisco Router** as the **Device Template**:

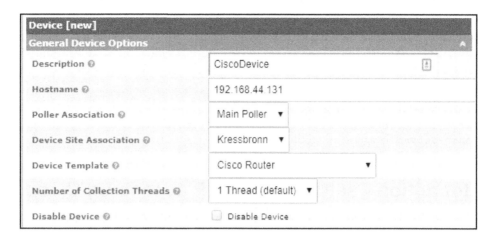

5. Select **Version 2** for the **SNMP Version** and enter the community name of your Cisco device.
6. Click **Save** at the bottom:

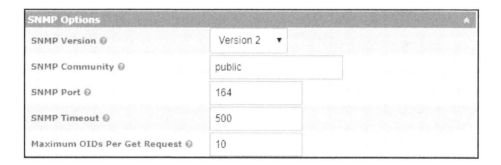

What just happened?

You just added your newly configured Cisco device to Cacti. You can now go on and monitor the different network interfaces and other statistics available on the device.

Configuring SNMP access on a Cisco PIX firewall

Cisco PIX Firewalls have some useful information on network performance and number of connections in use on the firewall. The following commands will enable a PIX firewall to be polled from a specific host. Each host needs to be entered separately, as there's no range command available on the PIX firewall:

```
snmp-server host inside 10.27.0.181
snmp-server location EMEA/Germany/Kressbronn/FW/+1/
snmp-server contact +49 0123 456789/IT-Group
snmp-server community public
```

Time for action - setting up SNMP access on Cisco PIX

Using the following steps enables the SNMP access on your Cisco PIX device.

1. Log on to your network device.
2. Go into enable mode:

   ```
   enable
   ```

3. Go into configure mode:

   ```
   configure terminal
   ```

4. Copy and paste or manually enter the previously listed.
5. Press *Ctrl + Z*.
6. Save the configuration:

   ```
   write mem
   ```

7. View the current configuration:

   ```
   sh run
   ```

What just happened?

You just configured a Cisco PIX firewall device to allow SNMP polls from your Cacti server.

Adding Cisco PIX firewall to Cacti

As with most host types, Cisco PIX devices aren't included as a host template with the base install of Cacti. If you don't have a host template yet, either go to the template repository on the Cacti site or download the Cisco PIX template from this book which has been tested against a Cisco PIX Firewall Version 6.3(5). For the next few steps, let's assume you're using the version from this book.

Time for action - adding a Cisco PIX firewall to Cacti

Let's go through the different tasks involved to add the Cisco PIX firewall templates and device to Cacti:

1. Download the `cacti_host_template_pix_firewall.xml` file.
2. Log in to Cacti as an admin user.
3. Go to **Import/Export** and click on the **Import Templates** link.
4. Select the downloaded file in the **Import Template from Local File Box**.
5. Click on the **Import** button:

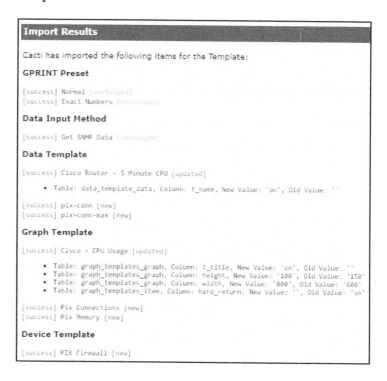

6. Go to **Management** and click on **Devices**.
7. Click the **Add** link in the top right corner.
8. Enter the `hostname` and **Description** of your Cisco PIX firewall.
9. Select **PIX Firewall** as the host template.
10. Select **Version 2** for the **SNMP Version** and enter the community name of your Windows system.
11. Click on the **Create** button.

What just happened?

You've just imported the Cisco PIX firewall template and used it during device creation. You can now select the different graphs and poll performance data from your PIX firewall.

Monitoring VMware ESX servers

The monitoring of VMware, or any other kind of virtualization servers, is as important as the guests running on it. Unlike with normal systems, performance problems on the virtualization hosts will affect many more systems and applications, therefore knowing the current, past, and possible future state of the host's performance is of great importance.

Preparing the SNMP access for VMware ESXi 6/6.5

To setup SNMP access on a VMware ESXi server, you'll need to have the SSH server enabled. On previous versions (VMWare ESXi 3.5 and Version 4), enabling the SNMP service was done through the VMware SDK. Later versions allow you to enable the SNMP service using the ESXCLI on the VMware host itself. If you have physical access to the VMware ESXi server, you do not need the SSH service to be enabled.

Time for action - enabling SSH access on a ESXi 6/6.5 server

The following steps will guide your through the process of enabling the SSH access on your VMware server:

1. Log in to the web-based VMware Management Console:

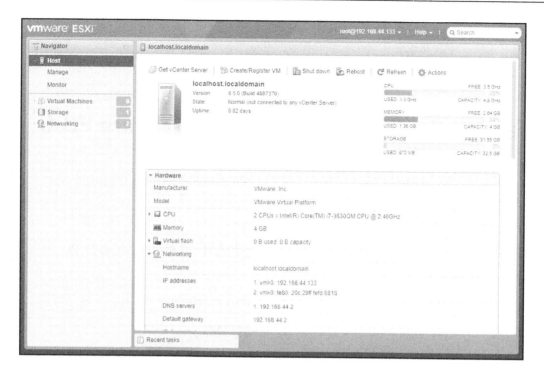

2. Go to the **Manage** section:

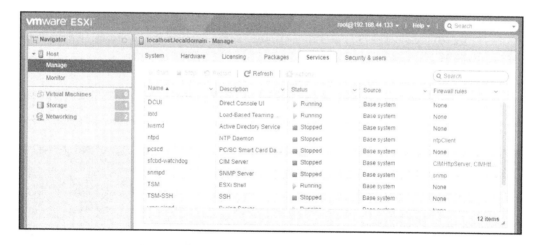

3. Select the **TSM-SSH** service and hit the **Start** button at the top.

What just happened?

You just enabled the SSH service in order to connect to your VMWare ESXi system remotely. Using the ESXCLI, you can now go ahead and enable the SNMP agent.

Enabling the SNMP service on a VMware ESXi 6/6.5 server

Now that you have enabled the SSH service, you can proceed with configuring and enabling the SNMP service of the VMware ESXi server.

Time for action - enabling the SNMP service on a VMware ESXi host

Now we can enable the SNMP service with the following steps:

1. Log on to your VMware ESXi server using SSH.
2. Execute the following commands:

```
esxcli system snmp set --communities public
esxcli system snmp set --enable true
esxcli network firewall ruleset set --ruleset-id snmp --allowed-all
true
esxcli network firewall ruleset set --ruleset-id snmp --enabled
true
/etc/init.d/snmpd restart
```

The following screen will be presented after executing the preceding commands:

```
192.168.44.133 - KiTTY                                                    —    □    ×
[root@localhost:~] esxcli system snmp set --communities public
[root@localhost:~] esxcli system snmp set --enable true
[root@localhost:~] esxcli network firewall ruleset set --ruleset-id snmp --allowed-all true
Already allowed all ip
[root@localhost:~] esxcli network firewall ruleset set --ruleset-id snmp --enabled true
[root@localhost:~] /etc/init.d/snmpd restart
root: snmpd Running from interactive shell, running command: esxcli system snmp set -e false.
root: snmpd setting up resource reservations.
root: snmpd opening firewall port(s) for notifications.
root: snmpd watchdog for snmpd started.
[root@localhost:~]
```

3. Go back to the VMware Management Console and start the **snmpd** service on there as well:

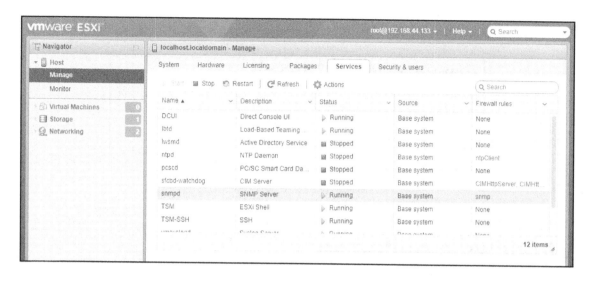

What just happened?

You just configured and enabled the SNMP agent on a VMware ESXi 6/6.5 server using the vSphere CLI.

Adding VMware ESX servers to Cacti

Now that you have enabled the SNMP agent on your ESX server, you can proceed with adding it to Cacti. There are some templates available on the Cacti website which work for version 5.5 of ESXi and later. They can be used to monitor the overall status of your ESXi server.

Time for action - adding a VMware ESX host to Cacti

Let's go through the steps of adding the VMware server to your Cacti system

1. Go to **Management** and click **Devices**.
2. Click the **Add** link in the top-right corner.
3. Enter the `hostname` and **Description** of your ESX server.

4. Select **Version 2** for **the SNMP Version** and enter the community name of your VMware ESX system.

5. Click the **Create** button:

6. You'll see the SNMP information on top showing the ESX version:

```
VmwareServer (192.168.44.133)

SNMP Information
System:VMware ESXi 6.5.0 build-4887370 VMware, Inc. x86_64
Uptime: 290835700 (33 days, 15 hours, 52 minutes)
Hostname:localhost.localdomain
Location:
Contact:
```

A sample SNMP output from a VMware 6.5 ESXi Server

Windows monitoring

There are several ways by which you can monitor a Windows host:

- Retrieving data using SNMP
- Retrieving data using WMI
- Collecting data with Windows PowerShell commands (for example, using the remote SSH command execution method)

Let's look into the SNMP and WMI methods in more detail using a Windows 2008 R2 server.

Windows SNMP setup

On a new Windows Server 2012 R2 server, by default the SNMP service is not installed. In order for Cacti to poll this server, you will need to enable this feature.

Time for action - enabling the SNMP server feature

Let's go through the steps to enable the SNMP service on your Windows server:

1. Log on to your Windows system as an administrator.
2. Go to **Control Panel** then to **Administrative Tools**.

3. Start the **Server Manager** and click on the **Add roles and features** link:

4. In the new window on the feature step, select the **SNMP features** as shown in the next image. Depending on your installation type or system setup, it may already be installed:

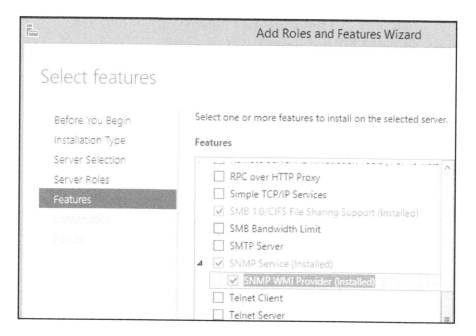

5. Click on **Next** , then on **Install**.
6. When the installation is finished, close the window and reboot the server.

What just happened?

You just installed and enabled the SNMP service on Windows. After rebooting, you'll be able to set security settings like community and allowed management stations. Changing these settings is your next step.

Configuration of the Windows SNMP service

After the installation of the SNMP feature, you'll not be able to poll the system for any performance data, because the default settings only allow the localhost system to access the SNMP service.

Time for action - configuring the Windows SNMP service

You'll now set some basic properties and add your Cacti server to the list of allowed hosts as well as configure a read-only community name for Cacti to use.

1. Log on to your Windows system as an administrator.
2. Go to **Start** then to **Administrative Tools** and click on **Services**.
3. Look for the **SNMP Service** and right-click on it.
4. Select **Properties** and make sure the **Startup type** is set to **Automatic**:

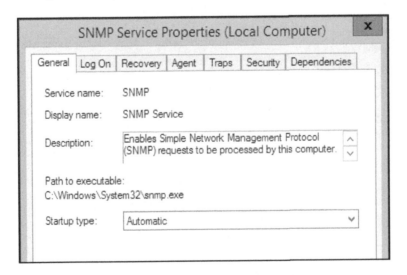

5. Select the **Agent** tab and enter the **Contact** and **Location** information:

6. Select the **Security** tab and add some community names and your Cacti servers IP address to the list at the bottom:

7. Click **Apply** then on **OK**.
8. Restart the SNMP service to activate the changes you made.

What just happened?

You just configured your Windows SNMP service. You can now add this Windows server to Cacti and start polling some of the basic SNMP information provided, like hard disk space and interface statistics.

WMI setup

WMI is secured by the normal Windows security methods; therefore, you'll need to create a dedicated WMI user and assign it the appropriate access rights to WMI. In this case, you're creating a local user account, but if the Windows server is part of an Active Directory domain it's possible to perform these steps (except 1-7) with a domain account.

Time for action - setting up a Windows WMI user

1. Log on to your windows system as an administrator.
2. Go to **Control Panel** then to **Administrative Tools** and double click **Computer Management**.
3. Click **Local Users and Groups** and click **Users**:

4. Click the **Action** menu and select **New User....**
5. Enter wmiuser as the **User name** and enter a password.

6. Set everything as shown in the following screenshot:

7. Click the **Create** button.
8. Edit the user and go to the **Member Of** tab.
9. Add the **Performance Log Users** and **Performance Monitor Users** group to the list:

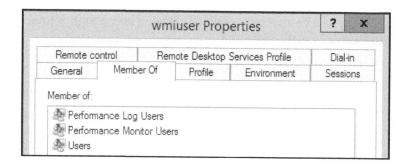

10. Click on **Apply** , then click **OK**.

11. In the left pane, expand the **Services and Applications** group and right click on **WMI Control**:

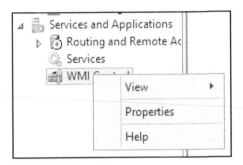

12. Select the **Properties** entry.

13. In the new dialog, click the **Security** tab and select **CIMV2** from the list:

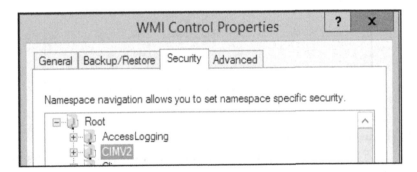

14. Click on the **Security** button.

15. Add the `wmiuser` you created earlier to the list and assign it **Enable Account** and **Remote Enable** permissions:

16. Click **Apply** and then click **OK**.
17. Now restart the Windows Management Instrumentation service in order to apply these changes.

What just happened?

You just added a user capable of doing remote WMI calls. You will be using this user to remotely poll performance data with the CactiWMI add-on from a Linux system.

> Make sure to enable WMI through the Windows Firewall. In contrast to the SNMP service, remote WMI request will not be allowed by default.

Installing the CactiWMI add-on

The WMI add-on available for Cacti provides a convenient data input method to access the WMI features provided by a Windows system. Let's move on and install it.

Installing the wmi.php Cacti interface

As already mentioned, the CactiWMI add-on comes with a script which is used by the different data input methods. The script needs to be placed in the appropriate directory and some minor configuration tasks need to be done.

The forum entry for the CactiWMI add-on can be found here:

```
http://forums.cacti.net/viewtopic.php?f=12t=30438
```

Time for action - installing the CactiWMI add-on - Part 1

Let's install the CactiWMI add-on on your Cacti server now:

1. Log on to your Cacti server.
2. Change to the /tmp directory:

   ```
   cd /tmp
   ```

3. Download the Cacti WMI add-on:

   ```
   wget -O CactiWMI.tgz
   http://forums.cacti.net/download/file.php?id=16949
   ```

4. Extract the files from the archive:

   ```
   tar -xzvf CactiWMI.tgz
   ```

5. Change into the created directory:

   ```
   cd 0.0.6.r101/
   ```

6. Run the following commands. They will copy the wmi.php script to the correct Cacti path, as well as creating the necessary directories. The chmod commands change the permissions of the files so Cacti is able to perform WMI calls:

   ```
   cp wmi.php /var/www/html/cacti/scripts
   mkdir -p /etc/cacti
   mkdir -p /var/log/cacti/wmi
   chown -R cactiuser:cactiuser /etc/cacti
   chown -R cactiuser:cactiuser /var/log/cacti/wmi
   chmod -R 700 /etc/cacti
   chmod -R 700 /var/log/cacti/wmi
   ```

7. Now create the `auth.conf` file which will contain your WMI user credentials:

   ```
   vi /etc/cacti/cactiwmi.pw
   ```

8. The file should have the following format:

   ```
   username=<your username>
   password=<your password>
   domain=<your domain>
   ```

What just happened?

You setup the files needed for the CactiWMI add-on. The `wmi.php` file provides the interface between Cacti and the program that talks to the WMI service on Windows servers.

Installing the wmic command

The `wmic` command is responsible for communication with the WMI service and is utilized by the `wmi.php` script.

Time for action - installing the CactiWMI add-on - Part 2

In this section, you will install the required the `wmic` command in order to poll the WMI interface on a Windows Server.

1. Log on to your Linux Cacti server with root privileges.
2. Download the latest version of the source files containing the `wmic` command:

   ```
   wget
   http://www6.atomicorp.com/channels/atomic/centos/7/x86_64/RPMS/wmi-
   1.3.14-4.el7.art.x86_64.rpm
   ```

3. Install the file:

   ```
   yum install wmi-1.3.14-4.el7.art.x86_64.rpm
   ```

4. Check where the `wmic` binary has been installed to:

   ```
   which wmic
   ```

5. Update the file `/var/www/html/cacti/scripts/wmi.php` to match the new path:

   ```
   $wmiexe = '/usr/bin/wmic'; // executable for the wmic command
   ```

What just happened?

You compiled the `wmic` binary which is needed to poll the WMI service of Windows systems. You've made sure that it compiled properly by running it with the version switch. You also copied the binary to a directory in your path.

Performance measurement with CactiWMI

Now you have all the pre-requirements for retrieving performance data using the WMI and SNMP interface.

Time for action - measuring performance with CactiWMI

Let's look into setting up a host with WMI:

1. Download the `cacti_host_template_wmi_-_all.xml` file from `https://github.com/neclimdul/CactiWMI/tree/master/templates`.
2. Log in to Cacti as an admin user.
3. Go to **Import/Export** and click on **Import Templates**.
4. Select the downloaded file for the **Import Template from Local File** box.
5. Click on **Import**:

```
Import Results

Cacti has imported the following items for the Template:

CDEF

[success] WMI - Disk I/O [new]
[success] WMI - Disk Used [new]
[success] WMI - Percentage Ratio [new]
[success] WMI - Memory [new]


[success] Surf Control 5.5 - Session Stats (WMI) [new]
[success] Enterprise Vault 2007 - Awaiting Backup (WMI) [new]
[success] IIS - Request Statistics (WMI) [new]
[success] Windows - Redirector Commands (WMI) [new]
[success] IIS - Connections (WMI) [new]
[success] Exchange 2003 - Total Mailbox Items (WMI) [new]

Device Template

[success] WMI - All [new]
```

6. Go to **Management** and click on **Devices**.
7. Click on **Add** in the top-right corner.
8. Enter the `Hostname` and **Description** of your Windows Server.
9. Select **WMI - All** as the Device Template:

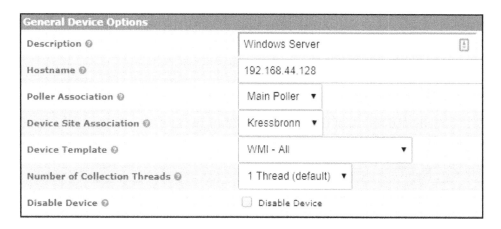

10. Select **Version 2** for the **SNMP Version** and enter the community name of your Windows system:

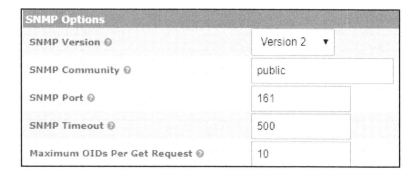

11. Click on **Create** at the bottom of the screen.

12. You'll now see some of the SNMP information you entered during the SNMP Service configuration:

```
Windows Server (192.168.44.128)
SNMP Information
System: Hardware: Intel64 Family 6 Model 58 Stepping 9 AT/AT COMPATIBLE -
Software: Windows Version 6.3 (Build 9600 Multiprocessor Free
Uptime: 296087 (0days, 0hours, 49minutes)
Hostname: WIN-TNQRTLT1R42
Location: EMEA/Germany/Kressbronn/DC/+1
Contact: +49 0123 456789/IT Group
```

13. You will also see all of the WMI-based data input methods currently associated with the selected host template:

Graph Template Name	Status	
1) Enterprise Vault 2007 - Awaiting Backup (WMI)	Not Being Graphed	✖
2) Exchange 2003 - Active Client Logons (WMI)	Not Being Graphed	✖
3) Exchange 2003 - Client RPC Latency (WMI)	Not Being Graphed	✖
4) Exchange 2003 - Database Performance (WMI)	Not Being Graphed	✖
28) Windows - Process Stats - Memory (WMI)	Not Being Graphed	✖
29) Windows - Processes (WMI)	Not Being Graphed	✖
30) Windows - Processor Queue Length (WMI)	Not Being Graphed	✖
31) Windows - Redirector Commands (WMI)	Not Being Graphed	✖
32) Windows - System Calls (WMI)	Not Being Graphed	✖

14. Click the **Create Graphs for this Host** link at the top.

15. Select some of the basic WMI graphs:
    1. Create: Windows - Available Disk Space (WMI).
    2. Create: Windows - CPU Usage - 1CPU (WMI).
    3. Create: Windows - Disk I/O (WMI).
    4. Create: Windows - Memory Usage (WMI).
    5. Create: Windows - Processes (WMI).

16. Click on the **Create** button. You will see the specific settings for each of the WMI graphs:

17. Confirm the settings on the following page and click on **Create**.

What just happened?

You just enabled WMI-based performance polling through Cacti. You can also configure some interface polling, by adding the **SNMP - Interface Statistics** dataquery to the **Associated Data Queries** list, as you've seen in previous chapters. Don't forget to add your new host to one of your Cacti trees.

Linux monitoring

Let's look into the SNMP configuration in more detail.

Linux SNMP setup

The net-snmp package is providing the required snmp daemon. During the installation of Cacti in Chapter 1, *Installing Cacti* you have installed this package already on your Cacti system.

Time for action - enabling SNMP on a Linux server

Let's look into configuring the SNMP access on your Cacti server:

1. Install net-snmpd if you have not done so already:

   ```
   yum install -y net-snmp
   ```

2. Now, edit the /etc/snmpd/snmpd.conf file:

   ```
   vi /etc/snmpd/snmpd.conf
   ```

3. Look for the following lines showing the default values on a CentOS 7 system:

```
####
# First, map the community name "public" into a "security name"

#          sec.name   source              community
com2sec notConfigUser  default            public

####
# Second, map the security name into a group name:

#          groupName          securityModel securityName
group    notConfigGroup v1                notConfigUser
group    notConfigGroup v2c               notConfigUser

####
# Third, create a view for us to let the group have rights to:

# Make at least  snmpwalk -v 1 localhost -c public system fast again.
#          name              incl/excl      subtree          mask(optional)
view     systemview    included   .1.3.6.1.2.1.1
view     systemview    included   .1.3.6.1.2.1.25.1.1

####
# Finally, grant the group read-only access to the systemview view.

#          group             context sec.model sec.level prefix read    write  notif
access   notConfigGroup ""         any          noauth    exact  systemview none none
```

4. As this will provide access to a limited part of the SNMP tree, you will have to change the view lines to the following:

```
# Make at least  snmpwalk -v 1 localhost -c public system fast again.
#          name              incl/excl      subtree          mask(optional)
view     systemview    included   .1
#view     systemview    included   .1.3.6.1.2.1.25.1.1
```

5. Now, restart the `snmp` daemon and make sure to enable it on system start:

```
systemctl enable snmpd
systemctl start snmpd
```

What just happened?

You have installed and configured the snmpd daemon of a Linux system. By enabling and starting it, you will now be able to poll information from this system.

Pop quiz - a few questions about Chapter 7

1. What do you need to use to configure the SNMP daemon on a ESXi 6.5 vSphere host?

   a) A SSH client
   b) The system management tool for the ESXi system
   c) The vSphere CLI client

2. How do you create a new graph with WMI performance items?

   a) Add the imported WMI graph template to the device
   b) Add a WMI data query to the device
   c) Add a SNMP community to the device

3. What do you need to edit when you change the password of the WMI user ID?

   a) `cactiwmi.pw` in `/etc/cacti`
   b) `config.php` in the include directory of the Cacti base directory
   c) `/etc/passwd`

Summary

You now have several guides at hand to configure your network devices, Windows servers and VMware ESX servers. Each of the different systems requires different methods and configuration tasks in order to poll the performance data.

Using the topics from this chapter, you are now able to configure Cisco based network and firewall devices to allow SNMP polling from Cacti. You have also learned how to set up and enable the SNMP daemon on VMware ESX 6/6.5 servers and looked into enabling the WMI polling feature for Windows servers.

You should now be able to extend your performance polling to a much broader range of systems including Windows servers and VMware ESX systems.

In the next chapter, you will be looking into the integrated Plugin Architecture of Cacti and how to install and configure new plugins.

8

Plugin Architecture

Now that you have learned about the basic Cacti features, you are ready to learn how to extend the capabilities of your Cacti instance with the available plugin architecture.

In this chapter, we are going to:

- Provide a short overview of the plugin architecture
- Configure the plugin architecture
- Learn how to extend Cacti with plugins
- Allow users to use the extended features of plugins

Let's start!

Introduction to the plugin architecture

Since Cacti 0.8.8, the plugin architecture has been an integrated part of Cacti. It extends the basic functionality of Cacti with the ability to call external functions and applications, also called plugins. In Cacti 1.x, several plugins have already been integrated into the core functionality such as, Thold, Aggregate, and Realtime.

Why plugins?

Plugins allow other external developers to implement open source and commercial features for Cacti without the need to change the core Cacti sources. Security patches for the core can also be safely applied without interfering with the functionality of the plugins.

Plugins allow end users to implement missing features or create specific enhancements needed for internal corporate use.

Plugin features

As already mentioned, plugins can have different functionalities. The following is a list of features implemented by some of the available plugins:

- **User interface enhancements**: For example, re-branding the login screen
- **Accessing the Cacti database**: Interaction with external tools
- **Manipulate RRD files**: Removing spikes from the graphs
- **Implementing caching/performance enhancements**: Providing support for very large Cacti deployments
- **Adding new functionality**: Such as reporting, syslog, or MAC tracking capabilities

As you can see, plugins can extend the functionality of Cacti beyond performance monitoring to a powerful, integrated network monitoring solution.

Common plugins

As there is quite a large list of plugins, not all of them are actively supported or still under development. Some of the plugins are quite old and are commonly known throughout the Cacti community. The following are some short descriptions of three well-known plugins.

MAC Track plugin

The MAC Track plugin adds MAC address tracking functionality to Cacti. It is able to track end devices based on their IP and/or MAC address and can help track down the root cause of, for example, virus attacks. If you do have a large network and need to know the location of your devices, this plugin is worth looking at.

Network Weathermap

The Network Weathermap plugin adds the ability to create your own network map to Cacti. Using this plugin, you can create building, site, or data center rack maps including graphical representations of link utilization and performance. The Network Weathermap plugin can create stunning graphs that tell a story in a single, easy to understand picture. Go and have a look at the *Show off your Weathermaps* thread in the forum: `https://forums.cacti.net/viewtopic.php?t=24433`.

Thold

Thold adds threshold monitoring and alerting to Cacti. Thresholds can be set on any kind of data stored within the RRD files, whether fixed thresholds or dynamic thresholds based on an automatic baseline calculation. Email alerts can be configured to be sent out to one or more recipients.

You will be installing and configuring the Thold plugin in the next chapter.

Configuring the plugin architecture

Once you have installed Cacti 1.x, you can assign the specific realm permissions to users who you want to allow.

Time for action - configuring the plugin architecture

Let's enable the access to the Plugin Management page for a user:

1. Log on to your Cacti web interface as an admin user.
2. Go to **Configuration | Users**.
3. Select the user who you want to allow to administer plugins.
4. Click on the **Permissions** tab.

5. Now select the **Plugin Management** box within the **System Administration** section:

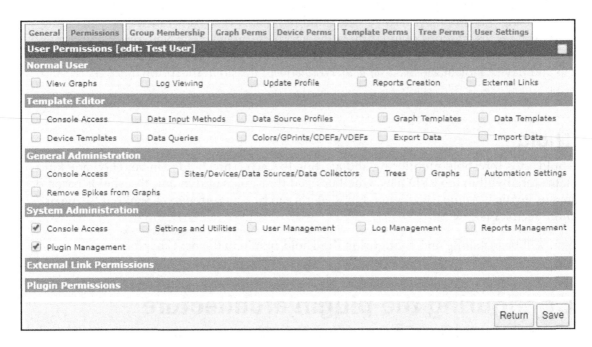

6. Click on the **Save** button.
7. The user should now notice a new menu called **Plugin Management** within the **Configuration** section:

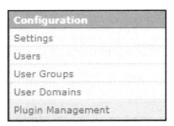

8. Click on the **Plugin Management** menu entry.

9. You will see a list of installed plugins. At the moment, this list should be empty, as shown in the following screenshot:

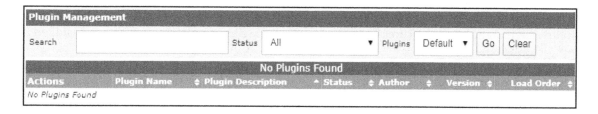

What just happened?

You just added permissions to install, enable, disable, and uninstall plugins to a user. By default, only the admin user will have this permission, so for any other user, you will have to provide this permission in order for them to be able to manage plugins.

Downloading and installing plugins

Now that you have successfully installed the plugin architecture, you can now go on and install some basic plugins. The plugins available can be divided into two categories: Plugins which that been created for Cacti 0.8.x, and plugins that are compatible with Cacti 1.x.

Cacti 1.x does not support any plugins created for previous versions of Cacti.

Plugin architecture (PIA) directory structure

Plugins have their own sub-directory within the Cacti directory tree. This special directory is named `plugins`.

Each plugin needs to be placed into this directory. The following files are needed as a minimum for each plugin to work properly:

- `setup.php`
- `index.php`
- `INFO`

The `index.php` file only contains a redirection to the main Cacti site in order to stop end users from browsing the plugin directory freely. The `setup.php` file contains the setup and enablement code, as well as code for the different plugin hooks. The `INFO` file contains the version of the plugin, as well as some additional descriptions and information. The following image shows the directory structure of the `plugins` directory with one installed plugin:

```
root@localhost:/var/www/html...          —    □    ×
[root@localhost plugins]# tree
.
├── gexport
│   ├── functions.php
│   ├── gexport.php
│   ├── INFO
│   ├── LICENSE
│   ├── locales
│   │   ├── index.php
│   │   ├── LC_MESSAGES
│   │   │   └── index.php
│   │   ├── po
│   │   │   └── cacti.pot
│   │   └── update-pot.sh
│   ├── poller_export.php
│   ├── README.md
│   ├── setup.php
│   └── website.template
└── index.php

4 directories, 13 files
[root@localhost plugins]#
```

Pre-Cacti 1.x plugins

Cacti 1.x changed the plugin architecture, which made all previous plugins written for the 0.8 versions incompatible with Cacti 1.x. Most plugins require only a small change to make them compatible with Cacti 1.x, but other plugins, such as Weathermap or CereusReporting, require a large amount of re-work. As several plugins have been abandoned over time, some old plugins will never be made available for Cacti 1.x.

Pre-Pia 2.x and Pia 2.x plugins

As mentioned, Cacti 1.x contains a completely new plugin architecture. Most of the pre-Pia 2.x plugins have been upgraded to the 2.x version, which didn't require the use of the `$plugin[]` array in order to enable plugins. PIA 1.x existed up until 0.8.7c and was replaced with PIA 2.x in Cacti 0.8.7g.

PIA 2.x enabled the admin user to install and activate plugins through the web console. PIA 3.x was then integrated into Cacti 0.8.8, still providing backwards compatibility to PIA 1.x plugins.

Old plugins for PIA 1.x, 2.x ,and 3.x do not run on Cacti 1.x anymore.

The plugin repository

Since the announcement and public availability of Cacti 1.x, a new plugin repository has been created on GitHub for officially supported plugins. Other plugins provided by third-party developers are still available from the old plugin repository on the Cacti webpage.

The new plugin repository for officially supported Cacti 1.x plugins is available at: `https://github.com/Cacti`.

Plugin requirements

The actual Cacti version requirements for the individual plugins can change frequently. You can check the compatibility by looking into the INFO file and checking the `compat` line, which defines the minimum Cacti version required.

The following screenshot shows a limited list of the available plugins and some information about the plugins from the old plugin repository:

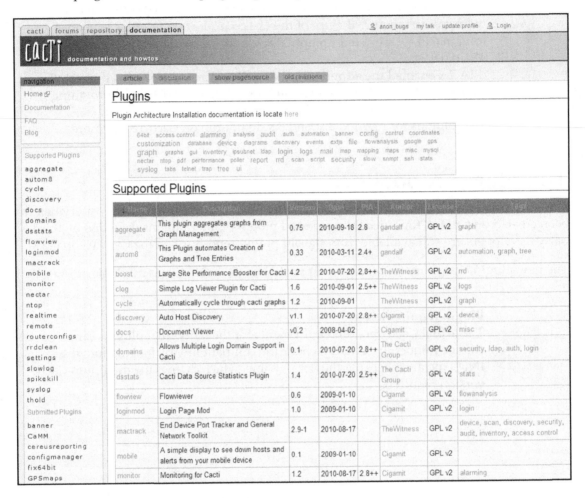

The old plugin repository can be found at the following webpage:

```
http://docs.cacti.net/plugins
```

The Graph Export (gexport) plugin

The gexport plugin replaces the integrated graph export functionality of Cacti. The core team decided to move this functionality to its own plugin as it was not used widely. As it's a basic plugin, we're going to use this one for exploring the basic installation process for plugins.

Time for action - installing the gexport plugin

The following steps show you how to install the gexport plugin:

1. Go to the plugins web page at: https://github.com/Cacti/plugin_gexport
2. Click on the **Clone or download** link.
3. Right-click on the **Download ZIP** link and copy the link target to the clipboard.
4. Log on to your Cacti installation as root using PuTTY.
5. Go to the new `plugins` directory using the following command:

   ```
   cd /var/www/html/cacti/plugins
   ```

6. Download the gexport plugin using the following command:

   ```
       wget -O gexport.zip
    https://github.com/Cacti/plugin_gexport/archive/develop.zip
   ```

7. Extract the archive:

   ```
   unzip gexport.zip
   ```

8. Rename the directory to the correct name of gexport:

   ```
   mv plugin_gexport-develop gexport
   ```

9. Log on to your Cacti web interface as a user with **Plugin Management** permissions.
10. Go to **Configuration | Plugin Management**.

11. You should now be able to see the gexport plugin in the list of available plugins, as shown in the following screenshot:

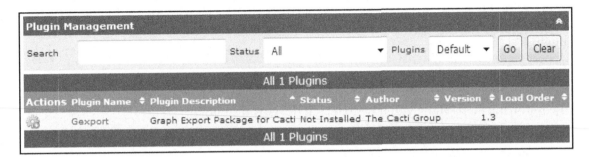

12. Click on the icon in the **Actions** column to install the plugin. The list of icons in the **Actions** column should change, as seen in the following screenshot:

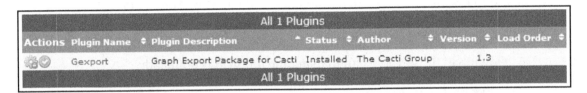

13. Click on the green icon in the **Actions** column to enable the plugin:

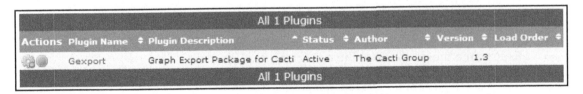

14. Now look at the **Utilities** section. You should see a new entry called **Graph Exports**. This entry is being provided by the gexport plugin:

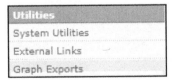

What just happened?

You just installed and enabled the gexport plugin. By enabling and installing the plugin, the plugin architecture ran the setup function of the plugin. This special function makes sure that all required files and database tables are created, and adds the necessary links to the hooks provided by the plugin architecture.

Removing a plugin

Sometimes you may just want to test a new plugin, and later decide to disable and remove it from your Cacti server. Let's look at the steps necessary to do so.

Time for action - removing the gexport plugin

Now that you have installed the gexport plugin, let's look at the steps required to remove it again.

1. Log on to your Cacti web interface as a user with **Plugin Management** permissions.
2. Go to **Configuration | Plugin Management**.
3. You should now be able to see the gexport plugin in the list of available plugins:

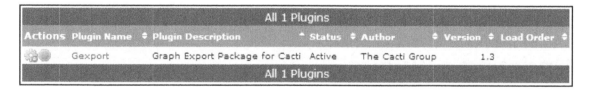

Actions	Plugin Name	Plugin Description	Status	Author	Version	Load Order
		All 1 Plugins				
	Gexport	Graph Export Package for Cacti	Active	The Cacti Group	1.3	
		All 1 Plugins				

4. Click on the red round icon in the **Actions** column to disable the plugin. The list of icons in the **Actions** column should change, as seen in the following screenshot:

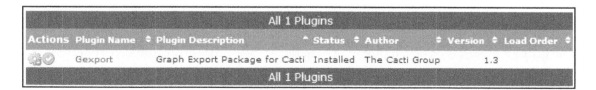

Actions	Plugin Name	Plugin Description	Status	Author	Version	Load Order
		All 1 Plugins				
	Gexport	Graph Export Package for Cacti	Installed	The Cacti Group	1.3	
		All 1 Plugins				

5. Click on the first gear icon in the **Actions** column to uninstall the plugin. You will see the default icon show up again:

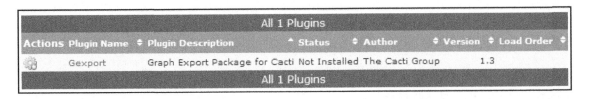

Actions	Plugin Name ⬍	Plugin Description	⬍ Status	⬍ Author	⬍ Version	⬍ Load Order ⬍
		All 1 Plugins				
🛠	Gexport	Graph Export Package for Cacti	Not Installed	The Cacti Group	1.3	
		All 1 Plugins				

6. Now log on to your Cacti installation as root using PuTTY.
7. Go to the `plugins` directory:

```
cd /var/www/html/cacti/plugins
```

8. Remove the `gexport` plugin using the following command:

```
rm -rf gexport
```

What just happened?

You successfully uninstalled and removed the gexport plugin from your Cacti installation. This will also remove any database tables or columns created. If a plugin used these tables to store data, then this data will be lost after the plugin is removed. Therefore, be careful when removing or disabling a plugin.

Updating a plugin

Now that you have learned how to add and remove a plugin in Cacti, what about the update of a plugin? The update of a plugin heavily depends on the plugin developer. In most cases, the update process simply involves extracting the new plugin and overwriting the existing files from the old plugin installation.

The plugin architecture provides some functionality to the plugin developer for checking for the existence of an older version and updating the old version accordingly.

The gexport plugin is one such plugin, where the update process only involves overwriting the existing files.

Before updating a plugin, make sure to read the readme files or ask within the specific plugin topics on the forum for help on the update process.

Adding plugin permissions

Some plugins add new realm permissions to the user management page. This allows you to grant access to one user group, but deny the usage of a plugin to another group. The following screenshot shows the new user realm permission **Export Cacti Graphs Settings** for the gexport plugin, which allows a specific user to configure automated graph export:

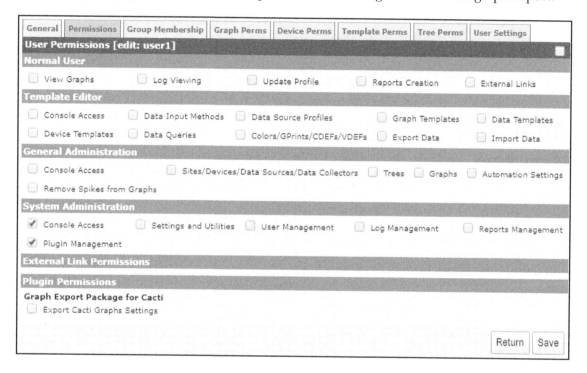

Pop quiz - a few questions about Chapter 8

1. What do you need to check if you are unable to see the **Plugin Management** link?

   a) The `config.php` file
   b) The Cacti log file
   c) The realm permissions of the user

2. How do you disable a plugin?

    a) Using the Plugin Management page
    b) Edit the `global.php` file
    c) Edit the `config.php` file

3. Which plugin should you use to find out where a specific computer is located?

    a) The Weathermap plugin
    b) The MAC Track plugin
    c) The Thold plugin

Summary

You now have successfully configured the PIA and are able to add new features and functionality to your Cacti instance using external plugins.

In this chapter, you have covered the different features and functionalities that plugins can provide. You have learned how to configure the plugin architecture and to provide access to plugin management for a specific user. You have walked through the different steps of installing, updating, and removing a plugin, as well as setting up specific plugin permissions for a user.

You should now be able to add other plugins and extend your Cacti installation with new features. In the following chapter, you will learn how plugins are structured and how to write your own plugin.

9
Plugins

Its integrated plugin architecture enables you to extend your Cacti installation by adding new functionality using the available plugins or by creating your own plugin.

In this chapter, we are going to:

- Provide an overview of general plugin design based on the cycle plugin
- Describe commonly used plugins
- Create our first plugin

Let's move on!

Plugin design

Let's look at how plugins communicate with Cacti and the plugin architecture.

The plugin architecture introduced several hooks into Cacti that can be used by plugins to:

- Display additional information
- Add functionality to a core Cacti function
- Manipulate data and graphs

Let's look at some of these hooks now.

Plugin hooks

Each plugin needs to register for a hook. Let's explore version 4.1 of the cycle plugin as it is one of the simpler plugins available.

> You can retrieve the latest version of the Cycle plugin from the following GitHub page:
>
> `https://github.com/Cacti/plugin_cycle`

Right at the top, the `setup.php` file contains the following function:

```
function plugin_cycle_install() {
  api_plugin_register_hook('cycle', 'top_header_tabs',
'cycle_show_tab',            'setup.php');
  api_plugin_register_hook('cycle', 'top_graph_header_tabs',
'cycle_show_tab',            'setup.php');
  api_plugin_register_hook('cycle', 'config_arrays',
'cycle_config_arrays',       'setup.php');
  api_plugin_register_hook('cycle', 'draw_navigation_text',
'cycle_draw_navigation_text', 'setup.php');
  api_plugin_register_hook('cycle', 'config_form',
'cycle_config_form',         'setup.php');
  api_plugin_register_hook('cycle', 'config_settings',
'cycle_config_settings',     'setup.php');
  api_plugin_register_hook('cycle', 'api_graph_save',
'cycle_api_graph_save',      'setup.php');
  api_plugin_register_hook('cycle', 'page_head',
'cycle_page_head',           'setup.php');
  api_plugin_register_realm('cycle', 'cycle.php,cycle_ajax.php', __('Plugin
-> Cycle Graphs', 'cycle'), 1);
  cycle_setup_table_new ();
}
```

This is the `install` function. It is called when you hit the **Install** button in the plugin management screen. As you can see, it calls the special `api_plugin_register_hook` function. This function registers some of the plugin functions with the plugin architecture hooks. Let us look into the `cycle_config_settings` and `cycle_show_tab` functions.

Plugin settings

Each plugin can have its own settings. Settings are normally used to let end users add special information needed for the plugin to work. In the case of the cycle plugin, this includes the export method, the frequency of the export, and many other settings.

The cycle_config_settings function

The `cycle_config_settings` function uses the special `config_settings` hook. This hook allows plugins to add fields, sections, and even a new tab to the Cacti settings page (the **Configuration | Settings** menu on the console). The following partial code provides this functionality:

```
function cycle_config_settings () {
  global $tabs, $settings, $page_refresh_interval, $graph_timespans;
  // ...
  $tabs['cycle'] = __('Cycle', 'cycle');
//...
  $temp = array(
    'cycle_header' => array(
      'friendly_name' => __('Cycle Graphs', 'cycle'),
      'method' => 'spacer',
      ),
    'cycle_delay' => array(
      'friendly_name' => __('Delay Interval', 'cycle'),
      'description' => __('This is the time in seconds before the next
graph is displayed.', 'cycle'),
      'method' => 'drop_array',
      'default' => 60,
      'array' => $page_refresh_interval
      )
    // ...
  );
  if (isset($settings['cycle'])) {
    $settings['cycle'] = array_merge($settings['cycle'], $temp);
  }else {
    $settings['cycle'] = $temp;
  }
}
```

This function uses two global variables, $tabs and $settings. The variable $tabs holds the different tabs available on the settings page. You can see these tabs in the following screenshot:

The $settings variable holds the current settings data. In order to append data to it, you will need to use these global variables.

The function starts by adding a **Cycle** tab to the list of tabs using the following code:

```
$tabs['cycle'] = __('Cycle', 'cycle');
```

The string to the right is the notation for translatable strings and will be displayed on the screen. The string on the left is a unique identifier used later again for the settings.

The function goes on to create a temporary array: $temp. This array holds the settings data to be displayed on the settings page. Cacti and the plugin architecture will take care of the database backend, so by adding fields here they will automatically be stored in the database when you hit the **Save** button on the settings page.

The cycle plugin adds several fields of which two are shown here, cycle_header and cycle_delay:

```
$temp = array(
  'cycle_header' => array(
    'friendly_name' => __('Cycle Graphs', 'cycle'),
    'method' => 'spacer',
    ),
  'cycle_delay' => array(
    'friendly_name' => __('Delay Interval', 'cycle'),
    'description' => __('This is the time in seconds before the next
graph is displayed.', 'cycle'),
    'method' => 'drop_array',
    'default' => 60,
    'array' => $page_refresh_interval
    )
  // ...
  );
```

The type of the field is defined in the special method variable. The cycle_header field is defined as a spacer that will create a new section on the **Cycle** tab. The cycle_delay field is defined as a drop-down taking a default list (array) of items as an argument.

The last part of the function checks for any already existing cycle settings and merges the new cycle settings with them. If none exist, then it simply adds the new cycle settings to the global settings array.

When installing the cycle plugin, you will see the new **Cycle** tab and the new fields that have been added to this tab:

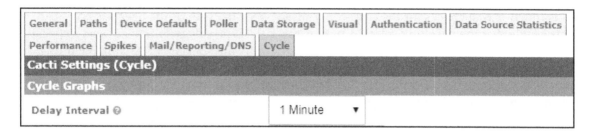

Displaying plugin data within Cacti

You have now seen how to add plugin-specific settings, but how can you actually use these settings and display some data within Cacti? Let's start with displaying an additional tab on the default Cacti interface next to the **graphs** tab:

The cycle_show_tab function

The `cycle_show_tab` function is registered to the two hooks `top_header_tabs` and `top_graph_header_tabs`. `top_graph_header_tabs` will be called when you click on the **graphs** tab and view at the Cacti graphs. `top_header_tabs` will be shown when you are in the Cacti **console** tab.

Look at the following code segment:

```
function cycle_show_tab () {
  global $config;
  if (api_user_realm_auth('cycle.php')) {
    if (substr_count($_SERVER['REQUEST_URI'], 'cycle.php')) {
      print '<a href="' . $config['url_path'] .
'plugins/cycle/cycle.php"><img src="' . $config['url_path'] .
'plugins/cycle/images/tab_cycle_down.gif" alt="' . __('Cycle') . '"></a>';
```

```
    }else{
        print '<a href="' . $config['url_path'] .
'plugins/cycle/cycle.php"><img src="' . $config['url_path'] .
'plugins/cycle/images/tab_cycle.gif" alt="' . __('Cycle') . '"></a>';
    }
  }
}
```

This function first checks for the correct permissions for the user. If the user has access, it checks whether the currently selected page is the `cycle.php` page or not and sets a special variable accordingly. In the last step, the function prints the special HTML link including the **cycle** tab image. Depending on the special variable set earlier, it either displays a blue tab image, or the red one, indicating that the current page is the `cycle.php` page. The final result on the screen can be seen on the following screenshot:

Commonly used plugins

Since the introduction of the plugin architecture, a lot of plugins for different functions have been created. There are specialized plugins that only provide one function and other more common plugins that act as a sort of container for several functions.

When creating new plugins, you should first check for already existing functionalities.

With Cacti 1.x several of the most commonly used plugins have been integrated into Cacti, including the settings, or the superlinks, plugin.

As the plugin architecture has changed, not all plugins are compatible with Cacti 1.x. While some plugin authors are working on adding Cacti 1.x compatibility, other plugins may never be migrated to the new plugin architecture.

The current list of supported compatible plugins can be found on GitHub at the following URL:
`https://github.com/Cacti`

Creating a new plugin

Now it is time for you to create your very first plugin. You will go through the different steps, from the concept of the plugin to its installation within Cacti.

The plugin will be quite simple, but will show you most of the common features and hooks of the plugin architecture.

File structure

All plugins should at least consist of `index.php`, `INFO`, and `setup.php` files. These files are the minimum requirement for any plugin to work properly, but of course you should also consider adding a README file as further documentation to your plugin. You can find some sample plugins, such as the maint plugin, on the following GitHub page:

`https://github.com/Cacti/plugin_maint`

Concept and design

Let's assume that you want to display additional data such as a table at the end of each host graph. The data that is being displayed has the following requirements:

- Display the hostname and IP address
- Show serial and warranty Information
- Display a contact address (email)
- Free text/HTML can be added

Based on this information, you will need to decide where you want to add the information. The following options are possible:

- Add fields to the host form offered by Cacti
- Add a separate form where this information can be entered

In order to show you the different types, you are going to use both options. You will add some of the fields to the host form, and you will also create a new form for adding those fields.

You will also need to think about the permissions of this plugin:

- **User permissions**: Users will be able to see the information
- **Admin permissions**: Admin users will be able to add the information

As you can already see , there are many ways to interact with Cacti using the plugin architecture.

The name of the plugin will be cbEnhancedInfo, where cb is an abbreviation for *Cacti Book*.

Now that you have a basic idea, let's look at the hooks we will need.

PIA hooks

The plugin architecture hooks allow a plugin to interact with Cacti. There are a lot of hooks available. Let's look at the hooks that we are going to use.

The tree_after hook

This special hook allows the displaying of additional information at the end of the graph display on the tree view page, which is the default view in a fresh installation of Cacti when you click the **graphs** tab. Using this hook allows you to display the information defined.

The draw_navigation_text hook

This special hook adds breadcrumb information when adding additional forms and webpages to the console. It's always a good idea to use this hook to fill the special $nav variable with data.

The config_arrays hook

This hook can be used to add new menu entries to the console menu. In general, this hook provides access to generic Cacti config arrays. You will add a new entry for your special form in here.

The config_settings hook

As you have learned earlier, this hook can be used to create plugin-specific settings tabs. You are going to add an option to the **Misc** tab to enable or disable the display of the special information.

The config_form hook

This hook allows the manipulation of the core Cacti forms. You will add some fields to the host form using this hook.

The api_device_save hook

As you have manipulated the host form, this hook allows you to actually store the data you have entered in your new host field.

No other plugin hooks are needed.

The plugin setup

Based on the concept and the hooks that you are going to use, let's start building the setup.php file. For better readability, the setup.php file will be split into the different functions used:

The plugin_cbEnhancedInfo_install function

This function is needed in order for the plugin architecture to register the hooks used and the realm permission setup. Let's look at the function for the cbEnhancedInfo plugin:

```
function plugin_cbEnhancedInfo_install () {
    api_plugin_register_hook('cbEnhancedInfo',
            'draw_navigation_text',
            'cbEnhancedInfo_draw_navigation_text',
            'setup.php');
    api_plugin_register_hook('cbEnhancedInfo',
            'config_arrays', '
            cbEnhancedInfo_config_arrays',
            'setup.php');
    api_plugin_register_hook('cbEnhancedInfo',
            'config_settings',
            'cbEnhancedInfo_config_settings',
            'setup.php');
```

```
api_plugin_register_hook('cbEnhancedInfo',
        'config_form',
        'cbEnhancedInfo_config_form',
        'setup.php');
api_plugin_register_hook('cbEnhancedInfo',
        'console_after',
        'cbEnhancedInfo_console_after',
        'setup.php');
api_plugin_register_hook('cbEnhancedInfo',
        'tree_after',
        'cbEnhancedInfo_tree_after',
        'setup.php');
api_plugin_register_hook('cbEnhancedInfo',
        'api_device_save',
        'cbEnhancedInfo_api_device_save',
        'setup.php');
cbEnhancedInfo_setup_table_new ();
}
```

This function registers all of the hooks mentioned earlier. As you can see, the hooks are matched to plugin functions that you still need to create.

Unfortunately, this function still lacks the permission setup. Let's look at how to add this.

Time for action - adding the realm permission functions

You're going to register two realms, one realm; allows the enhanced information to be viewed, the other one allows it to be created. You're going to use the files from Example 1 for this part:

1. Open the setup.php file from the cbEnhancedInfo directory.
2. Go the end of the first function named plugin_cbEnhancedInfo_install.
3. A comment is displayed:

   ```
   /* The realm permission are missing here --->*/
   /* <--- */
   ```

4. Between these two errors, enter the following line:

```
api_plugin_register_realm('cbEnhancedInfo',
        '',
        'Plugin - cbEnhancedInfo - View Information',
        1);
```

5. This line will register the permission realm, which allows a user to view the enhanced info on the tree view page.

6. After the code you just entered, add the following additional lines:

```
api_plugin_register_realm('cbEnhancedInfo',
'cbEnhancedInfo_listInformation.php,cbEnhancedInfo_addInformati
on.php',
'Plugin - cbEnhancedInfo - Add Information',
1);
```

7. This code allows a user to add the enhanced information on a separate management page described later in this chapter.

8. Now save the file.

9. Upload the `cbEnhancedInfo` directory to your `plugins` directory and change the permissions using the following command from the `plugins` directory:

```
chown -R apache cbEnhancedInfo
```

7. Now you can install and enable the plugin. You will be able to see the new plugin permission showing up in the **Plugin Permissions** tab in the user management screen:

What just happened?

You just added the realm permissions needed to allow users to add and view the enhanced information. Realm permissions are automatically checked when a user calls one of the PHP files.

The cbEnhancedInfo_draw_navigation_text function

This function adds some navigational text to the PHP files you are about to create. Let's have a look at it:

```
function cbEnhancedInfo_draw_navigation_text ( $nav ) {
    // Report Scheduler
    $nav["cbEnhancedInfo_listInformation.php:"] = array(
```

```
"title" => "Enhanced Information List",
"mapping" => "index.php:",
"url" => "cbEnhancedInfo_listInformation.php",
"level" => "1"
);
$nav["cbEnhancedInfo_addInformation.php:add"] = array(
"title" => "(Add)",
"mapping" => "index.php:,?",
"url" => "cbEnhancedInfo_addInformation",
"level" => "2"
);
$nav["cbEnhancedInfo_addInformation.php:update"] = array(
"title" => "(Edit)",
"mapping" => "index.php:,?",
"url" => "cbEnhancedInfo_addInformation.php",
"level" => "2"
);
return $nav;
}
```

As you can see, there are three entries for the special $nav variable. The first one adds a navigation entry for the listInformation view. The other two add some navigation entries for adding and updating information.

Each entry contains several fields. Only the title and level fields are important. The title field is the text being displayed on the navigational bar. The level field tells Cacti where to put the text.

For example, Home > Level 1 > Level 2.

The cbEnhancedInfo_config_form function

This function adds two fields to the host screen: Serial and Warranty. In order to add fields to a host, you will need to manipulate the special $fields_host_edit variable by adding more elements to it:

```
function cbEnhancedInfo_config_form() {
    global $fields_host_edit;

    $fields_host_edit2 = $fields_host_edit;
    $fields_host_edit3 = array();
    foreach ($fields_host_edit2 as $f => $a) {
     $fields_host_edit3[$f] = $a;
    if ($f == 'disabled') {
        $fields_host_edit3["ebEnhancedInfo_serial"] = array(
```

```
    "method" => "textbox",
    "friendly_name" => "Serial Number ",
    "description" => "The serial number of this device.",
    "value" => "|arg1:ebEnhancedInfo_serial|",
    "max_length" => "255",
    "form_id" => false
    );
    $fields_host_edit3["ebEnhancedInfo_warranty"] = array(
    "method" => "textbox",
    "friendly_name" => "Warranty",
    "description" => "The end date of the warranty of this device",
    "value" => "|arg1:ebEnhancedInfo_warranty|",
    "max_length" => "255",
    "form_id" => false
    );
} // end $f == disabled
} // end foreach
$fields_host_edit = $fields_host_edit3;
}
```

The new fields are added right after the disabled field, as shown in the following screenshot:

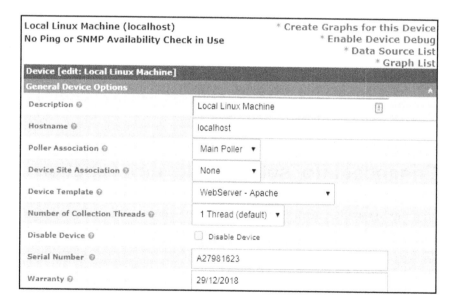

The cbEnhancedInfo_api_device_save function

This function is responsible for storing new host fields in the Cacti database. In order to do so, it populates the special $save variable with the new information. The following code shows this functionality using the ebEnhancedInfo_serial field as an example:

```
function cbEnhancedInfo_api_device_save ($save) {
        if (isset($_POST['ebEnhancedInfo_serial'])) {
        $save["ebEnhancedInfo_serial"] =
        form_input_validate($_POST['ebEnhancedInfo_serial'],
         "ebEnhancedInfo_serial",
         "",
         true,
          255
          );
        } else {
        $save['ebEnhancedInfo_serial] =
        form_input_validate('',
         "ebEnhancedInfo_serial",
         "",
         true,
          255
          );
        }
    }
```

Depending on the information provided by you when saving the device, the $save variable is populated differently. If you did not provide any input, the variable will hold an empty string for the ebEnhancedInfo_serial field. Otherwise, the field will be filled with the data you provided.

The cbEnhancedInfo_setup_table_new function

This is a special function called when installing the plugin. It takes care of modifying existing Cacti tables as well as adding new tables. Let's look at this function in a bit more detail:

```
function cbEnhancedInfo_setup_table_new () {
    global $config, $database_default;
    include_once($config["library_path"] . "/database.php");

    // Check if the cbEnhancedInfo tables are present
    $s_sql = 'show tables from `' . $database_default . '`';
    $result = db_fetch_assoc( $s_sql ) or die ( mysql_error() );
    $a_tables = array();
```

```
foreach($result as $index => $array) {
  foreach($array as $table) {
    $a_tables[] = $table;
  }
}
```

This first part prepares some variables that will be needed later on to check for the existence of the plugin table. It uses the standard MySQL database access to connect to the MySQL database and executes the `show tables` SQL statement on the Cacti database. Let's move on.

Time for action - adding additional fields to the host table

Besides serial information, the plugin is also going to store warranty information. You're not going to store this information in a new table; instead, you'll just add new columns to the existing host table. Let's look at how you can achieve this. You're going to use Example 2 for this. As a preparation, you should now disable and uninstall the plugin from Example 1:

1. Open the `setup.php` file from Example 2.
2. Go to the `cbEnhancedInfo_setup_table_new` function.
3. Search for the following code:

```
/* The additional columns are missing here --->*/
/* <--- */
```

4. Between these two lines, enter the following code. This code will append two columns to the `host` table that are going to be filled once you add some enhanced information on the host page and click the **Save** button.

```
api_plugin_db_add_column ('cbEnhancedInfo',
        'host',
        array('name' => 'ebEnhancedInfo_serial',
        'type' => 'varchar(1024)',
        'NULL' => true,
        'default' => ''
        )
        );
    api_plugin_db_add_column ('cbEnhancedInfo',
        'host',
        array('name' => 'ebEnhancedInfo_warranty',
        'type' => 'varchar(1024)',
        'NULL' => true,
        'default' => ''
```

```
    )
    );
```

5. Now uninstall the current plugin from Example 1, upload the cbEnhancedInfo directory from Example 2 to your `dir` and `install` plugins, and `enable` the plugin.

6. You will now be able to save serial and warranty information so, once you edit the host again, this information should be displayed to you.

What just happened?

Each of the two statements adds a new column to the default Cacti host table. They are given an empty string as default values and also can be NULL values. These fields can now be used to store and retrieve the enhanced information that you can provide when adding or updating a host. When you uninstall the plugin, the plugin architecture will make sure to also remove these additional fields from the host table.

Now let's look at the actual table creation:

```
if (!in_array('plugin_cbEnhancedInfo_dataTable', $a_tables)) {
    // Create Report Schedule Table
    $data = array();
    $data['columns'][] = array('name' => 'Id',
            'type' => 'mediumint(25)',
            'unsigned' => 'unsigned',
            'NULL' => false,
            'auto_increment' => true);
    $data['columns'][] = array('name' => 'hostId',
            'type' => 'mediumint(25)',
            'unsigned' => 'unsigned',
            'NULL' => false,
            'default' => '0');
    $data['columns'][] = array('name' => 'contactAddress',
            'type' => 'varchar(1024)',
            'NULL' => false);
    $data['columns'][] = array('name' => 'additionalInformation',
            'type' => 'text',
            'NULL' => true);
    $data['primary'] = 'Id';
    $data['keys'][] = array('name' => 'hostId', 'columns' => 'hostId');
    $data['type'] = 'MyISAM';
    $data['comment'] = 'cbEnhancedInfo Data Table';
    api_plugin_db_table_create ('cbEnhancedInfo',
'plugin_cbEnhancedInfo_dataTable', $data);
    }
```

As you can see, this part first checks whether the table already exists, and only creates the table if it does not. The table creation consists of creating a special `table` array and adding the different columns as arrays to it. If you have some experience with database table creation, this should be easy for you.

The cbEnhancedInfo_config_settings function

As we saw earlier, this function will add some plugin-specific settings to the **Misc** tab:

```
function cbEnhancedInfo_config_settings () {
  global $tabs, $settings;
  $tabs["misc"] = "Misc";
  $temp = array(
          "cbEnhancedInfo_header" => array(
    "friendly_name" => "cbEnhancedInfo Plugin",
    "method" => "spacer",
    ),
      "cbEnhancedInfo_showInfo" => array(
              "friendly_name" => "Display enhanced information a the tree
view",
              "description" => "This will display enhanced information
after the tree view graph.",
              "method" => "checkbox",
              "max_length" => "255"
          ),
  );

        if (isset($settings["misc"]))
                $settings["misc"] = array_merge($settings["misc"], $temp);
        else
                $settings["misc"] = $temp;

}
```

The function will add two entries to the **Misc** tab; one is only a separator, the other entry adds a checkbox where you can turn the enhanced information display on the tree view page on and off. Look at the following screenshot to see the results of this code:

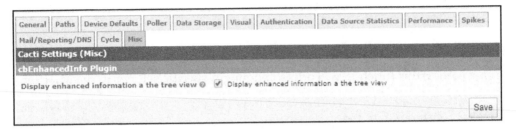

The cbEnhancedInfo_config_arrays function

This function enables you to create special menu entries on the **console** menu:

```
function cbEnhancedInfo_config_arrays () {
  global $menu;
  $temp = array(
"plugins/cbEnhancedInfo/cbEnhancedInfo_listInformation.php" => "Enhanced
Info"
  );
  if (isset($menu['CactiBook Plugins'])) {
    $menu['CactiBook Plugins'] = array_merge($temp,
    $menu['cbPlugins']);
  } else {
    $menu['CactiBook Plugins'] = $temp;
  }
```

As you can see, this function adds an array of links/title pairs. It then checks the special $menu variable for the existence of the CactiBook Plugins menu. You can add the links to already existing Cacti core menus, but for demonstration purposes let's create a new menu section. If the menu exists, the $temp array is merged with the existing menu, otherwise the $temp array will be assigned to the new menu item. The result on the console menu can be seen in the following screenshot:

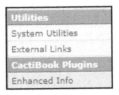

Data presentation

There's one large function left now, the cbEnhancedInfo_tree_after function. This function creates HTML data to be presented after the last graph on the tree view page.

Retrieving data from the database

One of the main tasks for data presentation is retrieval of data. The cbEnhancedInfo_tree_after function will retrieve data from the Cacti database, so let's take a look at the relevant section. This is going to use the files from Example 3. As preparation, you should remove Example 2 from Cacti and install and enable the plugin contained in Example 3. You should also add some sample data to the localhost device.

Time for action - retrieving data from the database

The main goal for the plugin is to present data to the user when they browse the tree view page in Cacti. Let's look at how to retrieve the required information from the database:

1. Open the setup.php file from Example 3.
2. Go to the cbEnhancedInfo_tree_after function.
3. Search for the following code:

   ```
   /* Example 3 - Data retrieval is missing here ---> */
   /* <--- */
   ```

4. Between these two lines, enter the following code:

   ```
   // Retrieve the enhanced information for that host from the table
   $host_contactAddress = db_fetch_cell("SELECT contactAddress FROM
   plugin_cbEnhancedInfo_dataTable WHERE hostId=$host_id");
   $host_additionalInformation = db_fetch_cell("SELECT
   additionalInformation FROM plugin_cbEnhancedInfo_dataTable WHERE
   hostId=$host_id");
       // Retrieve the host specific information from the host table
   $host_serial = db_fetch_cell("SELECT ebEnhancedInfo_serial FROM
   host WHERE id=$host_id");
   $host_warranty = db_fetch_cell("SELECT ebEnhancedInfo_warranty FROM
   host WHERE id=$host_id");
   ```

5. Save the file.

6. These lines are going to fetch enhanced information from the database. Let's see what these values actually look like.

7. Log on to your Cacti system and start the MySQL client using the following command:

```
mysql -u root -p
```

8. If you have followed the book closely, the preceding command will ask for a password. Enter it and you will be presented with the MySQL client prompt.

9. Enter the following command to change to the Cacti database:

```
use cacti;
```

10. The following line will retrieve country information from the localhost device. By default, the localhost device should have the id set to value 1, as it's automatically added as the first device by Cacti itself:

```
MariaDB [cacti]> SELECT ebEnhancedInfo_serial FROM host WHERE id=1;
+-----------------------+
| ebEnhancedInfo_serial |
+-----------------------+
| A27981623             |
+-----------------------+
1 row in set (0.00 sec)
```

11. As you can see in this example, the $host_serial variable is the going to have A27981623 as it's value.

What just happened?

The code you've entered uses the default database function to retrieve the relevant host-specific data from the cacti database. As the enhanced information data is distributed between the host table and the newly created plugin_cbEnhancedInfo_dataTable, the data needs to be retrieved from each of these tables accordingly.

With this information stored in the $host_ variables, you can now go on and look at the actual data presentation.

Presenting data on the tree view page

As a matter of fact, data that will be presented using the `tree_after` hook needs to be embedded within a table row element `<tr>`. Let's look into the `setup.php` file from Example 3 again to see how this can be achieved.

Time for action - presenting data on the tree view page

You're going to present enhanced information as a table embedded in a table row:

1. Go to the `cbEnhancedInfo_tree_after` function again and search for the following code:

   ```
   /* Example 3 - Data presentation is missing here ---> */
   /* <--- */
   ```

2. As you can see, there's already some data between these two lines. If you now go to the tree view page for your localhost device, you should actually see some data being displayed.

3. Replace the lines between the two code lines with the following code:

   ```
   ?>
         <tr bgcolor='#6d88ad'>
       <tr bgcolor='#a9b7cb'>
           <td colspan='<?php echo $columns;?>'
   class='textHeaderDark'>
             <strong>Enhanced Information</strong>
           </td>
       </tr>
       <tr align='center' style='background-color: #f9f9f9;'>
           <td align='center'>
         <?php
         print "<table>n";
         print "   <tr>n";
         print "      <td align=left><b>Contact Address</b></td>n";
         print "      <td
   align=left>".$host_contactAddress."</td>n";
         print "   </tr>n";
         print "   <tr>n";
         print "      <td align=left><b>Serial</b></td>n";
         print "      <td align=left>".$host_serial."</td>n";
         print "   </tr>n";
         print "   <tr>n";
         print "      <td align=left><b>Warranty</b></td>n";
         print "      <td align=left>".$host_warranty."</td>n";
   ```

```
print "   </tr>n";
print "   <tr>n";
print "       <td align=left><b>Additional
Information</b></td>n";
print "       <td
align=left>".$host_additionalInformation."</td>n";
print "   </tr>n";
print "</table>n";

print "</td></tr></tr>";
```

4. Save the file.
5. If you have not done so already, edit the localhost device and add some data for serial and warranty information.
6. Now go back to the tree view page and look at the localhost page again.
7. You should now be able to see something similar to the following screenshot. If you do not see the table, enable the **Display enhanced information in the tree view** option in the **Configuration | Settings | Misc** tab:

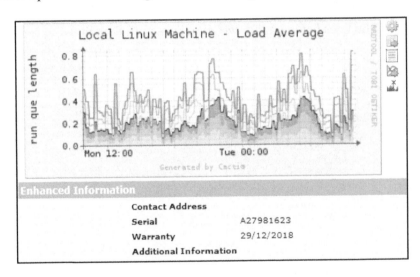

What just happened?

You just created an HTML table containing previously defined variables. This table is embedded in a parent table row. As the tree_after hook is always executed at the end of the parent table presentation, the additional table you just created is going to be appended to the last shown graph, as seen on the previous screenshot.

Creating the table list web page

There are still two items missing, the Contact address and the Additional Information fields. Through Examples 1 to 3, you have added fields to the device page. As Cacti not only allows you to add fields to existing pages, but also enables you to create new maintenance screens and pages, you are now going to add some new forms for managing these two new fields.

Let's start with the maintenance screen first using Example 4. The next section will look at the cbEnhancedInfo_listInformation.php file in Example 4.

In general, each Cacti web page that lists specific items comes with an action part (for example, to delete items), a data retrieval part, and the data display part. Let's look into the action part.

The action section

This section deals with actions that are executed on one or more selected items from the table list. The main action that all lists come with is the delete action.

Deleting data

Actions normally come with some data posted. In the case of the delete action, this data is a list of items that needs to be deleted. Let's look at this action about enhanced information data:

```
function form_delete() {
    /* loop through each of the selected tasks and delete them */
    while (list($var,$val) = each($_POST)) {
        // Check $var for the  number part and store the number in
        // the matches array
        if (preg_match("/^chk_([0-9]+)$/", $var, $matches)) {
        /* ================= input validation =============== */
        input_validate_input_number($matches[1]);
        /* ================================================== */
            db_execute("
              DELETE FROM
                `plugin_cbEnhancedInfo_dataTable`
              WHERE
                `Id`='" . $matches[1] . "'"
            );
        }
    }
}
```

```
        // when done, redirect the end-user to the listing page
        header("Location: cbEnhancedInfo_listInformation.php");
    }
```

This function analyzes all HTTP post variables and checks for any variable whose name starts with chk_ and ends with a number ([0-9]+). If you select one or more items on the web page, then this variable will hold the selected items. The number that is retrieved from the variable name is the actual database ID of the selected item.

After validating the number, it calls a database function to delete the item from the database.

What just happened?

Generally speaking, action functions are used to work on data. This can be as simple as deleting an item, or more complex, such as updating an existing set of data. The form_delete function described here is used to delete one or more existing items.

The data retrieval section

This section deals with retrieving data from the database. As you are able to sort the HTML table from the web page, sorting the data needs to taken care of, too.

Time for action - sorting and retrieving data

1. Let's look at the following code part. This code is made up of two parts; the first part takes care of preparing the sorting statement by looking into the sort_column and sort_direction items. Using these, it builds an ORDER BY SQL statement.

   The second part then selects different fields from two combined tables and returns the items in the requested sorting order by using the previously defined SQL statement:

```
        // Take care of the sorting, did the user select any column
        // to be sorted ?
        if ( isset_request_var('sort_column') )
        {
        // Did the user select a column that is actually sortable ?
          if (
              ( get_request_var("sort_column") == 'Id' )
              || ( get_request_var("sort_column") == 'hostId' )
```

```
                    || ( get_request_var("sort_column") == 'contactAddress' )
                    )
        {
          // What direction should the table be sorted, ascending or
          // descending ?
          if (
            ( get_request_var("sort_direction") == 'ASC' )
              || ( get_request_var("sort_direction") == 'DESC' )
          ) {
          // Finally, we can build the sort order sql statement
              $where_clause  .= ' ORDER BY ' .
                 get_nfilter_request_var("sort_column") .
          ' ' .get_nfilter_request_var("sort_direction");
          }
        }
      }
    // Select all data items from the table. The data will be stored
      // in an array. Note the $where_clause being used
      $a_enhancedInfos = db_fetch_assoc("
          SELECT
            `plugin_cbEnhancedInfo_dataTable`.`Id`,
            `host`.`description` as hostDescription,
            `plugin_cbEnhancedInfo_dataTable`.`contactAddress`,
            `plugin_cbEnhancedInfo_dataTable`.`additionalInformation`
            FROM
            `plugin_cbEnhancedInfo_dataTable`
            INNER JOIN
            `host`
            ON
        `plugin_cbEnhancedInfo_dataTable`.`hostId` = `host`.`Id`
        $where_clause
      ");
```

But why use such a complicated SQL statement when you could just do a SELECT
* as previously seen? Let's compare these statements.

2. Run the following SQL statement on the MySQL CLI, assuming you've entered
    the data already:

```
mysql> SELECT * FROM plugin_cbEnhancedInfo_dataTable;
```

3. You will see a screenshot similar to the one previously shown:

```
+----+--------+----------------+-----------------------+
| Id | hostId | contactAddress | additionalInformation |
+----+--------+----------------+-----------------------+
|  5 |      1 | Sample Contact | Sample Information     |
+----+--------+----------------+-----------------------+
1 row in set (0.00 sec)
```

4. Look at the host Id column. There's only a number being displayed. Now execute the following:

```
mysql> SELECT
    `plugin_cbEnhancedInfo_dataTable`.`Id`,
    `host`.`description` as hostDescription,
    `plugin_cbEnhancedInfo_dataTable`.`contactAddress`,
    `plugin_cbEnhancedInfo_dataTable`.`additionalInformation`
    FROM
    `plugin_cbEnhancedInfo_dataTable`
    INNER JOIN
    `host`
    ON
    `plugin_cbEnhancedInfo_dataTable`.`hostId` = `host`.`id`
    ORDER BY
    `hostId` DESC;
```

5. This time you will see the following:

```
+----+---------------------+----------------+-----------------------+
| Id | hostDescription     | contactAddress | additionalInformation |
+----+---------------------+----------------+-----------------------+
|  5 | Local Linux Machine | Sample Contact | Sample Information     |
+----+---------------------+----------------+-----------------------+
1 row in set (0.00 sec)
```

As you can see, the host Id column has been replaced with the hostDescription column, which provides more useful information than a host Id number. As you have joined together two databases, a SELECT * statement would return all fields from both databases, which in this case would be more than 30 fields.

You will see how to actually get down to the column data in the next section.

What just happened?

In this section, you have seen how to retrieve data from a database and how to order the data using the ORDER BY SQL statement. You have seen that you can join tables to retrieve more useful information and to replace database IDs with more descriptive values such as a hostname. Now that you have the data prepared, let's move on with the actual data presentation.

Data presentation

This section displays data using some Cacti-integrated functions and some HTML-based code.

Time for action - presenting the data

If you look into the code section, you will see that the code segment first starts off by creating the form that is needed for the action items to work. It then goes on to check the size of the array created earlier. If the array contains items, it continues with creating the table header ($menu_text).

Let's look into the relevant part for actually displaying the data you retrieved in the previous step. This part can be found in the cbEnhancedInfo_listInformation.php file for Example 4:

```
// The html header will contain a checkbox, so the end-user can
// select all items on the table at once.
html_header_sort_checkbox($menu_text,
  get_nfilter_request_var("sort_column"),
  get_nfilter_request_var("sort_direction"));
// This variable will be used to create te alternate colored
// rows on the table
$i = 0;
// Let's cycle through the items !
foreach ($a_enhancedInfos as $a_enhancedInfo)
{
  // Data presentation is missing here
}
html_end_box(false);
```

You can see that this code is made up of three sections. The first one creates the table header using the html_header_sort_checkbox function. The second section cycles through the data and the last part closes the table.

Let's look into the second section. As you can see, this lacks the data presentation part, so let's look into what needs to be in there:

1. Open the `missing_data_presentation_part.txt` file. You will see several function calls. For better readability, the following call is not displaying all of the items contained in the file:

```
form_alternate_row_color ($colors["alternate"],
   $colors["light"],
   $i,
   'line' . $a_enhancedInfo['Id']);
$i++;
...
form_selectable_cell ($a_enhancedInfo['Id'], $a_enhancedInfo["Id"
]);
form_checkbox_cell ('selected_items', $a_enhancedInfo["Id"]);
form_end_row ();
```

2. Copy all of the lines and paste them into the `cbEnhancedInfo_listInformation.php` file.

The code starts off by creating a table row using alternate row colors by using the `form_alternate_row_color` function. It then goes on to add each of the data items previously retrieved using the `form_selectable_cell` function. The `form_checkbox_cell` function adds a special cell to the table allowing the user to mark the row in order to choose an action for it. The `form_end_row` makes sure the table row is ended properly.

The following image shows the resulting table along with an item, the action drop-down box, and the page header:

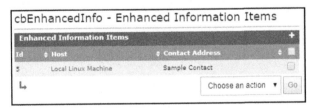

What just happened?

Using the functions provided by Cacti and the data retrieved previously, you created a table containing all the data. As you have seen, Cacti functions take care of the actual HTML code generation and also provide the functionality for creating alternate colored table rows.

Creating the add items form

The add items form will be displayed when you click the add link or select an already existing item from the list page. A form page where you can add or update items always uses at least two functions; one function that displays the form and one additional function that handles saving and updating the `cacti` database. Let's look at the functions used on your form in more detail.

Then next section will explore the `cbEnhancedInfo_addInformation.php` file for Example 4.

The form_display function

The `form_display` function handles data retrieval in the case of updating an item, and displaying the add/update form.

The data retrieval section

Data retrieval is nearly the same as for the list page you created earlier. This time you need to check whether the `form_display` function is called in update mode or a new item will be added. When in update mode, you will need to retrieve the already existing data from the database to be displayed in the form fields so you can see and change the data on the web page later:

```
// Initiate the default variables
$i_defaultHostId = 0;
$s_defaultContactAddress = '';
$s_defaultAdditionalInformation = '';
// Are we in the update mode?
if ( $dataId > 0 )
{
  // Yes we are, so retrieve the existing data
  // from the database:
    $a_items = db_fetch_assoc("
      SELECT
        `plugin_cbEnhancedInfo_dataTable`.`Id`,
        `plugin_cbEnhancedInfo_dataTable`.`hostId`,
        `plugin_cbEnhancedInfo_dataTable`.`contactAddress`,
        `plugin_cbEnhancedInfo_dataTable`.`additionalInformation`
      FROM
        `plugin_cbEnhancedInfo_dataTable`
      WHERE Id='$dataId'
      ");
```

```
    // Let's populate the default variables with the data
    // we retrieved from the database:
    foreach ($a_items as $a_item)
    {
      $i_defaultHostId =   $a_item['hostId'];
      $s_defaultContactAddress = $a_item['contactAddress'];
      $s_defaultAdditionalInformation =
          $a_item['additionalInformation'];
    }
}
```

When calling this function without a dataId, the first if function is skipped and the initial variables will be used to populate the form fields.

The data presentation section

This section handles displaying the different form fields. Cacti provides several types of form field that can be used. Some of the common ones that you'll need often are:

- form_text_box
- form_hidden_box
- form_dropdown
- form_checkbox
- form_radio_button
- form_text_area
- form_save_button

Let's look at how to use the form_text_box, form_text_area, and form_dropdown functions and how to start the update/add form:

```
// Let's start with displaying the form
?>
<form method="post" action="cbEnhancedInfo_addInformation.php"
enctype="multipart/form-data">
<?php
// What mode are we in ?
$s_mode = '[new]';
if ( $dataId > 0 ) {
  $s_mode = '[update]';
}
// Display the html start box
html_start_box("<strong>Enhanced Information Data</strong> ".$s_mode,
"100%", $colors["header"], "3", "center", "");
```

This part should be straightforward. It starts the HTML form and displays the mode in the HTML start box, as shown in the following screenshot:

Enhanced Information Data [new]

Now let's look at the actual form elements. The first entry is using the `form_dropdown` function to display a list of all available Cacti hosts. The list of hosts is retrieved directly from the database as an `id => name` array. This array is provided to the `form_dropdown` function, which creates the actual dropdown box on the web frontend. The form field data is going to be stored in the `hostId` variable and contains the select database ID for that host:

```
form_alternate_row_color($colors["form_alternate1"],$colors["form_alternate
2"],0); ?>
    <td width="50%">
        <font class="textEditTitle">Device Name</font><br>
        The device this data set is for.
    </td>
    <td>
        <?php
        $a_hosts = db_fetch_assoc("
            SELECT
                id,
                CONCAT(description,' [',hostname,'] ') as name
            FROM
                host
        ;");
        form_dropdown("hostId",$a_hosts, "name", "id", $i_defaultHostId, ""
,$i_defaultHostId ,"","");
        ?>
    </td>
</tr>
```

Now a `form_text_box` element is added to the frontend:

```
<?php
form_alternate_row_color($colors["form_alternate1"],$colors["form_alternate
2"],0); ?>
    <td width="50%">
        <font class="textEditTitle">Contact Address</font><br>
        A name, email or any other contact information.
    </td>
    <td>
        <?php
form_text_box("contactAddress","",$s_defaultContactAddress,255); ?>
```

```
        </td>
    </tr>
```

As you can see, the `form_text_box` function takes the initial variable for the contact address as an argument and limits the input to 255 characters. The data is going to be stored in the `contactAddress` variable.

Finally, let's have a look at a text area element:

```
<?php
form_alternate_row_color($colors["form_alternate1"],$colors["form_alternate
2"],1); ?>
    <td width="50%">
        <font class="textEditTitle">Additional Information</font><br>
        Some additional information for this device.
    </td>
    <td>
        <?php
form_text_area("additionalInformation",$s_defaultAdditionalInformation,5,50
,""); ?>
    </td>
</tr>
```

The `form_text_area` element provides enough space for larger information to be entered. This function displays an area box of 5 lines that can hold 50 characters each. The text entered is going to be stored in the `additionalInformation` variable once you click the **save** button.

The last part of the form presents the **save** button to end users. Depending on the mode of this form, some additional hidden fields need to be created, too:

```
if ( $dataId > 0) {
    form_hidden_box("update_component_import","1","");
    form_hidden_box("dataId",$dataId,"");
} else {
    form_hidden_box("save_component_import","1","");
}
html_end_box();
form_save_button("cbEnhancedInfo_listInformation.php", "save");
```

The existence of the different hidden fields will make sure that the `form_save` function knows whether the data provided is going to be used for updating an existing entry, or creating a new one.

The final form page can be seen in the following screenshot:

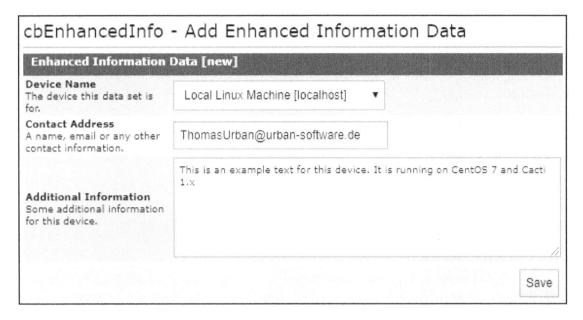

The form_save function

The `form_save` function takes care of creating new items or updating existing ones, depending on the hidden fields created earlier.

Time for action - retrieving data from the form post

When you press the **Save** button, the form values are posted to the server. The `form_save` function needs to retrieve these values and store them in the database.

Let's look at how the different parts of this function work.

As the data is going to be used for updating the `cacti` database, it's always a good idea to make it more secure by using the special prepared statement functions of Cacti 1.x:

```
// Retrieve the data from the form post
/* Add hostId statement here */
if ( isset_request_var('contactAddress') ) {
  $s_dataContactAddress =
    get_nfilter_request_var('contactAddress');
}
```

```
if ( isset_request_var('additionalInformation') ) {
   $s_dataAdditionalInformation =
   get_nfilter_request_var('additionalInformation');
}
```

The special requests variable is checked for the existence of the form data using the special isset_request_var function. If it is set, then the corresponding variable is set accordingly.

As you can see, there's a comment telling you the hostId statement is missing. Open the cbEnhancedInfo_addInformation.php file from Example 5 and add the following statement right after this comment.:

```
if ( isset_request_var('hostId') ) {
  $s_dataHostId= get_nfilter_request_var('hostId');
}
```

What just happened?

You just created the necessary statements to retrieve posted data from the form described earlier. Using the special isset_request_var function, you checked for the existence of the posted data and set the variables using the GET function.

The variables can now be used to update an existing item or to add a new item to the database. Let's look into how to create new items.

Time for action - creating a new database item

Creating a new item is done by using an INSERT SQL statement. The following code adds a new item to the cacti database using the more secure prepared version of the database function:

```
db_execute_prepared("
   INSERT INTO `plugin_cbEnhancedInfo_dataTable`
      (`hostId`, `contactAddress`, `additionalInformation`)
   VALUES
      (?, ?, ?)
   ", array(
      $s_dataHostId,
      $s_dataContactAddress,
      $s_dataAdditionalInformation
   )
);
```

If you look into the cbEnhancedInfo_addInformation.php file from Example 5, you will see that this code is actually missing. You can add this code right after the comment in the following section:

```
if ( ( isset_request_var('contactAddress') )
    && (isset_request_var('save_component_import') ) ) {
        /* Add Save statements here */
}
```

As you can see the, the code checks for the existence of the save_component_import and contactAddress form fields before creating the new item. This will make sure that the function is only creating a new item (save) if data has been entered for the contactAddress field.

Let's explore how this command will look with real data. Open a MySQL CLI and execute the following statement:

```
MariaDB [cacti]> INSERT INTO
`plugin_cbEnhancedInfo_dataTable`
(`hostId`, `contactAddress`, `additionalInformation`)
VALUES
(1, 'My Sample Contact Address','This is a test');
```

You will see the following text:

```
Query OK, 1 row affected (0.00 sec)
```

Let's look at the database table:

```
MariaDB [cacti]> SELECT * FROM plugin_cbEnhancedInfo_dataTable;
```

Output similar to the following screenshot will be displayed:

```
+----+--------+--------------------------+-----------------------+
| Id | hostId | contactAddress           | additionalInformation |
+----+--------+--------------------------+-----------------------+
|  7 |      1 | My Sample Contact Address | This is a test        |
+----+--------+--------------------------+-----------------------+
1 row in set (0.00 sec)
```

What just happened?

As you can see, the function uses the SQL INSERT statement to add data to the `cacti` database. The function will only use this statement, if the `save_component_import` field has been set and the user entered some text in the `contactAddress` field.

Let's look at how an update to an existing dataset is done.

Time for action - updating an existing item

When updating a new item, the special UPDATE SQL keyword can be used. The following code updates an existing item:

```
db_execute_prepared("
  UPDATE `plugin_cbEnhancedInfo_dataTable`
  Set
    hostId=?,
    contactAddress=?,
    additionalInformation=?
WHERE
    Id=?",
    array(
        $s_dataHostId,
        $s_dataContactAddress,
        $s_dataAdditionalInformation,
        $dataId
    )
);
```

As with the creation of a new item, this code is also missing from the file. You can enter this code after the comment in the following section:

```
if ( (isset_request_var('contactAddress'))
&& (isset_request_var('update_component_import') ) ) {
    /* Add Update statements here */
}
```

Let's explore how the `db_execute` command will look with real data. Open a MySQL CLI and execute the following statement. You may have to change the `Id` to match your database data from the `SELECT *` statement of the previous section:

```
MariaDB [cacti]> UPDATE `plugin_cbEnhancedInfo_dataTable`
  Set
    hostId=1,
    contactAddress='New Contact Address',
    additionalInformation='not available'
  WHERE
    Id=7;
```

You will see the following output:

```
Query OK, 1 row affected (0.01 sec)
Rows matched: 1  Changed: 1  Warnings: 0
```

Let's look at the database table again to see the changes:

```
MariaDB [cacti]> SELECT * FROM plugin_cbEnhancedInfo_dataTable;
```

Output similar to the following screenshot will be displayed:

```
+----+--------+---------------------+-----------------------+
| Id | hostId | contactAddress      | additionalInformation |
+----+--------+---------------------+-----------------------+
|  7 |      1 | New Contact Address | not available         |
+----+--------+---------------------+-----------------------+
1 row in set (0.00 sec)
```

As you can see, the item has been updated accordingly.

What just happened?

You just created the update section that takes care of updating existing items. As you can see, the only difference between the update section and the section for creating new items is the SQL statement being used.

You now have created all relevant parts of the plugin.

Installing the plugin

You can install this plugin using the default methods. You have created all the relevant parts that are needed for plugin management to install and enable the plugin within Cacti.

Publishing

If you've created a cool new plugin that you want everyone to know about, you can publish it on the `cacti.net` webpage.

Simply go to `http://docs.cacti.net/plugins.guidelines` and follow the guidelines published there or ask in the Cacti forums for help.

Pop Quiz - A few questions about Chapter 9

1. When adding new fields to a host, which plugin hook do you need to register for?

   a) The `api_device_save` hook
   b) The `config_arrays` hook
   c) The `config_settings` hook

2. How do you add new tables to the database using the plugin architecture?

   a) `api_plugin_db_table_create`
   b) `api_plugin_db_table_modify`
   c) `api_plugin_db_table_add`

3. What can you use the `tree_after` hook for?

   a) You can execute some functions after you create a new Cacti tree
   b) You can display additional information at the end of the graph tree view page
   c) You can display additional fields on the Cacti tree creation page

Summary

During this chapter, you have learned quite a lot about creating your own plugin. You have looked into installing and using the cycle plugin and how to create a concept for your own plugin. You have gone through the creation of the main `setup.php` file and learned the different steps involved in actually presenting data within Cacti.

You have also looked at adding a new web page for viewing a list of enhanced information items and learned how to create the necessary forms to add these new enhanced information items

You should now be able to create your own personal Cacti plugins. In the next chapter, you're going to install and configure a threshold monitoring plugin to further enhance Cacti.

10
Threshold Monitoring with Thold

Now that you've installed several plugins and know how to create your own, let's look at how one of the more complex plugins can help you monitor your devices and send out alerts based on thresholds.

In this chapter, we are going to:

- Provide an overview of the Thold plugin
- Describe the different threshold types available
- Create a threshold
- Create a threshold template and assign it to a data source

Let's start with some basics!

Threshold monitoring

With the addition of a threshold monitoring plugin, Cacti increasingly becomes a performance management tool. Setting thresholds on gathered performance data for alerting allows you to:

- Repair hardware problems before users are impacted
- Identify performance issues before there are real problems
- Identify virus outbreaks

With thresholds set, you do not have to look at all your graphs every day to identify these items.

Thold

Thold is a threshold monitoring and alerting plugin for Cacti that dates back as far as December 2004, but has since been replaced by the currently available plugin. Thresholds can be created per device and data source but Thold also supports threshold template creation.

Differences between Thold and Icinga

Thold and Icinga both create alerts based on reaching different thresholds. While Thold relies on Cacti to poll data, Icinga is using its own plugins and connection methods to retrieve data. Although Icinga offers more configuration possibilities such as the parent concept as well as creating network maps, in contrast to Thold Icinga lacks the capability to build a threshold using historical data. Up until the release of Thold for Cacti 1.x, Thold was not able to scale well, so it was limited to a small number of thresholds for monitoring. With the release of the Thold daemon, this limitation is now gone.

Installing Thold

Lets start by installing the Thold plugin.

Downloading and installing Thold

Thold is not published on the `cacti.net` page, but is freely available from the common GitHub-based plugin page: https://github.com/Cacti/plugin_thold.

Time for action - installing Thold

The following steps will install the latest Thold version for Cacti 1.x

1. Log on to you Cacti installation as root.
2. Go to the new plugins directory:

```
cd /var/www/html/cacti/plugins
```

3. Download the Thold plugin using the following command:

```
wget -O thold.zip
https://github.com/Cacti/plugin_thold/archive/develop.zip
```

4. Extract the archive:

```
unzip thold.zip
```

5. Rename the directory to the correct name of thold:

```
mv plugin_thold-develop thold
```

6. Log on to your Cacti web interface using a user with **Plugin Management** permissions.
7. Go to **Configuration** -> **Plugin Management**.
8. You should now be able to see the Thold plugin on the list of available plugins:

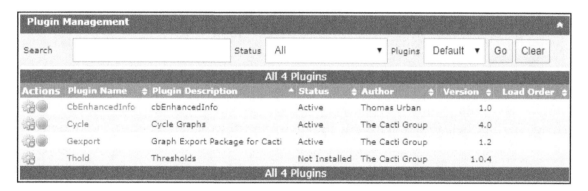

What just happened?

You installed the Thold plugin, thereby enabling you to set thresholds on values of RRD data and send out alerts if your thresholds are breached. Before moving on, make sure you don't forget to enable the plugin through the **Plugin Management** page.

Configuring Thold

As with most complex plugins, Thold comes with its own configuration tab on the Cacti settings page. Let's look at the various options for Thold.

General options

The general settings area contains some very basic options. The following screenshot shows their default values:

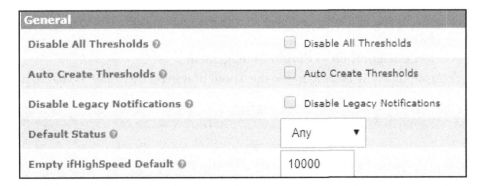

Most of these settings are self-explanatory, allowing you to specify the generic behavior of Thold. The little help icon next to each line allows you to see a more specific description of these settings.

Default alerting options

The default alerting options area lets you define logging settings as well as some exemptions and triggers. Look at the following screenshot showing the default values:

Logging	
Log Threshold Breaches @	☐ Log Threshold Breaches
Show Data Source in Log @	☐ Show Data Source in Log
Log Threshold Changes @	☐ Log Threshold Changes
Debug Log @	☐ Debug Log
Alert Log Retention @	1 Month ▼
Threshold Daemon	
Enable Threshold Daemon @	☐ Enable Threshold Daemon
Maximum Concurrent Threshold Processes @	4
Alert Presets	
Weekend exemptions @	☐ Weekend exemptions
Default Trigger Count @	1
Re-Alerting @	12
Baseline Presets	
Baseline Time Range Default @	▼
Baseline Trigger Count @	2
Baseline Deviation Percentage @	20

As you can see, there is a new section available called **Threshold Daemon**. This new feature in Thold for Cacti 1.x allows the delegation of Thold-related tasks to a dedicated daemon. This daemon can also run on a different system to reduce the load on the Cacti poller. More information on this new feature will be provided later in this chapter.

Default email options

The default email options section lets you define the appearance of alert emails as well as the generic content of these emails. Look at the following screenshot for the default values:

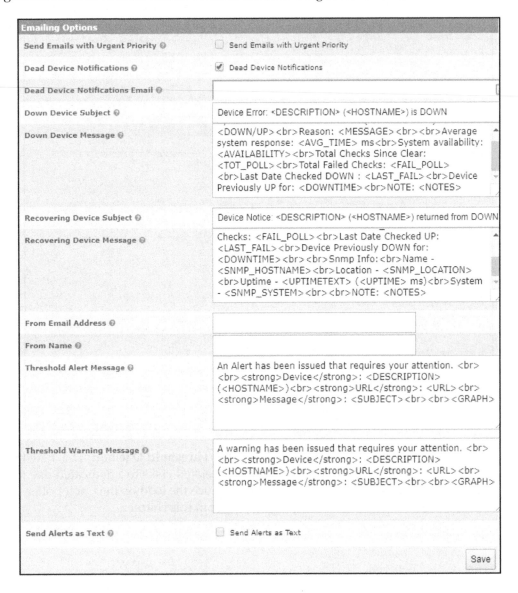

There are two fields that need an explanation: **DeadDeviceNotifications** and **DeadDeviceNotificationEmail**. By default, Cacti doesn't immediately mark a device as being down if it was unreachable. If you look at the **Device Defaults** tab and scroll down to the bottom of that page, you will see the following settings:

This means that Cacti will try to poll the device twice before marking it as down, while waiting three polling cycles before marking the device as being recovered. Based on the default poller interval of five minutes, the total times these values represent are 10 and 15 minutes, respectively.

As Thold uses the internal Cacti mechanism, a dead device notification will also be sent out after two polling cycles.

You've also seen that Thold accepts an e-mail address to receive the dead device notification message. The new Thold version for Cacti 1.x now also allows you to set this email on a per-device basis or by defining a notification list.

Default baseline options

Thold has the ability to trigger alerts by doing some baseline analysis. The default baseline options define time ranges and triggers to take into account when calculating a threshold breach. The default values can be seen in the following screenshot:

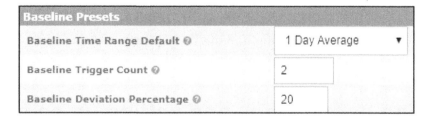

Syslog and SNMP notification

The new Thold version now also offers the ability to send out SNMP Notifications. If you want to use this, you will have to set up SNMP receivers under **Utilities | System Utilities | SNMP Notification Receivers**:

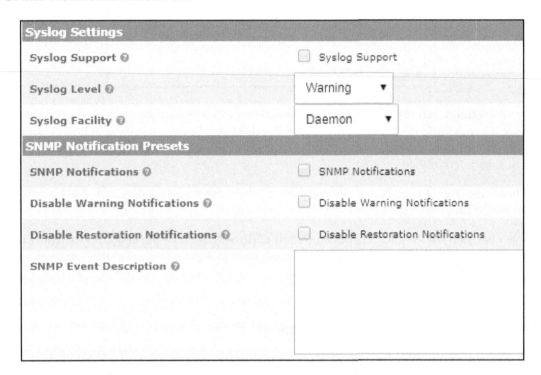

Using Thold

Now that you have installed and configured the Thold plugin, let's move on and assign Thold permissions to a user and create some thresholds.

Assigning permissions and setting up an email address

First, you'll have to assign permission for Thold to a user. For alerting to work properly, you should also define an email address for the user.

Time for action - giving permission to a user

The following steps guide you through the process of adding Thold permissions to a user:

1. Log on to Cacti as a user with administrative rights.
2. Click the **Console** tab and go to **Configuration** | **Users**.
3. Click the user who should have access to the plugin.
4. Add an email address for the user in the new **Email Address** field:

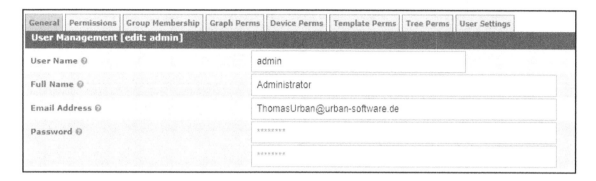

5. On the **Permissions tab**, tick the checkbox next to
   Configure Threshold Templates, **Configure Thresholds**, **Manage Notification Lists**, and **View Thresholds** as seen in the following screenshot:

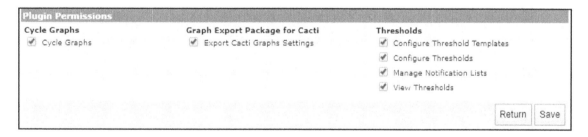

6. Click the **Save** button.

What just happened?

You just gave a user permission to create threshold templates and individual thresholds, to view thresholds within Cacti, and to create new notification lists.

Creating a notification list

One new feature is the ability to create notification lists, which allows you to define different email targets for the threshold alerts. These can be set on a device, threshold template, or a specific threshold.

Time for action - creating a notification list

Let's look at how to define a notification list:

1. Log on to Cacti as the user you changed in the previous step.
2. Click **Notification Lists** under the **Management** menu:

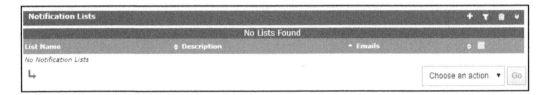

3. Click the plus sign at the top right to add a new list.
4. Define a name for the list and enter a description as well as a comma-separated list of email addresses:

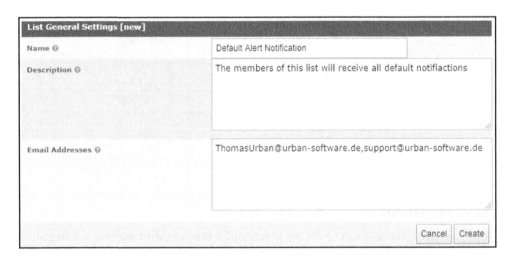

5. Click the **Create** button to save your new list.

What just happened?

You've defined your first notification list, which you can use in your threshold template definition and as a dead device notification target within specific devices.

Creating a threshold

Thresholds can be set on a per-data-source basis, but this can be tedious in large environments; thankfully, the plugin provides an easy way of creating thresholds using a shortcut icon on the graph view pages.

Time for action - creating your first threshold - Part 1

The following steps will guide you through the process of setting up a threshold:

1. Log on to Cacti as the user you changed in the previous step.
2. Click the **graphs** tab and go to a device or graph.
3. On the right of the graphs, there are a number of small icons. Click the one showing a small document with a checkmark in it, as seen in the following screenshot:

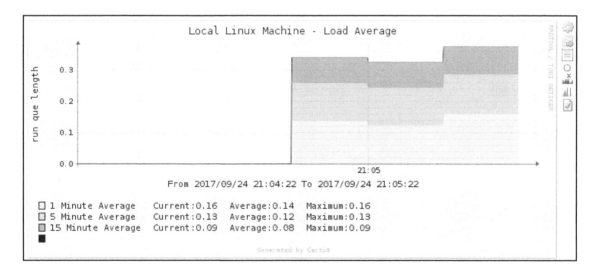

4. On the next page, select **Create a new Threshold** from the drop-down box and click the **Continue** button, as shown in the following screenshot:

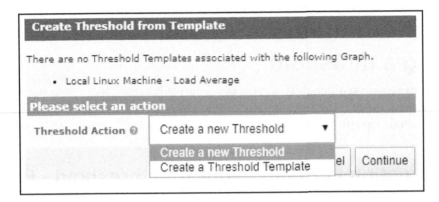

5. On the next page, the **Device** and **Graph** drop-down boxes should already be filled in. Now select **load_15min** as the **Data Source** for which you want to create a threshold. The following screenshot displays the information for the **Localhost-Load Average** graph:

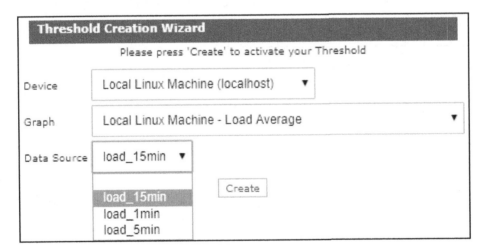

6. Click the **Create** button.
7. You'll now see a page where you can define the threshold for the specific data source you've selected. Let's stop here for a moment and look at this page in more detail.

What just happened?

You just walked through the first steps of creating a threshold. You selected the device and graph for which you're going to create a threshold as well as the data source that will be monitored for threshold breaches. You are now presented with the actual threshold creation page.

The threshold creation page

The threshold creation page can be divided into three main parts:

- Basic and mandatory settings
- Threshold setup
- Alert setup

Depending on the number of data source items that make up the graph, you will also see a tab at the top for changing between them.

Template and General Settings section

In the **Template** and **General Settings** section you can define Thold's functionality. If this threshold is based on a threshold template, which will cover shortly, then you can enable or disable the propagation of settings from the parent template here. Look at the following screenshot for the default settings of each field:

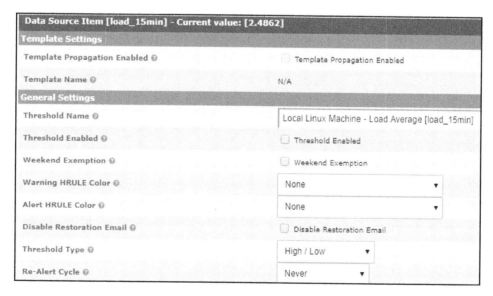

The **Re-Alert Cycle** field allows you to enable email alerts to be sent out regularly as long as a threshold is breached. This will remind the appropriate person that there is an ongoing issue to be resolved. The default value of **Never** will make sure that a threshold breach alert will only be sent once.

In this section, you can also change the **Threshold Type** to one of the following types:

- **High/Low**: The threshold is breached if the value is above or below these numbers.
- **Baseline Deviation**: A time range from the past is used to calculate acceptable minimum and maximum values. The threshold is breached if the values deviate by this amount, as a percentage.
- **Time Based**: Similar to the high/low threshold, a time-based threshold is defined by setting high and low numbers. In order to trigger the threshold, it must be breached x number of times within the last y minutes (for example, twice within the last 30 minutes).

The type of threshold you choose here changes the content of the following section.

Threshold setup section

This section provides fields for setting up the actual threshold. Depending on the **ThresholdType** you chose earlier, this section changes.

The following screenshot displays the section seen when you choose the **High/Low** type:

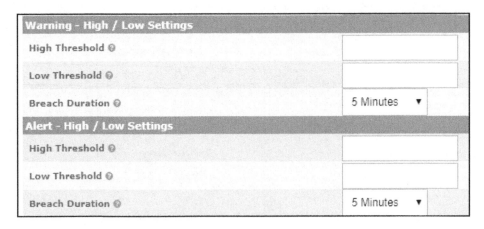

As mentioned earlier, **High/Low** thresholds are the simplest type. A value has to be at fault for a consecutive number of times (**Breach Duration**) for an alert to be issued. A new feature that was integrated in Thold is the ability to define a warning threshold that sends out specific warning notifications.

The **Baseline Deviation** threshold type provides more fields for you to fill in, as shown in the following screenshot:

Baseline Settings	
Time range ❷	1 Day Average ▼
Deviation UP ❷	
Deviation DOWN ❷	
Baseline Trigger Count ❷	2

As not all data sources can be defined with a fixed threshold limit, the **Baseline Deviation** threshold provides an automated way of creating a threshold for these kinds of data source.

Let's assume that you have a system with an average load of 5% during working hours from Monday to Friday and, due to backups and/or heavy reporting functions running at night, it goes up to 15%. If you now set a high threshold of 15%, then you would probably not notice an unusual load during working hours, when a virus outbreak increases the average load to 10%.

This is where the **Baseline Deviation** threshold comes in handy. By setting the reference point for the threshold to the value from a day ago and choosing a decent but not too large time range, you can define a dynamic threshold by using the **Deviation UP** and **Deviation DOWN** fields. The **Baseline** threshold will then alert you when the average load increases to, for example, 10% during working hours but will also alert you during the night when the average load increases beyond 15%.

You can take care of smaller usage spikes by also defining a **TriggerCount**.

The last threshold type available is the **Time Based** threshold, so let's look at its settings:

Warning – Time Based Settings	
High Threshold ❓	
Low Threshold ❓	
Breach Count ❓	1
Breach Window ❓	5 Minutes ▾
Alert – Time Based Settings	
High Threshold ❓	
Low Threshold ❓	
Breach Count ❓	1
Breach Window ❓	5 Minutes ▾

As described earlier, **Time Based** thresholds have fixed high and low threshold values but, in contrast to the simple **High/Low** type, this one is able to check for the number of threshold breaches within a specific time range.

When would you use this? Let's assume you are counting the number of failed logins for the root user to your system. As sometimes happens, you type in the wrong password, and you do not want to be alerted for every single failed login, so you set the **HighThreshold** to 2. If someone tries to log in to your system twice within five minutes, then you will get an alert. However, if someone tries to log in to your system 288 times in a span of 24 hours, or on average once every five minutes, then you will never get an alert.

Time Based thresholds will allow you to define a case that would cause the threshold to alert when the value is breached twice (**Breach Count**) during the last 60 minutes (**Breach Window**). In the example with the failed logins, you will now get an alert telling you that someone tried to log on 7 times during the last 60 minutes.

Other Settings section

The **Other Settings** section allows you to define the recipients of the alert. As you have already set up an email address for a user, it should show up in the **Notify accounts** list.

Your previously defined notification list should show up within the drop-down boxes for the warning and alert notification list.

If you have external users in need of this information, have systems that create tickets, or if you take action on an alert, you can define some extra email addresses in the **AlertEmails** and **Warning Emails** boxes.

The following screenshot shows the alert section and a description of the fields:

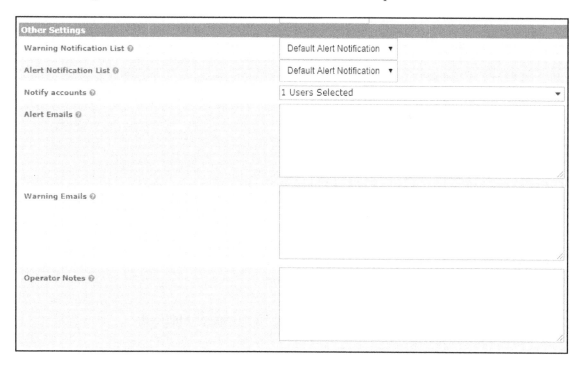

Time for action - creating your first threshold - Part 2

Now let's get back to work and continue with defining the threshold.

1. You are now going to define a **High/Low** threshold, so select **High/Low** as the **Threshold Type**.

2. Look at the sample graph at the top of the page and set a good **HighThreshold** that is relatively near or just below the maximum limit of your graph. This will allow you to check the functionality of the alerting later on. In the following graph example, the **HighThreshold** value for your **Warning** should be set to 0.6. The value for the **Alert** should be set to 1:

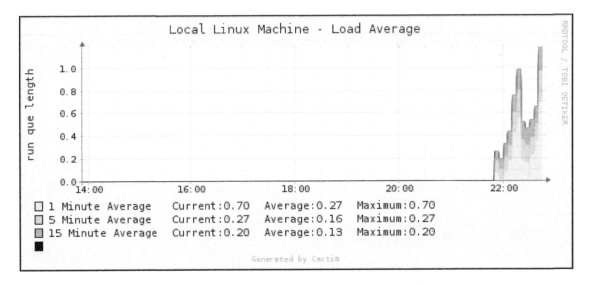

3. Select **5 minutes** as the **Breach Duration**.

4. Leave **Data Type** as **Exact Value**.

5. Select the account that shows up in the **Notify accounts** field.

6. Click the **Save** button.

What just happened?

You've finished creating your first threshold. By selecting a high threshold value that's near your normal average load, you should receive an email alert when there's a high load on your system.

As you may have noticed, you skipped the **DataType** field, leaving it at the default value. What's the purpose of this field? Depending on the data source type, you can use different methods to extract a value from the data source. Remember when you created graph templates? You sometimes had to use a CDEF to turn bits into bytes or make numbers negative. The same principle applies here. The values returned from the data source are not always the same values you displayed on the graph and for some of these data sources you had to use a CDEF to make them appear as you want.

You can also choose to convert values to a percentage compared to another data source. An example for this would be memory calculations, where you may want to set a threshold of the free memory available as a percentage of the total system memory. You can of course use a fixed low value with the minimum free memory, but this threshold will only be valid for a limited number of systems. Defining these thresholds as a percentage will be much better when defining threshold templates that will apply to a large set of dissimilar systems with different memory footprints.

Testing the threshold

Now that you have defined a threshold, how can you test whether everything is working? On Linux systems, you can use commands to create an artificial load on the system.

Time for action - creating an artificial load

Let's look at how you can create a load on the system at which the threshold should be triggered:

1. Log on to your CentOS Linux system as the root user.
2. Execute the following command, causing 3 cores to be utilized for 60 seconds:

```
seq 3 | xargs -P0 -n1 timeout 60 yes > /dev/null
```

3. Go back to Cacti and look at the average load graph. It should show a much higher average load than when you set up the threshold:

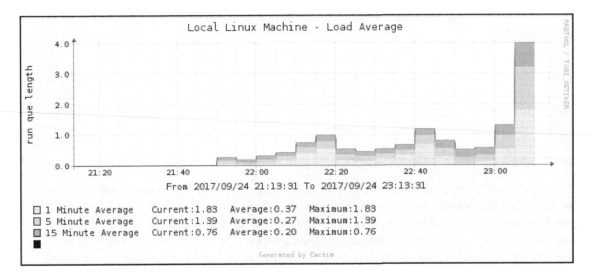

4. Check your email account for the threshold alert.
5. In the event you did not receive an email, check the configuration of the settings plugin. There may be a misconfiguration or a missing entry there.

Viewing threshold breaches

As you have created your first threshold and forced it to breach by using the stress tool, let's look at how you can view these breached thresholds.

Time for action - viewing breached thresholds

The following steps will show you how to view any breached thresholds:

1. Log on to Cacti as a user with **ViewThresholds** permissions.
2. Go to the **thold** tab
3. You should be presented with a page listing all threshold breaches, like the one shown in the following screenshot:

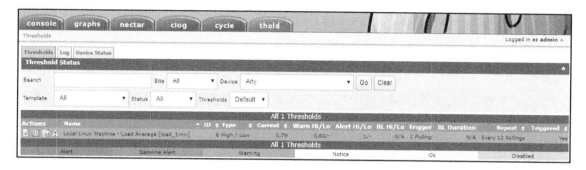

4. Click the second button (with the red background and the white circle in it) to disable the threshold:

5. Click the green button to enable it again:

6. You can edit the threshold by clicking the first icon, viewing the graph for the threshold, or viewing the threshold history by clicking on the last icon.

What just happened?

You just looked at the threshold page that is available to all users with **ViewThresholds** permissions. Depending on what other permissions you have, not all icons will appear.

Creating threshold templates

Now that you have created a single threshold, let's look into creating a threshold template with baseline support for the average load threshold.

Time for action - creating your first threshold template

Let's look into the tasks involved in creating a threshold template:

1. Log on to Cacti as a user with administrative rights.
2. Go to the **Console** tab and click **Threshold** under the **Templates** section.

3. You should see an empty table, as seen in the following screenshot:

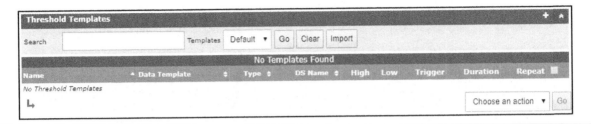

4. Click the plus link, +, in the top-right corner.
5. Select **Unix - Load Average** from the **Data Template** drop-down box.
6. Select **10min (10 Minute Average)** from the **Data Source** box, as seen in the following screenshot:

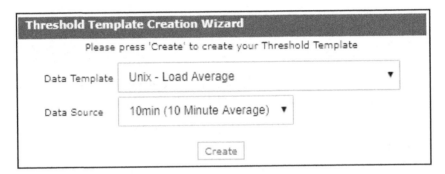

7. Click the **Create** button.
8. On the next screen, change the **Threshold Type** to **Baseline**.
9. In the **Baseline monitoring** section, select 30 Minutes as **Time reference in the past**.

The Time reference drop-down is based on the Data Profile being used. The High Collection Rate has 15 Minutes (Average), 1 Hour (Average), and 4 Hour (Average). The System Default shows the 30 Minute (Average), 2 Hour (Average), and 1 Day (Average)

10. Add **10** for **Baseline deviation UP**.
11. Add **10** for **Baseline deviation DOWN**.

12. Leave everything else in this section at the default values, as shown in the following screenshot:

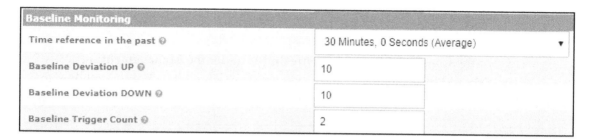

13. Change the **Re-Alert Cycle** and **Notify accounts** to suit your needs.
14. Click the **Save** button to save your template.
15. Go back to the **Template** page under the Template section and check the table for the existence of your new template:

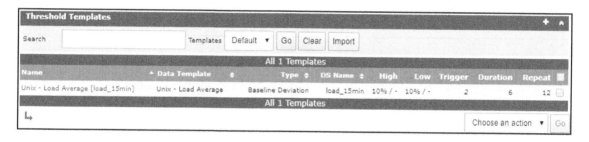

What just happened?

You just created your first baseline-based threshold template. As you may have noticed, the data source you selected was the 10 min Average data source, but the **DS Name** on the table shows **load_15min** as the name. This is because the data template for the **Unix - Load Average** assigns the **10min - 10 Minute Average** output field to the **load_15min** internal Data Source Name.

Assigning threshold templates

Now that you have created a template for the **Load Average** threshold, you can assign this template to the previously-created **Load Average** threshold for your localhost device.

Time for action - assigning a threshold template

Having created the template, you should now assign it accordingly. The following steps will show you how to do this:

1. Log on to Cacti as a user with administrative rights.
2. Go to the **Console** tab and click **Thresholds** under the **Management** section.
3. You should see a table with all your currently-defined thresholds, as shown in the following screenshot:

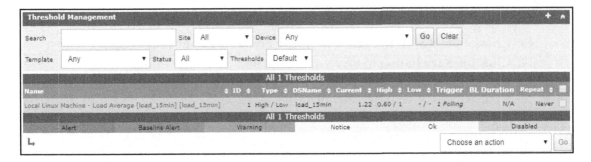

4. Check the checkbox to the right of the **Load Average** threshold.
5. Choose **Delete** from the drop-down box at the bottom and click the **Go** button. This will make sure that this threshold does not exist anymore, as existing thresholds cannot be migrated to those based on a template.
6. Click the **graphs** tab and select the device where you created the **Load Average** threshold earlier.
7. Click the Create Threshold icon next to the **Load Average** graph.
8. From the following screen, select the **Unix - Load Average [load_15min]** template, as seen in the following screenshot:

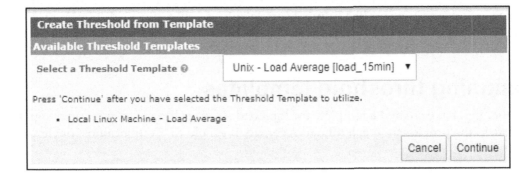

9. Click **Continue** to save your selection.
10. Go to the **Console** tab and click **Thresholds** under the **Management** section.
11. Click **Localhost - Load Average [load_15min]** to open the threshold definition page.
12. The **Template Propagation Enabled** checkbox should be checked and all other fields disabled, as seen in the following example screenshot:

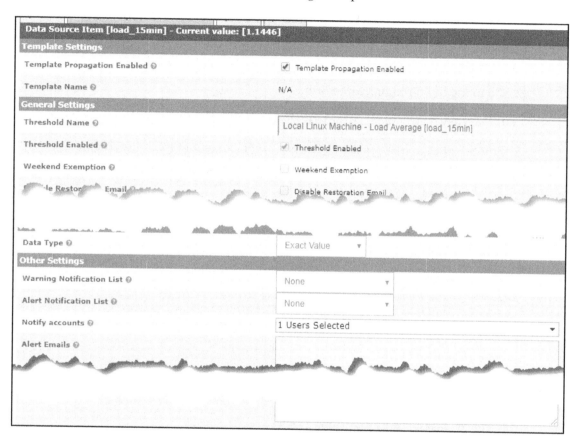

What just happened?

You just assigned your first threshold template to a data source. Every time you change the base threshold template, the changes will propagate to the assigned thresholds. Please note that notification email recipients are also stored in the template, so for different alert recipients you will need to create different templates.

Thold daemon

The thold daemon is a new feature allowing you to separate threshold detection from the poller, allowing you to have alerting without impacting the performance of the poller itself. Let's look how to set up the daemon on your Cacti box.

Time for action - enabling the thold daemon

The following steps will show you how to enable the thold daemon:

1. Log on to the cacti system as root.

2. Go to the thold plugins directory:

   cd /var/www/html/cacti/plugins/thold/

3. Edit the thold_daemon.service file and change it to the following:

   ```
   [Unit]
   Description=Cacti Thold Daemon.
   After=mariadb.service
   AssertPathExists=/var/www/html/cacti/plugins/thold/

   [Service]
   User=cacti
   Group=cacti
   Type=simple
   ExecStart=/usr/bin/php
   /var/www/html/cacti/plugins/thold/thold_daemon.php -f

   [Install]
   WantedBy=multi-user.target
   ```

4. Copy the service file to the system directory:

   cp thold_daemon.service /usr/lib/systemd/system/

5. Enable the thold_daemon:

   systemctl enable thold_daemon

6. Start the thold daemon:

   systemctl start thold_daemon

7. Now log on to Cacti as a user with administrative rights.
8. Go to the **Console** tab and click **Settings** under the **Configuration** section.
9. Now go to the **Thresholds** tab and check the **Enable Threshold Daemon** checkbox.
10. Hit the **Save** button.

What just happened?

You just enabled the thold daemon to start after the MariaDB service at boot time. You also made sure that thold is using the daemon instead of going through the poller to check for any threshold breaches.

Pop quiz - a few questions about Chapter 10

1. When are baseline thresholds best used?

   a) When performance values stay the same
   b) When performance values vary between different days
   c) To identify performance issues

2. Where do you define the alert email addresses?

   a) In the user management screen
   b) In the alert setup screen
   c) In both screens

3. What happens if you change the notification email address in a threshold template?

   a) Nothing happens
   b) The notification email address gets propagated to the actual thresholds
   c) A confirmation email is sent out to that address

Summary

You have learned quite a lot about thresholds, baselines, and other parts of the Thold plugin. You have covered the basic steps of installing and configuring the Thold plugin and created your first threshold via the graph view page. You have learned about the differences between the three threshold types and created a baseline deviation-based threshold template. During the final part of this chapter, you assigned the threshold template to a data source and enabled the Thold daemon for increased threshold-monitoring performance.

You should now be able to create a set of thresholds and templates to monitor your network and receive alerts when performance issues occur. In the next chapter, you're going to learn how to create reports containing specific Cacti graphs and how to send them to your customers using scheduled email.

11
Enterprise Reporting

You have created a solid foundation when it come to graphs, so it's now time to learn how you can create reports and send them to your users. This chapter is going to show you how to define reports with the integrated Nectar add-on and the commercially supported CereusReporting plugins.

In this chapter we are going to:

- Provide an overview of Nectar and CereusReporting
- Describe the process of creating a report
- Schedule a report to be sent via email
- Describe the advanced reporting features of CereusReporting

It's time for reporting!

Overview of Nectar and CereusReporting

In Cacti 1.x, Nectar has become an integrated part of Cacti and added some missing reporting capabilities to it. Nectar allows you to send out one or more graphs via email to multiple recipients. In contrast to Nectar, CereusReporting allows you to define a sophisticated report using the PDF format, allowing you to define enterprise-looking reports, including Weathermap reports, SmokePing graphs, and other data. Let's look at these in more detail.

Nectar

Nectar is the *true* descendant of the *reports* plugin, which in the early days of Cacti had the ability to email graphs and text on a scheduled basis. As support and development for the reports plugin was abandoned some time ago, one of the Cacti developers created a new plugin called **Nectar**. This plugin was integrated into the core of Cacti 1.x. Nectar is capable of creating reports containing Cacti graphs and some text, and then sending these graphs as inline images within emails.

Nectar supports:

- Scheduling report generation
- Basic formatting of the reports using HTML and CSS code
- Sending reports based on Cacti graphs via email

CereusReporting

The CereusReporting plugin has been rewritten and re-designed for Cacti 1.x. It is a commercial product and offers a free Standard Edition for on-demand report generation and backwards compatibility with Cacti 0.8.8h.

CereusReporting allows the creation of PDF-based reports and supports report scheduling, mail delivery, and report archiving.

CereusReporting offers the following features:

- On-demand report generation from the graphs tab
- Scheduled PDF report generation and emailing
- Report templating and customization
- Report archiving

At the time of writing, the most current version is 3.01.

Nectar

Let's look into Nectar and how to create and schedule reports using this new integrated plugin. Please make sure that your user has the **Reports Creation** and **Reports Management** permissions.

Report generation

Now that you have installed the Nectar plugin, let's look into how to create your first report.

Time for action - create your first Nectar report

The following steps will create your first Nectar report:

1. Log on to your Cacti web interface.
2. Click on the **nectar** tab.
3. You should see an empty table. Click on the **+** link in the top-right corner.
4. You will see a new page where you can define your Nectar report. Enter `My New Report` as the **Report Name** and check the **Enable Report** checkbox.
5. Within the **Email Frequency** section, check the **Next Timestamp for sending Mail Report** field and choose the date/time you want your first report to be sent out.
6. Select **Day(s)** as the **Report Interval** so your report will be sent out daily, at the time you scheduled your first report, as seen in the following screenshot:

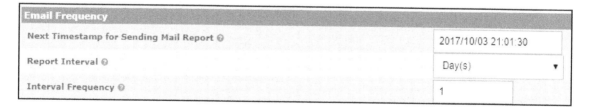

Email Frequency	
Next Timestamp for Sending Mail Report ❷	2017/10/03 21:01:30
Report Interval ❷	Day(s) ▾
Interval Frequency ❷	1

7. Go to the **EmailSender/Receiver Details** section and fill in your email details.
8. Once you are done, click the **Create** button.

What just happened?

You have just created your first report. This report is still empty as you still have to add report items to it.

Important note:

Check the regional settings for your MySQL database. Some instances actually use the dash sign "-" as the date separator, and not a forward slash "/".

Time for action - adding report items

Let's add some items to your report:

1. You should now see several new tabs as seen in the following screenshot:

2. Click on the **Items** tab.
3. A new page opens with an empty table. Click on the + link at the top-right of the table.
4. As seen in the following screenshot, the new page offers several drop-down boxes to choose from. Select **Graph** as the **Type** and select one of your existing graphs to be added to the report:

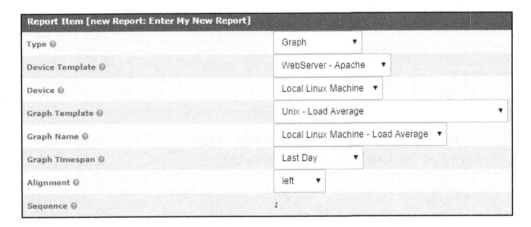

5. Once you've selected an item from each drop-down box, you will see the graph displayed underneath. Click on the **Save** button to continue.

6. The table should now list your previously added graph.

7. Click on the **Preview** tab to see a preview of your report.

8. On the **Events** tab, you can see the next date and time that your report will be generated and sent out.

9. In order to test your report, click on the **Send Report** link to the far right of the tabs. An email similar to the one shown in the following screenshot will be sent to you:

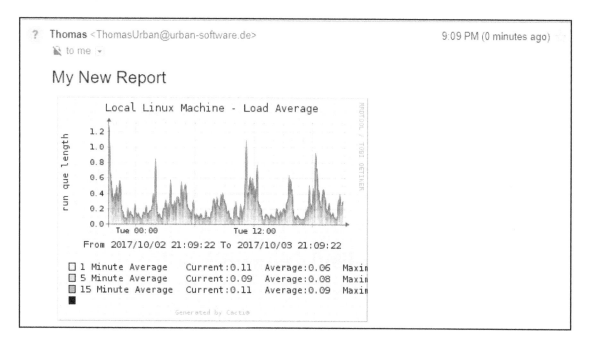

What just happened?

You've just added a graph item to your report and scheduled it to be sent via email on a regular basis. The email contains the Cacti graphs as inline images and can be forwarded to other people.

CereusReporting

CereusReporting allows the creation of PDF reports and comes as a free Standard Edition as well as commercial Professional and Business Editions.

Installation

The Standard, Professional, and Business Editions share the same code, so let's install the Standard Edition now.

You can get the latest version from the CereusReporting product page at the following website:

```
https://www.urban-software.com/products/cereusreporting-professional-pdf-
reports-for-cacti/cr-downloads/
```

This example is going to be based on the v3.01 version with Cacti installed on CentOS 7.

Installing the right IonCube loader:

Make sure you install the correct version. You can find out your current running PHP version using the command `php -v` and your extension directory using `php -i | grep extension_dir`

Time for action – installing CereusReporting

Let's look into the different steps of installing the CereusReporting plugin on a CentOS 7 version running PHP 5.4:

1. Log on to your Cacti installation as root.
2. If you have not yet installed the `php-gd` and `php-mbstring` modules, do this now:

```
yum install php-gd php-mbstring
```

3. The CereusReporting plugin is encrypted with the IonCube software. In order to load the plugin, you need to install the PHP loader for it. The following commands will install the required module:

```
cd /tmp
wget
http://downloads2.ioncube.com/loader_downloads/ioncube_loaders_lin_x86-64.t
ar.gz
tar -xzvf ioncube_loaders_lin_x86-64.tar.gz
cp ioncube/ioncube_loader_lin_5.4.so /usr/lib64/php/modules
```

4. You now have to tell PHP to load this module:

```
echo "zend_extension=/usr/lib64/php/modules/ioncube_loader_lin_5.4.so"
> /etc/php.d/ioncube.ini
```

5. Restart the web server so it loads the new module:

```
systemctl restart httpd
```

6. Now change to the tmp directory again:

```
cd /tmp
```

7. Download the latest installer version:

```
wget -O cereusreporting-3.01-64.run
'https://www.urban-software.com/?ddownload=2808'
```

8. Make the file executable:

```
chmod +x cereusreporting-3.01-64.run
```

9. Execute the installer:

```
./cereusreporting-3.01-64.run
```

10. Accept the license:

```
-----------------------------------------------------------
Welcome to the CereusReporting Setup Wizard.
-----------------------------------------------------------
Please read the following License Agreement.
You must accept the terms of this agreement before continuing with the
installation.
...
Press [Enter] to continue:
Do you accept this license? [y/n]: y
```

11. Make sure you select the correct plugins directory:

```
Please specify the directory where CereusReporting will be installed.
Installation Directory [/var/www/html/cacti-1.1.28/plugins]:
/var/www/html/cacti/plugins
```

12. Keep the remaining default values. The installer should finish with the following message:

```
Setup has finished installing CereusReporting on your computer.
```

13. Download the license.txt file for the Standard Edition:

```
cd /var/www/html/cacti/plugins/CereusReporting/config
wget -O license.txt 'https://www.urban-software.com/?ddownload=2959'
```

14. Now log on to your Cacti web interface and enable the plugin.

15. Next, add CereusReporting permissions to your user:

16. You should now be able to see the **Cereus** tab at the top as shown in the following screenshot:

What just happened?

You have just installed and enabled the CereusReporting Standard Edition along with its basic requirements. This edition allows you to create simple on-demand reports and create pre-defined reports. Do not forget to give the appropriate realm permissions to your users.

Plugin configuration

Before creating your first report, you will need to configure the CereusReporting plugin. There are several basic settings that are essential for the plugin to work properly. Let's set up the plugin now.

Time for action - configuring CereusReporting

In the following steps, you set some basic configuration for the plugin:

1. Go to **Configuration | Settings**.
2. Select the **CereusReporting** tab.
3. Check the **Print Header/Footer to PDF** box.
4. Enter the URL for your Cacti web interface in the **Cacti Host/Server URL** field.
5. Check the **Archive Directory**.

6. You can leave the rest of the settings as they are. Your settings should now look as shown in the following screenshot:

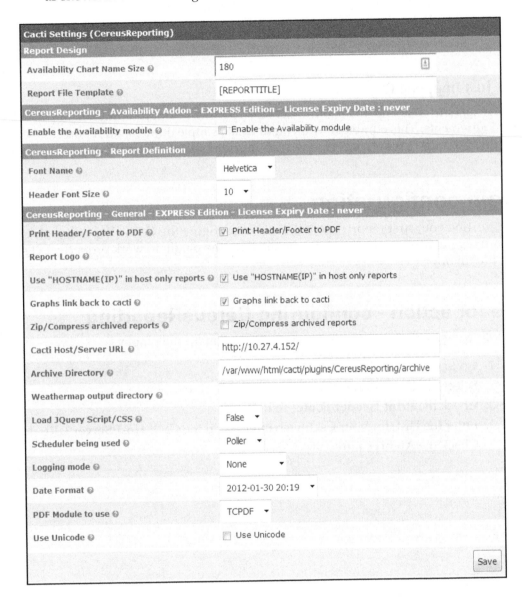

7. Click on the **Save** button.

What just happened?

You just defined the basic settings for the CereusReporting plugin.

Report generation

The CereusReporting plugin is able to create instant PDF reports from the graph tree-view page as well as allowing the user to create a pre-defined report collection.

On-demand report generation

On-demand reports can be enabled for every user, allowing them to create instant PDF reports while viewing the Cacti graph tree-view pages.

Time for action - creating an on-demand report

On-demand reports are generated from the graphs tab. Let's see how you can do this:

1. Log on to your Cacti web interface.
2. Click on the **graphs** tab. You should notice some new icons between the **Graph Filters** and the actual Cacti graphs:

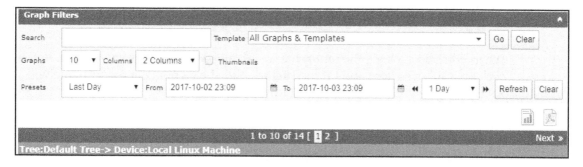

3. Non-admin users will not see the left **Add graphs to report** button.
4. Select a host that you want to generate a report for.

5. Click on the PDF icon to the far right. You will be presented with a new dialog that allows you to include any **Sub-Leafs** of the currently selected tree, or email the report to an email address:

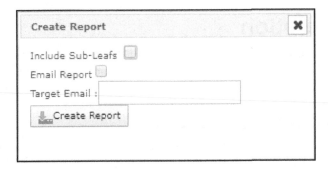

6. If you just hit the **Create Report** button you will see a notification that the report is being generated. After a while, the final report will be downloaded as a PDF file:

7. When you select a host, the report name will always have the same format. If you click on a sub-tree item and hit the **Include Sub-Leafs** box, the report name will have the name you entered on the settings page.

What just happened?

You just created your first instant PDF report using the CereusReporting plugin. The graphs included within the report show the exact timeframe that you selected in the Cacti tree-view page. You are able to select single graphs by clicking on the small checkbox next to each graph, or create a report of a whole sub-tree by enabling the **Include Sub-Leafs** checkbox on the dialog.

Let's now look at how you can create a pre-defined report.

Pre-defined report generation

Pre-defined reports are a collection of graphs from one or more hosts that can also come from different Cacti trees. This allows you to add graphs of a specific type (for example, hard disk space on servers) to one report.

Time for action - creating a pre-defined report

Let's go through the different steps involved in creating your first pre-defined report:

1. Go to the **console** tab.
2. Click on **CereusReporting | Manage Reports**.
3. An empty table will be shown. Click on the **+** link at the top-right of that table.
4. When the new page is shown, enter `Test Report` as the **Report Name**.
5. Enter a short **Report Description** of the report. This description will be shown at the beginning of the final PDF report.
6. Select the **ColorCircle Template** as the **Report Template**.
7. Select **1 Day** as the **Default Report Timespan**.
8. Enable the **Add the Header to the report** and **Add the Footer to the report** checkboxes.
9. Retain the remaining default entries.
10. Click on the **Save** button. You will be redirected back to the report overview table:

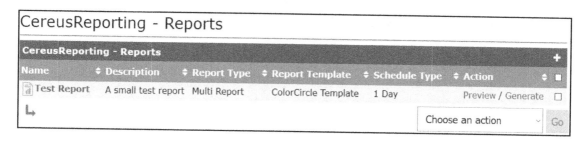

11. Click on the report name. You will see a new toolbar at the bottom of the report:

12. Click on the **Chapter** button. In the dialog window enter `Single Hosts` and hit the **Add** button.
13. Now click on the **Host** button. From the new dialog select **Local Linux Machine** and hit the **Add** button.
14. Click on the **Chapter** button again. In the dialog enter `Load Averages` and hit the **Add** button.
15. Now click on the **RegExp** button. Select the **Default Tree** as the tree. Select **Filter on graph title** from the filter type and add `/Load Average/` as the regular expression:

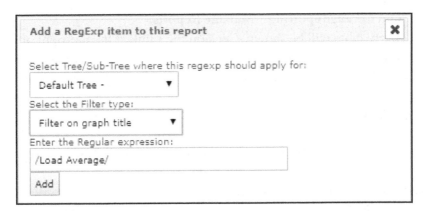

16. The report items should now look like this:

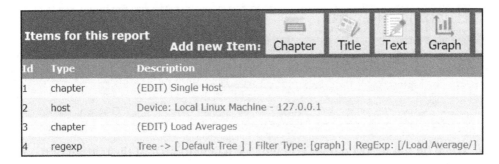

17. Go back to the **Manage Reports** page.

18. Click on the **Generate** link next to your **Test Report**.

19. You will see some information about your report and be able to select a start and end time for your report data. The start and end time is always based on the **Default Report Timespan** that you defined for that particular report as seen in the following screenshot:

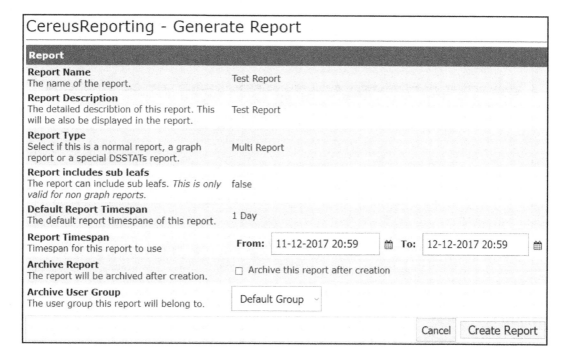

[297]

20. Click on the **Create Report** button to create your report. The report will contain all the graphs that you added previously, as well as the report description you defined. The following screenshot shows part of the first page of such a report:

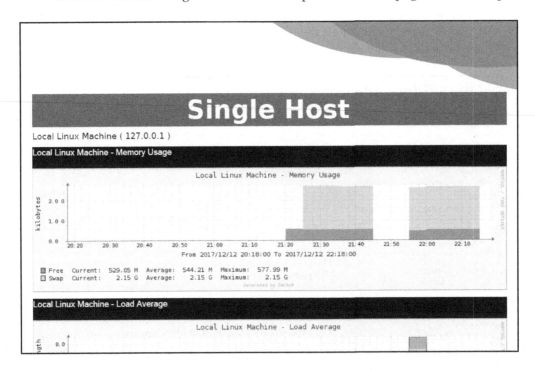

What just happened?

You just created your first pre-defined PDF report. You can use this kind of report to group similar graphs into one report for easier comparison.

Scheduling a report

Let's look into how you can schedule a report to be sent out via email. For this, you will have to request a trial license for the scheduling module.

Time for action - scheduling a pre-defined report

Let's create a schedule for your report now:

1. Log on to your Cacti web interface.

2. Go to **CereusReporting | Manage Report Schedule**.
3. In the empty table, click on the + link in the top-right. A new page will show up.
4. Enter `Daily Test Report` as the **Schedule Name**.
5. Select the previously defined **Test Report** as the **Report** to be scheduled.
6. Enter `This is a daily test report` as the **Report Schedule Description**.
7. Select **daily** as the **Recurring frequency**.
8. Set the **Report Schedule** to **00:00** hours of the next day.
9. Enter your email address in the **Report Recipients** list.
10. Enable all checkboxes on this **Report Schedule** as shown in the following screenshot:

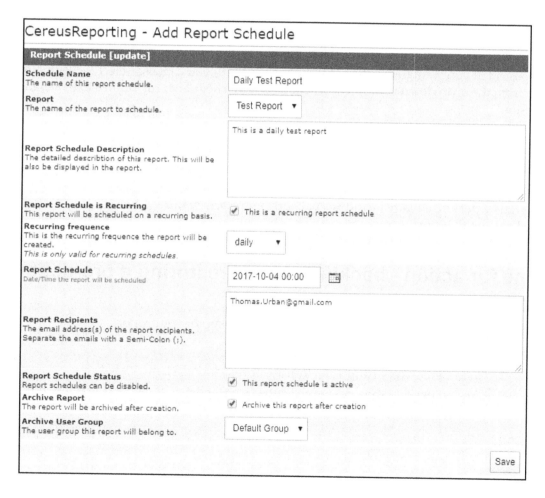

11. Click on the **Save** button.
12. You will be redirected to the **Report Schedules** table. Here you should see your new report schedule as shown in the following:

What just happened?

You just scheduled your first report. You will receive the report once the initial date/time has passed. If you want to test the schedule functionality you can also select the **Run Now** item from the drop-down menu, which will force the schedule to run at the next available timeslot.

Report backup and restore

Once you create a large report, you may want to create a backup of it. The Standard Edition of CereusReporting already includes a backup and restore feature, which creates XML-based backup files of your reports.

Time for action - backing up and restoring a pre-defined report

The following steps show the process of creating a backup of your report:

1. Log on to your Cacti web interface.
2. Go to **CereusReporting** | **Backup/Restore**.
3. Click on the checkbox next to the **Interface Report** as shown in the following screenshot:

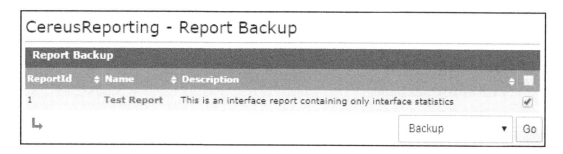

4. Select **Backup** from the drop-down box and hit the **Go** button at the top to create a backup file.

5. A new table will be displayed at the bottom of the page as shown in the following screenshot:

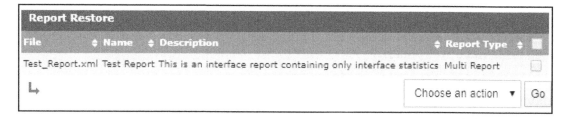

6. Click on the checkbox next to the `Interface_Report.xml` file.

7. Click on the **Go** button at the bottom to restore the report. The CereusReporting plugin never overwrites existing reports, but will create a new report with the same data as the original one as shown in the following screenshot:

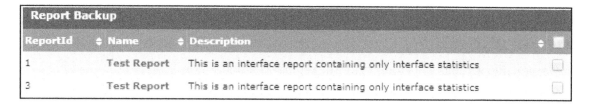

What just happened?

You just created a backup of your **Interface Report** and also restored it. The XML backup file contains all the necessary information to fully restore the report, including:

- General report settings
- Defined report items
- Defined report schedules

Moving the report to another system will not be possible as the report items refer to item IDs within the local Cacti database. Normally these IDs will be different on other systems.

Report scheduling and polling performance

Report generation requires some fine-tuning. Depending on the report type, size, and report generation settings, scheduled report generation can have a negative impact on polling time when being run by the poller.

Using the poller mode is fine for relatively small reports, but should be avoided when running large reports.

In order to reduce the performance impact of report generation, the CereusReporting plugin does provide the ability to run report generation as a cron job.

Let's look how you can enable such cron-based report generation.

Time for action - setting up cron-based report generation

Let's look into setting up a cron job for the report scheduler:

1. Log on to your Cacti server.
2. Create a new file in /etc/cron.d to run the report generation:

```
vi /etc/cron.d/reportScheduler
```

3. Add the following one line to this file:

```
*/1 * * * * cactiuser /usr/bin/php
/var/www/html/cacti/plugins/nmidCreatePDF/cron_pdf_scheduler.php >
/dev/null 2>&1
```

4. Save the file by hitting *ESC* and entering :x.
5. Now log on to your Cacti web interface.
6. Go to **Configuration | Settings**.
7. Click on the **CereusReporting** tab.
8. Select **Cron** as the **Scheduler being used**.
9. Click the **Save** button.

What just happened?

You just changed your scheduler from the poller-based version to a cron-based one. This will allow the Cacti poller to concentrate on polling performance data while the operating system deals with report generation.

Advanced reporting features of CereusReporting

CereusReporting has some advanced reporting features. It adds support for graph generation via the DSSTATS plugin, and creates availability and SLA reports. This section provides you with an overview of these advanced features.

TCPDF report engine

The TCPDF report engine is an advanced reporting engine capable of adding bookmarks or Unicode support to PDF files. This is the default report engine for CereusReporting version 3.0.

Cacti Data Source Statistics (DSSTATS) reports

The DSSTATS reports feature allows the creation of graphical charts for the raw data provided by the DSSTATS plugin. The DSSTATS plugin tracks peak and average values for all data sources. It does not store all the data from RRD files, but you will be able to retrieve the values for hourly, daily, weekly, monthly, and yearly time periods.

DSSTATS reports use simple SQL queries to generate pie, bar, or simple line charts, which can then be added to a PDF report.

A simple example of such a DSSTATS chart is shown as follows:

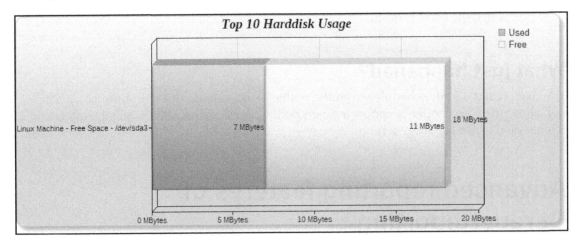

Availability reports

A new feature introduced with the release of the CereusReporting .0 version is the ability to create availability reports. Device availability is calculated using Cacti internal polling statistics. The following functionality is provided with this feature:

- The ability to define a global- or host-based SLA timeframe (for example, 8h x 5 days SLA report)
- Global and/or per-host definable SLA

An example of an availability chart with a 8x5 defined SLA timeframe can be seen in the following screenshot:

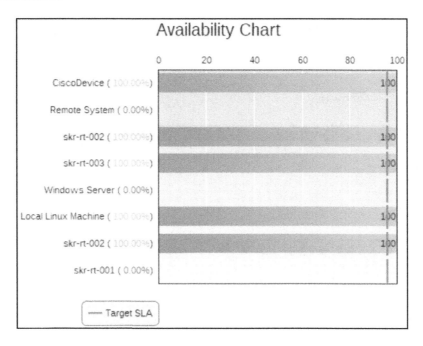

SmokePing reports

CereusReporting allows the integration of SmokePing graphs by utilizing the free nmidSmokeping plugin:

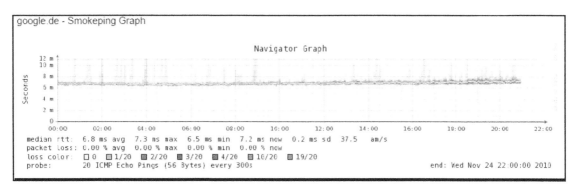

Report templates

You can create your own report templates by using your favorite word processor and exporting your corporate or customer-specific report design to a PDF file. The PDF file can be used to create the look and feel of PDF reports as seen in the following screenshot:

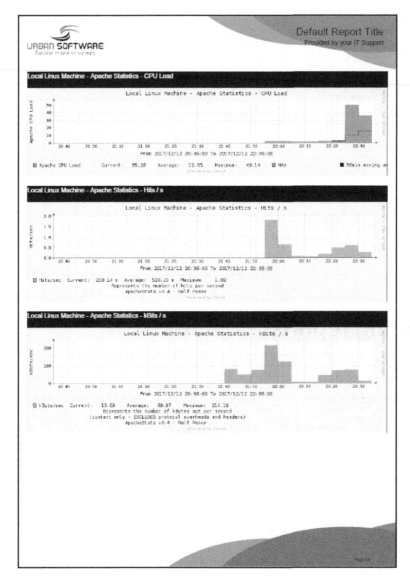

A sample PDF report

Pop quiz - a few questions about Chapter 11

1. What type of report can you generate using Nectar?

   a) HTML report
   b) CSV report
   c) HTML email containing the report
   d) All of the above types

2. Where can you disable a report in Nectar?

   a) By going to the **nectar** tab
   b) By editing the report
   c) By disabling the nectar plugin

3. What plugins and extensions does the CereusReporting plugin support?

   a) The SmokePing tool
   b) The DSSTATS plugin
   c) Availability reports
   d) All of the above

Summary

In this chapter, you learned how to create HTML- and PDF-based reports to send out to your colleagues, management, or customers. You have seen two different plugins capable of creating, scheduling, and mailing reports.

Specifically, you installed the CereusReporting plugin and created your first custom report with Nectar. You learned how to schedule reports using Nectar and created an instant PDF report with the CereusReporting plugin. The chapter described the different steps involved in creating pre-defined reports and how to schedule these using the CereusReporting plugin.

You should now be able to define new reports and schedule them to be sent out to a list of email recipients. Now, you not only have a performance monitoring solution, but a performance reporting solution as well!

In the next chapter, you're going to learn how to use the Cacti CLI and the autom8 plugin to automate your Cacti instance.

Cacti Automation for NOC

In a large environment, adding users and managing devices and graphs can become a time-consuming job. With the availability of the Cacti CLI, most of these manual tasks can be automated, but selecting and creating meaningful graphs for devices still involves quite a lot of effort. This chapter will show you how to use the CLI to automate device management and how to create rules for adding graphs to a device using the new automation functionality.

In this chapter we are going to:

- Provide an overview of Cacti automation
- Describe the process of using the CLI to add permissions, devices, and trees
- Configure the graph and device automation feature

Let's automate Cacti!

Overview of Cacti automation

Automation of the many administrative Cacti tasks can be done using the Cacti CLI, the automation feature (formerly Autom8 plugin), or using both in combination. Let's look into the different functionalities that the Cacti CLI and the new integrated automation feature have to offer.

What happened to Autom8?

With Cacti 1.x, Autom8 has been integrated into the core Cacti code under the Automation section. The functionality and features mostly remained the same.

The Cacti CLI

The Cacti CLI was the first tool to automate the different Cacti tasks. As its name suggests, it is a CLI-based set of PHP files that interact with Cacti core functions and the database. The Cacti CLI can be used to create scripts for integrating external tools such as an asset management tool into Cacti. NOC environments usually have a central inventory management system holding detailed device information and the Cacti CLI will help you import devices into Cacti using this information. What else does the Cacti CLI offer you?

Users

Cacti users can be created using the CLI by copying an existing user with a new user ID. You've already done this in `Chapter 4`, *User Management* when you imported a list of users into Cacti.

Permissions

When you created a user, the user had the same realm permissions as the template user being used during the copy or import process. If you want to give additional permissions to a user you can use the Cacti CLI to do so. Unfortunately, only the adding of permissions is supported, the Cacti CLI does not allow the removal of permissions.

Trees

A special CLI script exists for managing the Cacti tree. You can add a new tree, or add different items to an existing tree, using the Cacti CLI.

Devices

As already mentioned, you can use the Cacti CLI to add new devices to Cacti. This is especially useful if you want to import a lot of devices into Cacti.

Graphs

As you can add devices to Cacti using the CLI, it also provides an interface for adding graphs to a device.

Overview of automation

Automation allows you to automate tree, item, and graph creation based on the device and graph details. This automation can be defined as rules that are triggered when a new device or new graph is created. Let's look at the different automation parts.

Trees

Automation doesn't create trees itself, but can create tree items, such as headings, or add host items to an existing tree. This function lets you automatically organize newly created devices and graphs without manual interaction. Automation rules can also be applied to existing devices.

Graphs

Graph rules automate the addition of graph templates to devices. They are applied whenever a device is added or index information (for example, for SNMP interfaces) is re-indexed. Graph rules can be created based on any of the graph data query fields, such as the operating status of an interface (**ifOperStatus**).

Using the Cacti CLI

Let's look at how you can use the Cacti CLI to manage user permissions and some basic administrative tasks.

Adding permissions

When copying a user, the user permissions of the original user are copied to the new user. Let's assume that you have set your original user to deny access by default for trees, devices, and graphs. Now if you want to add further permissions to the new user, you can use a special script from the Cacti CLI.

Time for action - adding permissions to a user

Let's look how this permission script works:

1. Log on to your Cacti system.
2. Change to the Cacti CLI directory:

   cd /var/www/html/cacti/cli

3. Execute the following command:

   php add_perms.php

4. You'll see a short overview of the available options for this command:

```
[root@localhost cli]# php add_perms.php
Cacti Add Permissions Utility, Version 1.1.23, Copyright (C) 2004-2017 The Cacti Group

usage: add_perms.php [ --user-id=[ID] ]
    --item-type=[graph|tree|host|graph_template]
    --item-id [--quiet]

Where item-id is the id of the object of type item-type

List Options:
    --list-users
    --list-trees
    --list-graph-templates
    --list-graphs --host-id=[ID]
```

5. As you can see, this tool requires the user ID so let's get a list of all available users:

   php add_perms.php --list-users

6. You'll be shown a list of all users together with their user IDs:

```
[root@localhost cli]# php add_perms.php --list-users
Known Users:
id        username          full_name
1         admin   Administrator
3         guest   Guest Account
4         turban  Thomas Urban
6         _CustomerA_user Template User for Customer A
7         Test User
13        user1   User Name1
14        user2   User Name2
15        user3   User Name3
16        user4   User Name4
```

7. Now let's assume you want to give access to a specific tree. The command for this is as follows:

```
php add_perms.php --user-id=[ID] --item-type=tree --item-id=[TREEID]
```

8. You already have the ID for the user so let's get the TREEID with the following command:

```
php add_perms.php --list-trees
```

9. As with the users list, you will see a list of the Cacti trees available together with their ID:

```
[root@localhost cli]# php add_perms.php --list-trees
Known Trees:
id        sort method                        name
1         Manual Ordering (No Sorting)    Default Tree
2         Manual Ordering (No Sorting)    Customer A
```

10. Now you are able to give or revoke access depending on your current default tree policy. Let's change the access to the Customer A tree for user user1:

```
php add_perms.php --user-id=13 --item-type=tree --item-id=2
```

11. When executed, you will not get any confirmation back:

```
# php add_perms.php --user-id=13 --item-type=tree --item-id=2
#
```

12. You can check the User Management page of that user for the result. When the **Default Tree Policy for this user** is set to **Deny**, you should see **Access Granted** as in the following image. If the **Default Tree Policy for this user** is set to **Allow**, then you will see **Access Restricted** instead:

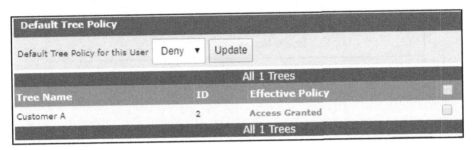

What just happened?

You just added permissions to an existing user to allow the viewing of a specific Cacti tree. In combination with an available permission request system, this script can be used to automatically add the requested permissions on approval, without the need for a Cacti administrator to manually add them.

Adding a Cacti tree

Although manually adding a Cacti tree itself does not involve lots of work, managing the items underneath does.

Time for action - adding a Cacti tree

Let's go through the steps of adding a new Cacti tree from the CLI:

1. Log on to your Cacti system.
2. Change to the Cacti CLI directory:

```
cd /var/www/html/cacti/cli
```

3. Execute the following command:

```
php   add_tree.php
```

4. You will see the different options for this command:

```
Cacti Add Tree Utility, Version 1.1.23, Copyright (C) 2004-2017 The Cacti Group

usage: add_tree.php  --type=[tree|node] [type-options] [--quiet]

Tree options:
    --name=[Tree Name]
    --sort-method=[manual|alpha|natural|numeric]

Node options:
    --node-type=[header|host|graph]
    --tree-id=[ID]
    [--parent-node=[ID] [Node Type Options]]

Header node options:
    --name=[Name]

Host node options:
    --host-id=[ID]
    [--host-group-style=[1|2]]
    (host group styles:
    1 = Graph Template,
    2 = Data Query Index)

Graph node options:
    --graph-id=[ID]

List Options:
    --list-hosts
    --list-trees
    --list-nodes --tree-id=[ID]
    --list-graphs --host-id=[ID]
```

5. As you can see, you can add trees, hosts, or even single graphs to a tree or sub-tree. Let's add the localhost device to a tree. Use the following command to retrieve a list of hosts:

```
php add_tree.php --list-hosts
```

6. Use the following command to get a list of existing trees:

```
php add_tree.php --list-trees
```

7. Now get a list of the nodes from a tree:

```
php add_tree.php --tree-id=2 --list-nodes
```

8. You will see a list of the existing nodes for that tree, as in the following screenshot:

```
[root@localhost cli]# php add_tree.php --list-trees
Known Trees:
id       sort method                    name
1        Manual Ordering (No Sorting)   Default Tree
2        Manual Ordering (No Sorting)   Customer A

[root@localhost cli]# php add_tree.php --tree-id=2 --list-nodes
Known Tree Nodes:
type     id     parentid        title    attribs
Header   1      N/A     Country A        Manual Ordering (No Sorting)
Header   2      1       Site A  Manual Ordering (No Sorting)
Device   9      2       192.168.44.131  Graph Template
Device   6      2       192.168.178.43  Graph Template
Device   3      2       192.168.178.161 Graph Template
Device   7      2       192.168.44.137  Graph Template
```

9. Now let's add the localhost device to Site A:

```
php add_tree.php --type=node --node-type=host --tree-id=2 --parent-node=2 --host-id=1
```

10. This will add the localhost device (--host-id=1) to the Site A node (--parent-node=2) under the Customer A tree (--tree-id=2):

11. You will see a confirmation once the item has been added, as seen here:

```
[root@localhost cli]# php add_tree.php --type=node -
Added Node node-id: (11)
```

What just happened?

You just added a device to a sub-tree within Cacti. This can be used to automatically add new devices to the correct sub-trees. You will later see how this can more easily be achieved using the automation feature.

Adding a device

Let's look into how you can use the Cacti CLI to automatically import a bunch of devices, but first let's look at the CLI commands you will need for the import process.

Time for action - adding a single device to Cacti

Let's add a new device to Cacti using the CLI:

1. Log on to your Cacti system.

2. Change to the Cacti CLI directory:

   cd /var/www/html/cacti/cli

3. Execute the following command:

   php add_device.php

4. You will see a list of all available options. Here you can see a short summary of these:

```
[root@localhost cli]# php add_device.php
Cacti Add Device Utility, Version 1.1.23, Copyright (C) 2004-2017 The Cacti Group

usage: add_device.php --description=[description] --ip=[IP] --template=[ID] [--notes="[]"] [--disable]
    [--poller=[id]] [--site=[id] [--external-id=[S]] [--proxy] [--threads=[1]
    [--avail=[ping]] --ping_method=[icmp] --ping_port=[N/A, 1-65534] --ping_timeout=[N] --ping_retries=[2]
    [--version=[0|1|2|3]] [--community=] [--port=161] [--timeout=500]
    [--username= --password=] [--authproto=] [--privpass= --privproto=] [--context=] [--engineid=]
    [--quiet]
```

5. Let's assume that you are using a global SNMP community that you have defined in the **General** section on the Cacti settings page. Then, you can add a device using the following syntax:

   php add_device.php --ip="192.168.178.53" --description="myCLIDevice" --template=2

6. This will add a `Generic SNMP Device` to Cacti as seen here:

```
[root@localhost cli]# php add_device.php --ip="192.168.178.53" --description="myCLIDevice" --template=2
Adding myCLIDevice (192.168.178.53) as "Generic SNMP Device" using SNMP v2 with community "public"
Success - new device-id: (9)
```

What just happened?

You just added a new device using the Cacti CLI. You can now build an import script to add a list of devices to Cacti.

Importing a list of devices into Cacti

Let's now look at the import script. The following code parses a special import file containing the device description, IP, SNMP version, and the community and host template:

```
$import_file = $_SERVER["argv"][1];
$dir = dirname(__FILE__);

print "Cacti Device Import Utilityn";
print "Import File: ". $import_file . "n";

/* Check if the import file exists */
if ( file_exists( $import_file ) ) {
    print "nImporting Devices...n";
    // read in the import file
    $lines = file( $import_file );
    foreach ($lines as $line)
    {
        // cycle through the file
        $line = rtrim ($line); // remove the line ending character
        $data = preg_split("/;/",$line);   // split at the ";"
        $device_description = $data[0];
        $device_ip = $data[1];
        $device_snmp_version = $data[2];
        $device_snmp_community = $data[3];
        $device_template = $data[4];
        // Check if the device template is a number
        // and if not, set the template to a generic device template
        if ( preg_match("/^d+$/",$device_template) == 0 ) {
          $device_template = 2; // Generic SNMP-enabled device
        }
        // Build the command
        $command = "php $dir/add_device.php ".
```

```
                    "--ip="$device_ip" ".
                    "--description="$device_description" ".
                    "--version=$device_snmp_version ".
                    "--community=$device_snmp_community ".
                    "--template=$device_template";
        $return_code = `$command`;
        print $return_code;
    }
  }
  else {
    die("Error: Import file [$import_file] does not exist!nn");
  }
```

As you can see, this import script uses the already existing `add_device.php` tool to actually add the device to Cacti. The import script only wraps the system call to this tool within a `foreach` loop, which cycles through every entry of the import file.

So, instead of adding every single device to Cacti, you can use a single text file containing the basic information about your devices.

Let's have a look at this import file:

```
myCiscoRouter;192.168.0.11;2;public;1
myOtherDevice;192.168.0.12;2;public;
```

Each line of this import file contains the following data:

```
description;ip;SNMP version;SNMP community;host template
```

The available host templates can be displayed with the command:

php add_device.php --list-host-templates

You can import a device list saved as `devicelist.txt` with the following line:

php import_devices.php devicelist.txt

You will see the following output on the command line:

```
[root@localhost cli]# php import_devices.php devicelist.txt
Cacti Device Import Utility
Import File: devicelist.txt

Importing Devices...
Adding myCiscoRouter (192.168.0.11) as "Cisco Router" using SNMP v2 with community "public"
Success - new device-id: (10)
Adding myOtherDevice (192.168.0.12) as "Generic SNMP Device" using SNMP v2 with community "public"
Success - new device-id: (11)
```

As you can see, by using the Cacti CLI and some additional scripting, you can integrate external inventory databases with Cacti.

Adding a graph to a device

Although adding a graph to a device is also possible using the CLI, it is recommended you use the automation functionality for this task.

Automation - true Cacti automation

Using the capabilities of the CLI to add devices to Cacti, you can use automation to automatically create graphs for that device and add them to a Cacti tree.

Automation rules

Automation uses rules that are triggered by special events such as:

- Adding a new device to Cacti
- Re-indexing the device

Rules are based on any item of the hosts table, so you can use SNMP fields such as `sysLocation` for your rules!

Tree rules

Let's have a look at creating a tree rule using some SNMP fields.

Time for action - adding a new tree rule

There are quite a few steps involved in creating a tree rule. Let's look into these now:

1. Log on to the Cacti web interface with admin privileges.
2. Go to **Automation | Tree Rules**.
3. You will see the following table with some default entries:

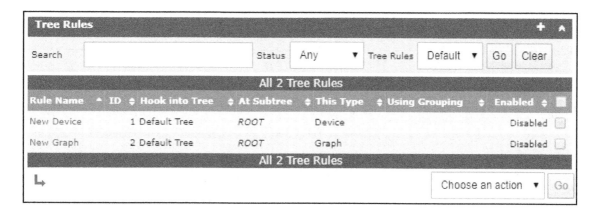

4. Click on the + link at the top-right of that page.
5. You should now see the new **Tree Rule Selection**.
6. Enter `Country A` as the **Name**.
7. Select **Customer A** as the **Tree**.
8. Select **Device** as the **Leaf Item Type**.
9. Select **Graph Template** as the **Graph Grouping Style**.
10. The form should look like the following screenshot now:

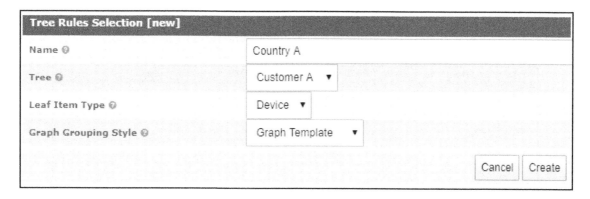

11. Click on **Create**.

12. Some additional tables and fields should show up as seen here:

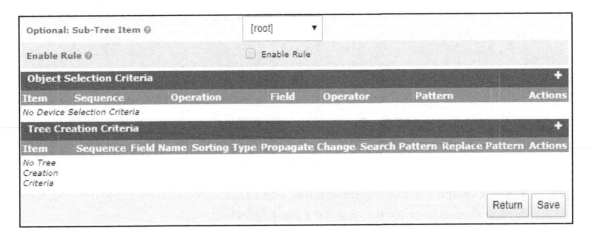

13. Click on the + link of the **Object Selection Criteria** table.
14. You can now create a new **Rule Item**.
15. Select **H: snmp_sysLocation** as the **Field Name**.
16. Select **contains** as the **Operator**.
17. Enter `Country A` as the **Matching Pattern**. This can also be a regular expression, depending on the **Operator** being used.
18. Your new rule items should now look like the following screenshot:

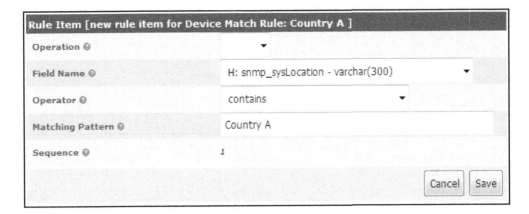

19. Click on the **Save** button.
20. Now you should define the action part. Click on the + link in the top-right of the **Tree Creation Criteria** table.
21. On this new **Rule Item**, select **Alphabetic Ordering** as the **Sorting Type**.
22. Select **H: snmp_sysLocation - varchar(300)** as the **Header Type**.
23. Enter . * as the **Matching Pattern** so your new rule looks like the following:

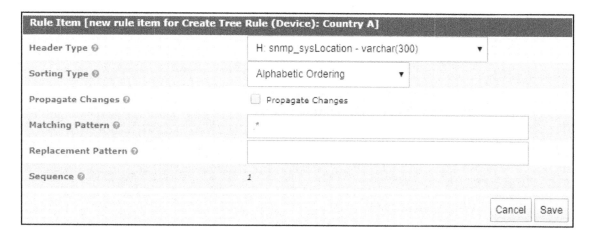

24. Click on the **Save** button.
25. In the main **Tree Rule Selection**, you will need to change some of the items now.
26. Select **Country A** as the **Sub-Tree Item**.
27. Click the checkbox next to **Enable Rule**.

28. Click on the **Save** button. Your **Tree Rule** should look identical to the following screenshot:

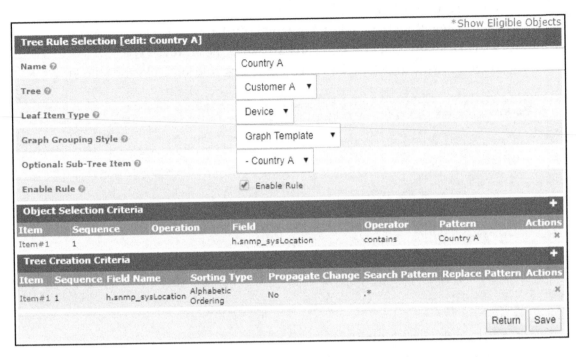

29. If you have defined the `sysLocation` field in a host to match **Country A**, you will see that host when you click on the **Show Eligible Objects** link at the top of that page:

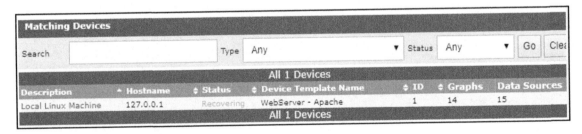

What just happened?

You just created your first **Tree Rule**. Now, every time you add a new device or re-index a device that contains **Country A** in the `sysLocation` field, that host will be added to the **Country A** Cacti tree.

Let's look at how you can apply this new rule to already existing devices manually.

Time for action - applying an automation rule to devices

Let's look at how to apply the new automation rules to your devices:

1. Go to **Management | Devices**.
2. Select the devices you want to apply the new automation rule to.
3. Select **Apply Automation Rules** from the action drop-down box as shown in the following screenshot:

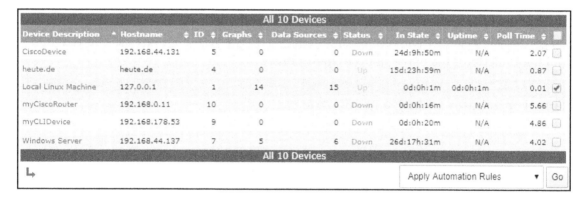

All 10 Devices									
Device Description	▲ Hostname	⬍ ID ⬍	Graphs ⬍	Data Sources ⬍	Status ⬍	In State ⬍	Uptime ⬍	Poll Time ⬍	☐
CiscoDevice	192.168.44.131	5	0	0	Down	24d:9h:50m	N/A	2.07	☐
heute.de	heute.de	4	0	0	Up	15d:23h:59m	N/A	0.87	☐
Local Linux Machine	127.0.0.1	1	14	15	Up	0d:0h:1m	0d:0h:1m	0.01	✔
myCiscoRouter	192.168.0.11	10	0	0	Down	0d:0h:16m	N/A	5.66	☐
myCLIDevice	192.168.178.53	9	0	0	Down	0d:0h:20m	N/A	4.86	☐
Windows Server	192.168.44.137	7	5	6	Down	26d:17h:31m	N/A	4.02	☐
All 10 Devices									
↳							Apply Automation Rules ▾		Go

4. Click on the **Go** button.
5. In the following confirmation dialog press the **Continue** button.
6. Now go to **Management | Trees**.
7. Click on the **Customer A** tree.

8. You should see your device show up under the **Country A** item as shown in the following screenshot:

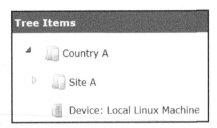

What just happened?

You just applied your new tree rule to a device. Automation then created a new tree item for that host under the **Country A** sub-tree, as defined in the rule.

Graph rules

Let's have a look at how you can use automation to create an In/Out Bits (64-bit Counters) graph for interfaces that have an up **ifOperStatus**.

Time for action - adding a graph rule

The following steps guide you through the process of creating a graph rule:

1. Go to **Automation | Graph Rules**.
2. Click on the + link at the top-right of the table.
3. Enter `IfOperStatus - UP - 64bit` as the **Name**.
4. Select **SNMP - Interface Statistics** as the **Data Query**.
5. Click on the **Create** button.
6. Select **In/Out Bits (64-bit Counters)** as the **Graph Type**.
7. Click on the checkbox next to **Enable Rule**.
8. Add some **Device Selection Criteria** so your rules look as follows:

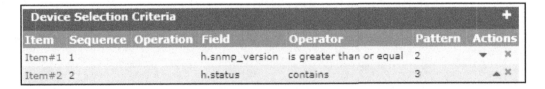

Item	Sequence	Operation	Field	Operator	Pattern	Actions
Item#1	1		h.snmp_version	is greater than or equal	2	▼ ✕
Item#2	2		h.status	contains	3	▲ ✕

9. Now click on the **Add** link in the **Graph Creation Criteria** table.
10. Select **ifOperStatus - Status** as the **Field Name**.
11. Select **contains** as the **Operator**.
12. Enter **up** as the **Matching Pattern**.
13. Click on the **Save** button.
14. Your new **Graph Rule** should now look like the following screenshot:

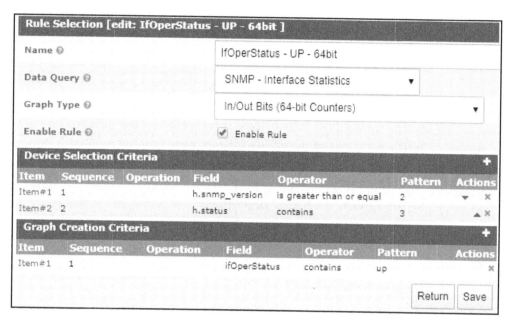

What just happened?

You just created a new **Graph Rule** to traffic graphs with 64-bit counters to any interface that is up. You can use the links in the top-right of the graph rule screen to check which hosts and interfaces match your selection.

You can now apply this rule by going back to the device management screen and applying the automation rule as you did with the **Tree Rule** your created earlier.

Further information

This chapter only provides a very short overview of the possibilities of the new automation feature.

Pop quiz - Let's test your knowledge about Chapter 12

1. What file and which parameters do you need to call to add a new Cacti tree?
    1. `php add_tree.php --function=new --type=tree --name="New Cacti Tree"`
    2. `php add_tree.php --type=tree --name="New Cacti Tree"`
    3. `php create_tree.php --type=tree --name="New Cacti Tree"`

2. What number represents the up status of a device?
    1. The up status of the device is represented by the number 1
    2. The up status of the device is represented by the number 2
    3. The up status of the device is represented by the number 3

3. What rule do you need to create to have all Cisco devices within a sub-tree?
    1. You can use the SNMP description
    2. You can use the host template name
    3. You can use both of the above

Summary

In this chapter you learned how to automate parts of Cacti.

You learned how to use the CLI to add realm permissions to a user and automate the import of new devices using the CLI and some custom code. You also learned how to create a new **Tree Rule** to automatically put devices into the correct Cacti tree. The chapter also showed you how to create a **Graph Rule** to add 64-bit counter traffic graphs to all interfaces that are up and are using SNMP version 2.

You should now be able to automate most of the common Cacti tasks by using the Cacti CLI and the new automation feature.

The information you've learned throughout this book allows you to install and manage your own Cacti instance. You've read how to extend Cacti with readily available plugins and how to create your own plugins. With the added reporting and automation functionality, you're able to offer a full set of automated services to your customers.

The next chapters will provide you with some further information on how to move your Cacti installation to a different system, and how to make use of the new multi-poller feature.

13
Migrating Cacti to a New Server

From time to time, it becomes necessary to move an existing Cacti installation to a new server. This may be due to hardware retirement, operating system upgrades, a technology move from Linux to a Windows system, or simply switching to a more powerful system. This chapter will provide you with the tools, commands, and processes to prepare and execute the migration of Cacti from one system to another system with minimal downtime.

In this chapter, we are going to:

- Provide an overview of the migration process
- Describe the differences between a 32-bit and 64-bit system
- Execute an actual migration between two systems

Let's migrate Cacti!

Overview of a Cacti migration

The migration of a Cacti installation not only consists of copying over files, but also includes the conversion of RRD files and the final tasks involved through the Cacti web-interface. Let's look at the different steps migration needs to take care of.

The Cacti files

The first step is the preparation of the Cacti files. You have several options for doing a migration. The simplest one is copying the Cacti files and the more complex one is doing a new Cacti install and executing an upgrade. In both cases, you will have to make sure you copy all the required files, including any scripts or configuration files, which may not reside in the Cacti main directory. Things such as the WMI configuration file may be residing in the /etc directory, while the spine configuration may be stored in a completely different area.

If you have worked this book and created a backup script already, then you should have a complete list of these files stored in the backup.

The database

The database holds all configuration data required to poll your devices or log on to the Cacti system. In most cases, you can simply back up the database and restore it on the new system without much preparation.

RRD files

RRD files are special, as these are not only architecture-dependant (32-bit versus 64-bit) but also operating system-dependant. RRD files created on a Linux system are not compatible with a Windows system, but need to go through a dumping and loading process in order to convert them to the architecture of the target system. There's a special procedure for this, that we will integrate into our backup script, so your backup can be restored on any system.

The poller

During the migration, the poller on the target system should be left off. The easiest way to do this is to stop scheduled tasks or cronjob that calls the poller.

Firewall/network settings

If you are migrating to a complete new system without re-using IP addresses, you will have to consider changing your firewall and access list settings on your network devices, so the new system is able to poll the devices.

Differences between a 32-bit and 64-bit system

As described earlier the main difference between a 32-bit and 64-bit system is the architecture of the RRD files. As these files are handled differently between these two system types you will always have to convert them when you want to migrate from one system to an other. This makes the migration between architectures and operating systems more complex than just copying over files as you have to take care of converting the RRD files first. Other than that, you will not have to take care of any of the other tools such as the MySQL database or the actual cacti files as these are system architecture and operating system-independent.

Cacti files

Now, let's start with backing up your Cacti files. If you have followed this book closely, you should already have a backup script set up. Let's change it so that it also takes care of the additional files we're added with WMI and other templates or PHP modules.

Enhancing the backup script

The original backup script only takes care of your plain Cacti files and some PHP configuration, but omits additional config files such as WMI settings or database configuration files. Now, let's review our backup script and add the missing files to the backup as well as make it a bit more version-independent by using a variable for the Cacti version.

Time for action - enhancing your Cacti backup

Using the original backup script, let's add the missing files and make the backup script more version-independent by using a defined variable:

1. Log on to your Cacti system.
2. Change to the backup Cacti directory:

   `cd /backup`

3. Edit the `backupCacti.sh` file and add the following line to the top of the script:

   `CACTIVER="1.1.28";`

4. Now add the ./etc/cacti/cactiwmi.pw file (as well as the path to the my.cnf file and my.cnf.d directory) to the TAR backup.

5. Finally, replace the version information with the newly added variable:

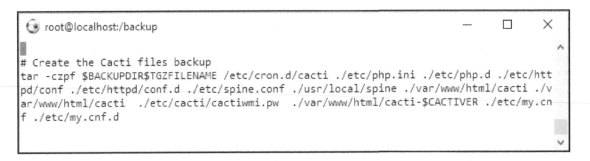

```
root@localhost:/backup                                    —      □      ×

# Create the Cacti files backup
tar -czpf $BACKUPDIR$TGZFILENAME /etc/cron.d/cacti ./etc/php.ini ./etc/php.d ./etc/htt
pd/conf ./etc/httpd/conf.d ./etc/spine.conf ./usr/local/spine ./var/www/html/cacti ./v
ar/www/html/cacti  ./etc/cacti/cactiwmi.pw  ./var/www/html/cacti-$CACTIVER ./etc/my.cn
f ./etc/my.cnf.d
```

What just happened?

You just added the WMI configuration as well as the MySQL/MariaDB configuration files to the backup. The newly added CACTIVER variable allows you to change the script quickly when you update your Cacti instance. These changes will allow you to easily restore the Cacti instance on the same system. Now, this backup also includes RRD files, which are system-and architecture-dependent. As we also want to use this backup to migrate to another system, we have to exclude these files from the backup.

Time for action - removing RRD files from your Cacti backup

Let's exclude RRD files from the backup as we have the XML files already:

1. Log on to your Cacti system.
2. Change to the backup Cacti directory:

   cd /backup

3. Edit the backupCacti.sh file and add --exclude='./var/www/html/cacti-$CACTIVER/rra' after the backup filename:

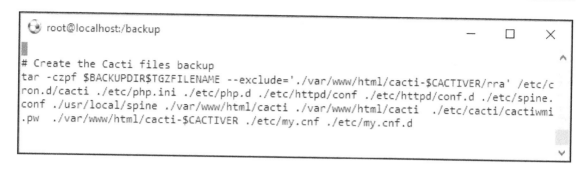

```
root@localhost:/backup                                    —    □    ×

# Create the Cacti files backup
tar -czpf $BACKUPDIR$TGZFILENAME --exclude='./var/www/html/cacti-$CACTIVER/rra' /etc/c
ron.d/cacti ./etc/php.ini ./etc/php.d ./etc/httpd/conf ./etc/httpd/conf.d ./etc/spine.
conf ./usr/local/spine ./var/www/html/cacti ./var/www/html/cacti ./etc/cacti/cactiwmi
.pw ./var/www/html/cacti-$CACTIVER ./etc/my.cnf ./etc/my.cnf.d
```

What just happened?

You have excluded the `rra` directory containing the RRD files. Don't worry, as you're going to add a more system-independent backup method for your RRD files later.

The RRD files

As you learned earlier, RRD files are system-dependent. This means that you cannot simply copy RRD files to a new system: you will have to convert them first. Luckily, this can be done using the XML dump function of the rrdtool.

Time for action - dumping and loading an RRD file

Let's test the process of dumping an RRD file and re-creating it using the resulting XML file from the dump.

1. Log on to your Cacti system.
2. Change to the `tmp` directory.
3. Copy any of the RRD files. In this example, you will use the `hdd_used` file for the local Linux machine:

   ```
   cp /var/www/html/cacti/rra/local_linux_machine_hdd_used_16.rrd /tmp
   ```

4. Now, dump the data from the RRD file to a new XML file:

   ```
   rrdtool dump local_linux_machine_hdd_used_16.rrd >
   local_linux_machine_hdd_used_16.xml
   ```

5. The resulting file is a plain-text XML file that can be looked at using the `more` command. Use the following command to display the XML file as seen in the following screenshot:

```
more local_linux_machine_hdd_used_16.xml
```

```
root@localhost:/tmp                                            —    □    ✕

<?xml version="1.0" encoding="utf-8"?>
<!DOCTYPE rrd SYSTEM "http://oss.oetiker.ch/rrdtool/rrdtool.dtd">
<!-- Round Robin Database Dump -->
<rrd>
        <version>0003</version>
        <step>300</step> <!-- Seconds -->
        <lastupdate>1510503511</lastupdate> <!-- 2017-11-12 17:18:31 CET -->

        <ds>
                <name> hdd_used </name>
                <type> GAUGE </type>
--More--(0%)
```

6. Now, remove the original RRD file:

```
rm local_linux_machine_hdd_used_16.rrd
```

7. Using the new XML file, you can now restore the original RRD file using the `rrdtool restore` command:

```
rrdtool restore local_linux_machine_hdd_used_16.xml
local_linux_machine_hdd_used_16.rrd
```

8. You can now look at the file using the `rrdtool info` command. The following screenshot shows the first few lines of the `rrdtool info | more` command output:

```
root@localhost:/tmp                                —    □    ×
filename = "local_linux_machine_hdd_used_16.rrd"
rrd_version = "0003"
step = 300
last_update = 1510503511
header_size = 5216
ds[hdd_used].index = 0
ds[hdd_used].type = "GAUGE"
ds[hdd_used].minimal_heartbeat = 600
ds[hdd_used].min = 0.0000000000e+00
ds[hdd_used].max = NaN
ds[hdd_used].last_ds = "8459564"
--More--
```

What just happened?

You used the `rrdtool` command to dump an existing RRD file into an XML file. Using this XML file, you restored the original RRD data. Using this mechanism allows you to create system- and architecture-independent backup files that can be used to migrate your Cacti installation easily to a new system.

Enhancing the backup script to dump RRD data

Now that you understand the process of creating system-independent XML data from your RRD files, you can use this to further enhance your backup script with the rrdtool dump feature.

Time for action - enhancing your Cacti backup

The next steps finalize the script for the Cacti backup

1. Log on to your Cacti system.
2. Change to the backup Cacti directory.

3. Edit the `backupCacti.sh` file and add the following lines before the `tar` command:

```
# Dump the rrd files to xml files
mkdir -p /tmp/xml
cd /var/www/html/cacti/rra
for i in `find -name "*.rrd"` ; do rrdtool dump $i > /tmp/xml/$i.xml;
done
cd /
```

4. This will dump all RRD files as XML into the `/tmp/xml` directory. Now you also have to add the path to the `tar` command, so it's included in the backup as shown in the following screenshot:

```
 root@localhost:/backup                                       —    □    ✕
# Dump the rrd files to xml files
mkdir /tmp/xml
cd /var/www/html/cacti/rra
for i in `find -name "*.rrd"` ; do rrdtool dump $i > /tmp/xml/$i.xml; done
cd /


# Create the Cacti files backup
tar -czpf $BACKUPDIR$TGZFILENAME --exclude='./var/www/html/cacti-$CACTIVER/rra'
 /etc/cron.d/cacti ./etc/php.ini ./etc/php.d ./etc/httpd/conf ./etc/httpd/conf.
d ./etc/spine.conf ./usr/local/spine ./var/www/html/cacti ./var/www/html/cacti
 ./etc/cacti/cactiwmi.pw   ./var/www/html/cacti-$CACTIVER ./etc/my.cnf ./etc/my.
cnf.d ./tmp/xml
```

What just happened?

You added the dump command to your backup script and made sure to include the XML files in the backup. The resulting backup file should now have everything included to do the actual migration to the new system.

Creating the initial cacti backup

Now that you have enhanced the backup script, you can finally create a backup that you will use to restore cacti as well as the cacti database on the new target system. This backup will contain the XML-converted RRD files, the actual Cacti files, and several configuration files. Not all of these will be required on the final system depending on the operating system type.

Time for action - creating the complete Cacti backup

The following steps will guide you through the process of creating a backup.

1. Log on to your Cacti system.
2. Change to the backup Cacti directory.

   cd /backup

3. Execute the backupCacti.sh file:

   bash backupCacti.sh

4. If this is your first backup, you will see the following output once the backup has completed:

```
[root@localhost backup]# ls
backupCacti.sh
[root@localhost backup]# bash backupCacti.sh
find: '/backup/cacti_*gz': No such file or directory
tar: Removing leading '/' from member names
[root@localhost backup]#
```

What just happened?

You created the initial backup containing all required files, which you can now move to the target system. The backup contains XML-converted RRD files as well as the completed Cacti files.

Preparing the target system

With all files backed up and converted, you can now start preparing the target system. Let's assume you're going to migrate from your current Cacti system to a Windows system. In Chapter 1, *Installing Cacti* you have learned about the BSOD2600 Windows Installer from the Cacti forum. By using this installer, you will have everything set on the new system for the migration to take place.

Restoring the Cacti files

The first step of the migration is to copy over the Cacti files and database backups. As the Linux backup is using TAR, you should install and use the 7Zip application to extract the files from the archive.

The 7Zip archive tool is open source software and distributed under the GNU LGPL. You can use this tool on any computer, including systems in a commercial organization, without paying any license fees.

7Zip is available from the following link:
http://www.7-zip.org/download.html

Time for action - restoring Cacti files

Let's look into restoring Cacti files to your Windows system

1. Log on to the new Windows system.
2. Go to the Windows Task Scheduler and disable the poller first:

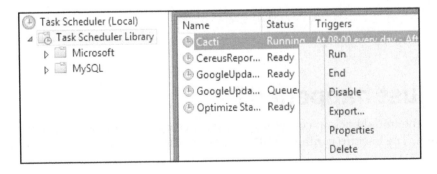

3. Go to the directory where you have put the backup files.

4. Extract both files. Make sure you extract the TAR archive within the `.tgz` file as well:

etc	11/14/2017 21:29	File folder	
tmp	11/14/2017 21:29	File folder	
usr	11/14/2017 21:29	File folder	
var	11/14/2017 21:29	File folder	
cacti_database_20171112.sql	11/12/2017 17:42	SQL-Script	8,450 KB
cacti_database_20171112.sql.gz	11/12/2017 17:42	GZ File	1,061 KB
cacti_files_20171112.tar	11/12/2017 17:42	TAR File	154,670 KB
cacti_files_20171112.tgz	11/12/2017 17:43	TGZ File	61,951 KB

5. In Explorer, open the Cacti directory: `C:Apache24htdocscacti`.

6. Rename the `config.php` file in the include directory and make a note of the database configuration contained within:

```
/* make sure these values refect your actual database/host/user/password */
$database_type = "mysql";
$database_default = "cacti";
$database_hostname = "localhost";
$database_username = "cactiuser";
$database_password = "DcdPwfnYlK";
$database_port = "3306";
$database_ssl = false;

/*
   Edit this to point to the default URL of your Cacti install
   ex: if your cacti install as at http://serverip/cacti/ this
   would be set to /cacti/
*/
//$url_path = "/cacti/";

/* Default session name - Session name must contain alpha characters */
//$cacti_session_name = "Cacti";
```

7. Delete all files from the `rra` directory:

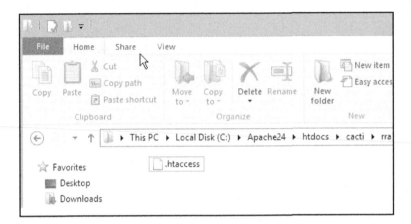

8. In a new Explorer window, open the newly created `Cacti_files` directory containing the backup Cacti files.

9. Now, copy all files from the backup to the `cacti` directory. Replace all files if asked to do so:

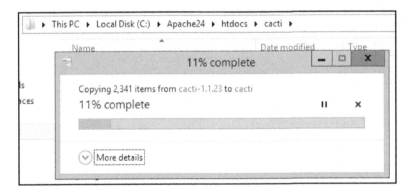

10. After the copying is finished, edit the `config.php` file, and change the username and password to match the credentials you noted down earlier.

What just happened?

You have extracted the Cacti backup using the 7Zip application and copied the Cacti files to the installation directory. This will make sure the Cacti installation on the target system contains the same files and scripts as your source system.

Considerations for plug-ins:

If you have any plug-ins installed that require special PHP modules to be loaded, then is not a good time to revisit the installation guides for these plug-ins. Especially for Windows systems, some of the PHP modules require additional steps to be considered.

You may also come across plug-ins that are designed to work on a specific operating system so as to make use of specific functionality only provided by this operating systems.

Restoring the database

In order to restore the Cacti database, you can use the MySQL client that is installed with the Windows-based Cacti installer.

Time for action - restoring the Cacti database

Let's look at how to restore the database backup using the MySQL CLI.

1. Log on to the new Windows system.
2. Start a command prompt.
3. Change to the MySQL bin directory:

```
cd C:Program FilesMySQLMySQL Server 5.6bin
```

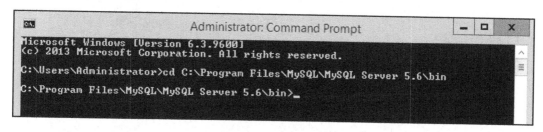

4. Start the MySQL client using the following command:

```
mysql -u root -p
```

5. Login to the local MySQL database on the Windows system using the credentials provided by the BSOD2600 Installer:

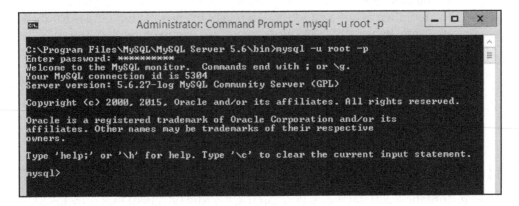

6. Drop the Cacti database:

```
drop database cacti;
```

7. Recreate the database and select it:

```
create database cacti;
use cacti;
```

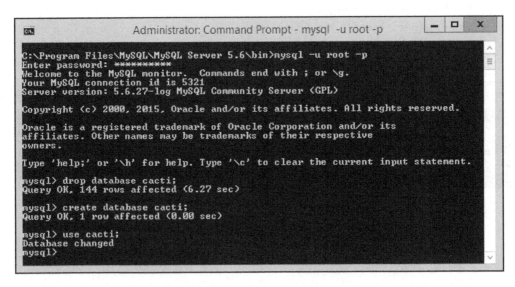

8. Now restore the backup SQL file. Let's assume you have placed it in a directory named `C:restore`:

```
Source C:restorecacti_database_20171112.sql
```

9. Once the restore is completed, you will be returned back to the MySQL command prompt:

```
Query OK, 0 rows affected (0.00 sec)
Query OK, 0 rows affected (0.00 sec)
Query OK, 0 rows affected (0.00 sec)
Query OK, 0 rows affected (0.00 sec)
mysql>
```

What just happened?

You have imported the Cacti database into the new system, overwriting any existing data. With the files and database backup restored, you will have an exact copy of the Linux system. This also includes the paths to the different tools still pointing to the Linux path. You will change these once the RRD files have been restored as well.

Restoring the RRD files

Now with the Cacti files and database restored, you're still missing the RRD files. As the new system is on Windows, you cannot use the for command, which we executed to create the original XML files. Luckily some forum members have provided Windows-based scripts, which you can utilize to restore the XML files easily.

The following post in the Cacti Forum provides some tools to dump and restore RRD files on Windows and Linux:

https://forums.cacti.net/viewtopic.php?t=24865

Time for action - restoring the RRD files

Let's look at how to restore XML files.

1. Log on to the new Windows system.

2. Download the following archive and extract the script to the Desktop of the target Windows system:

   `https://www.urban-software.com/wp-content/uploads/rrdRestore.zip`

3. Open it and check the configuration directories on the top. Make sure they match your system:

```
File  Edit  Format  View  Help
'Set the Variables
strComputer = "."
strInputDir = "C:\xml"
strCactiDir = "C:\Apache24\htdocs\cacti"
strLogFile = "C:\xml\Restored.txt"
```

4. Close the script and double-click on it to start the conversion. Several DOS Windows will pop up during the process.

5. Once completed, you can check the RRD files in `C:Apache24htdocscactirra`.

6. There's also a short log file that you can review. The name and path to the file have been set using the `strLogFile` variable in the script.

What just happened?

You have restored RRD files from XML files. The target system now has all files, the RRD data as well as the database, restored. As mentioned earlier, you still have to take care of some configuration settings within Cacti to make sure it can find all the required tools.

Updating the Cacti configuration

During the installation of Cacti, you were asked for the paths to different tools such as rrdtool or snmpwalk. These settings are also stored in the Cacti database and need to be changed to match the new paths on the Windows system.

Time for action - updating the Cacti configuration

The following steps show you how to change the different settings to match your Windows setup:

1. Log on to the Cacti system using your admin credentials.
2. Go to **Console | Configuration | Settings** and then to the paths page.
3. As you can see, all of the paths shown are marked as invalid or nonexistent:

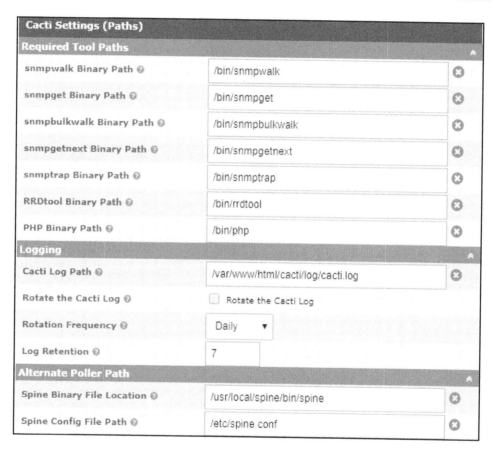

4. Change the paths to match the default Windows paths for the BSOD2600 Installer:

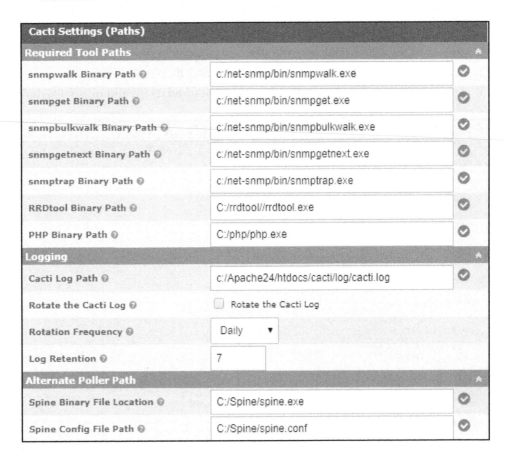

5. Save the new settings.

What just happened?

You adapted the paths to match the new Windows settings. This will allow Cacti to find all the files and tools required to poll devices and display graphs. The only task left for now is re-enabling the Cacti scheduler.

Further information

This chapter only provides a very short overview of the migration process and tasks involved. Depending on your source Cacti installation, there are numerous other things to take care of. The WMI polling interface, for example, is quite different between a Linux and Windows system. Also, some scripts may not work due to being written in Bash or Perl, which require additional tools to be installed. The main difference right now is the localhost device, which changed from being a Linux system to a Windows system with different drives, network devices, and SNMP settings.

In the event you run into any issues, you should check the Cacti forum for any information regarding your issue and ask for help if required.

Pop quiz - let's test your knowledge

1. What file and which parameters do you need to call to add a new Cacti tree?

   a) `php add_tree.php --function=new --type=tree --name="New Cacti Tree"`
   b) `php add_tree.php --type=tree --name="New Cacti Tree"`
   c) `php create_tree.php --type=tree --name="New Cacti Tree"`

2. What is the number for the up status of a device?

   a) The status of an up device is represented as the number "1"
   b) The status of an up device is represented as the number "2"
   c) The status of an up device is represented as the number "3"

3. What rule do you need to create to have all Cisco devices within a subtree?

   a) You can use the SNMP description
   b) You can use the host template name
   c) You can use both of the above

Summary

In this chapter, you learned how to migrate a Cacti system from a Linux to a Windows server.

You enhanced the backup script created earlier to create an architecture-independent complete backup. You also learned how to prepare a target Windows system for migration and restore the Cacti database. Finally you completed the migration by changing Linux-specific paths to new Windows paths.

You should now be able to plan, prepare, and execute the migration of a Cacti system to a new platform.

The final chapter will provide you with more information on how to implement the new remote poller feature.

14
Multiple Poller with Cacti

The ability to use more than one polling server has been introduced with Cacti 1.x. This new feature, called **remote poller concept**, finally allows the distribution of the actual polling to multiple systems. Previous versions of Cacti were limited by the hardware setup or additional tools and plugins like the multipoller plugin and the commercially-available CereusAgent were required to be used in order to implement this functionality. This chapter will show you how to set up a multipoller environment with one master system for the configuration and a data display part and two systems providing the actual polling functionality.

In this chapter, we are going to:

- Provide an overview of the multiple poller architecture
- Set up a master Cacti system
- Set up two polling Cacti systems

Overview of the remote poller architecture

The new remote poller architecture of Cacti 1.x is essentially running a full Cacti in a remote location with a set of devices assigned and synced to it. The remote poller Cacti will go and poll devices, even in the case of an unreachable master server, and will report back the data to the master server to be added to the RRD files. The RRD files themselves only reside on the master Cacti system. As of November 2017, only a few plugins do support the remote poller concept. One of these is the Thold plugin.

The master server

The master server contains all configuration data and adds the polled data to the RRD files. It is providing the user interface to the graphs to end-users. As long as the network connection between the remote poller and the master system is available and the remote poller is online, data from the remote poller will be written directly to the master server database. The master server can also be used to poll devices.

Any configuration change that's happening on the master server is being populated to the remote poller. You will see this later in this chapter.

The remote poller server

In the setup which you are going to build, the remote poller does all of the polling work. It needs a direct connection to the master server and needs to be able to populate the master database server. The remote poller concept also ensures that no data is lost if this connection isn't working, by caching the data locally. The remote poller needs to have the same scripts and resources available as the master server. No RRD files will be created on the remote poller, so the I/O load is far less then on a normal Cacti system.

The network

Although the concept is called remote poller, reports from the Cacti forum indicate that the current version of the remote poller functionality is having performance issues when placed remotely with high-latency connections between the master server and the remote poller. This is due to the constant database connections being made between these systems. You should therefore place the master server and the remote poller close to each other.

The database

As previously mentioned, the database is taking a key role in the remote poller concept. As the data from the remote poller is being transferred to the master server, the database of the master server should be running on a high I/O capable filesystem. By default, Cacti configures some critical I/O intense tables to be memory tables; so, you should take care to have enough memory available on the master server. Configuration changes from the master server are stored in the database and transferred to the remote poller database when changes happen.

Firewall/network settings

In contrast to a single Cacti instance, the remote poller concept requires you to allow every poller to connect and query the devices. This not only includes access lists on network devices, but also firewall setting and the distribution of SSH keys or WMI credentials for login purposes.

Setting up the master system

As you should have a working Cacti system already, you are going to change this single system to act as a master system. In our setup, there are several new commands that need to be executed so the remote poller is able to connect to the master system. Before you begin, make sure you have the latest version of Cacti installed on your server.

In the example, you will use the following IP setup:

- Master Server: 192.168.44.134
- Remote Poller 1: 192.168.44.129
- Remote Poller 1: 192.168.44.130

Make sure to change these to match your setup.

Time for action – configuring the master system

Let's look into the steps involved for preparing the master system:

1. Log on to your Cacti system.
2. Now, grant database access from remote poller to the cacti database and the MySQL timezone information. Note down the username and password which you have used, as you will need these when setting up the remote poller:

```
    GRANT ALL ON cacti.* TO rcactiuser@192.168.44.129 IDENTIFIED BY
'MyV3ryStr0ngRemotePassword';
    GRANT ALL ON cacti.* TO rcactiuser@192.168.44.130 IDENTIFIED BY
'MyV3ryStr0ngRemotePassword';
    GRANT SELECT ON mysql.time_zone_name TO rcactiuser@192.168.44.129
IDENTIFIED BY 'MyV3ryStr0ngRemotePassword';
    GRANT SELECT ON mysql.time_zone_name TO rcactiuser@192.168.44.130
IDENTIFIED BY 'MyV3ryStr0ngRemotePassword';
```

3. Add the following new firewall zone and rules to allow the two remote pollers to connect to your database:

```
firewall-cmd --new-zone=remotepoller --permanent
firewall-cmd --reload
firewall-cmd --zone=remotepoller --add-source=192.168.44.129/32
firewall-cmd --zone=remotepoller --add-port=3306/tcp
firewall-cmd --zone=remotepoller --add-source=192.168.44.130/32
firewall-cmd --zone=remotepoller --add-port=3306/tcp
firewall-cmd -reload
```

4. Now, log on to the Cacti interface and enable the boost option. Go to **Console|Configuration | Settings** and click on the **Performance** tab. Then, enable the **Enable On-demand RRD Updating** and **Enable direct population of poller_output_boost table** option:

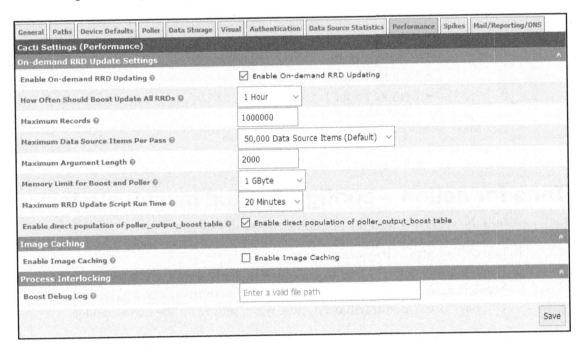

What just happened?

You have prepared the master system to allow remote connections to the master database. This is required for the actual remote poller setup and will be checked during the installation process. The connection is required for the remote poller to transfer the data to the master system, for it to be added into the RRD files. You have also enabled the boost option, which is a requirement for the remote poller concept to function properly.

Setting up the remote poller system

As mentioned earlier, the remote poller is essentially a full Cacti system. Hence, your initial task is to install a new Cacti system on the new server.

Time for action – setting up the remote poller system

The following steps will prepare a new remote poller server:

1. Follow the installation guide from `Chapter 1`, *Installing Cacti* but skip the web-based installation.

2. Now you have to add the remote poller specific settings. Edit the spine configuration file in vi editor:

   vi /etc/spine.conf

3. Change the `RDB_` variables to match the database settings of your master server:

```
RDB_Host           192.168.44.134
RDB_Database       cacti
RDB_User           cactiuser
RDB_Pass           MyV3ryStr0ngPassword
RDB_Port           3306
```

4. Now, edit the `include/config.php` file and change the `rdatabase` variables accordingly:

```
$rdatabase_type     = 'mysql';
$rdatabase_default  = 'cacti';
$rdatabase_hostname = '192.168.44.134';
$rdatabase_username = 'rcactiuser';
$rdatabase_password = 'MyV3ryStr0ngRemotePassword';
$rdatabase_port     = '3306';
$rdatabase_ssl      = false;
```

5. For the installation, you will have to make the `config.php` file writeable by the webserver:

```
chmod 660 /var/www/html/cacti/include/config.php
chown apache.cacti var/www/html/cacti/include/config.php
```

6. Add some new firewall rules so the master server can access the database on the remote poller by executing the following:

```
firewall-cmd --new-zone=remotepoller --permanent
firewall-cmd --reload
firewall-cmd --permanent --zone=remotepoller --add-source=192.168.44.134/32
firewall-cmd --permanent --zone=remotepoller --add-port=3306/tcp
firewall-cmd --reload
```

7. Allow the master server to access the remote poller database. Log on to the MySQL database on the remote poller and execute the following commands:

```
GRANT ALL ON cacti.* TO mcactiuser@192.168.44.134 IDENTIFIED BY 'MyV3ryStr0ngMasterPassword';
FLUSH PRIVILEGES;
```

8. Now, start the web-based installer and go to the **Installation Type** step. Select **New Remote Poller** and confirm that no errors show up:

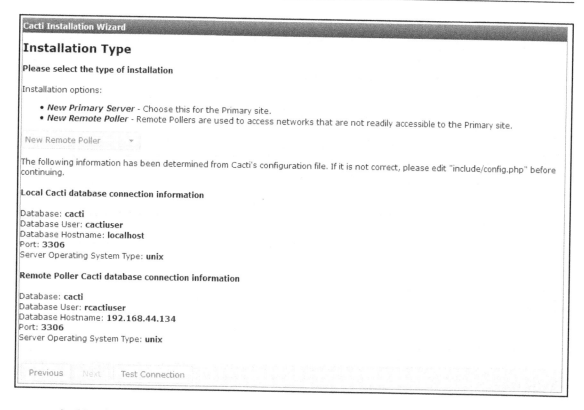

9. Hit the **Test Connection** button to confirm that the database settings are correct, and hit **Next**.

10. Finish the installer. You should see the following screen afterwards:

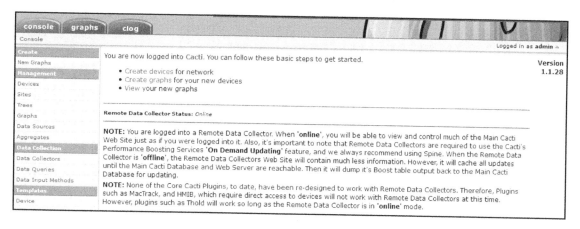

11. As the write access to the `config.php` file isn't required anymore, you can remove it now:

chmod 440 /var/www/html/cacti/include/config.php

12. Log on to the master server and confirm that the new remote poller shows up by going to the **Console | Data Collection | Data Collectors**:

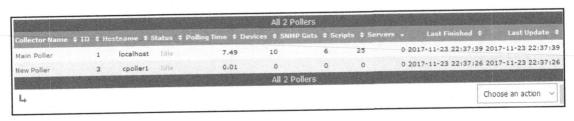

					All 2 Pollers					
Collector Name	ID	Hostname	Status	Polling Time	Devices	SNMP Gets	Scripts	Servers	Last Finished	Last Update
Main Poller	1	localhost	Idle	7.49	10	6	25	0	2017-11-23 22:37:39	2017-11-23 22:37:39
New Poller	3	cpoller1	Idle	0.01	0	0	0	0	2017-11-23 22:37:26	2017-11-23 22:37:26
					All 2 Pollers					
↳									Choose an action ⌄	

What just happened?

You have successfully set up a new remote poller and configured it to connect to the master system. You have made all required changes to the spine poller and confirmed that this new poller is showing up on the master system. Now, go ahead and repeat the steps to set up a second poller.

Prepare the remote poller

After having set up the remote poller, you will have to check the configuration and make an initial full sync to the remote system.

Time for action – setting up the remote poller system

The following steps describe how to setup the remote poller in Cacti:

1. Log on to the master Cacti system.
2. Got to the **Console | Data Collection | Data Collectors**. You should see a list of available pollers:

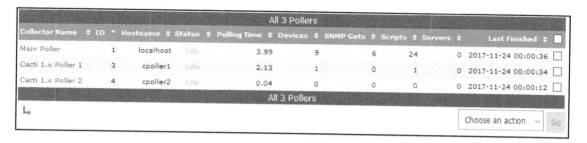

3. The default **Collector Name** is **New Poller**, which you can change by clicking on the name:

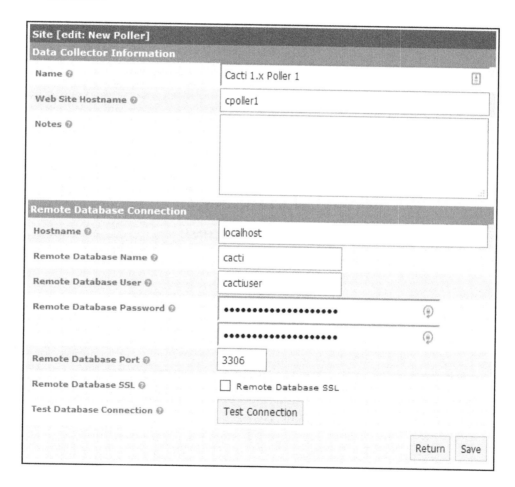

4. Note that the **Hostname** is listed as `localhost`, which should be changed to the actual IP of the remote host. In the example, poller 1 should be `192.168.44.129`. After the change, test the connection:

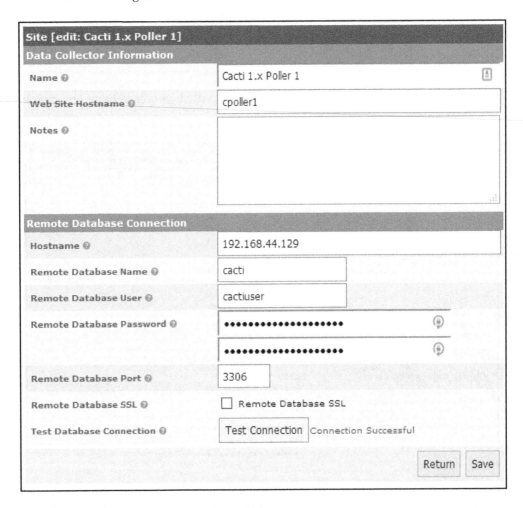

5. Now, return to the overview and select both poller. Choose the **Full Sync** option from the drop-down box and hit **Go**:

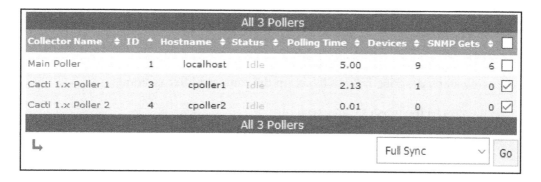

Collector Name	⬍	ID	▲	Hostname	⬍	Status	⬍	Polling Time	⬍	Devices	⬍	SNMP Gets	⬍	☐
Main Poller		1		localhost		Idle		5.00		9		6		☐
Cacti 1.x Poller 1		3		cpoller1		Idle		2.13		1		0		☑
Cacti 1.x Poller 2		4		cpoller2		Idle		0.01		0		0		☑

All 3 Pollers

| ↳ | | | | Full Sync ⌄ | Go |

6. The initial **Full Sync** will take a bit of time. If there's an error with the connection, you will see an error message appearing to the top of the screen.

What just happened?

You have finalized the remote poller setup by confirming the configuration and executing an initial **Full Sync**.

Final configuration of the master poller

As you have seen in the screenshots, the master poller has its hostname set to localhost as well. While this does not have any negative effect on the functionality of the remote poller, it has an impact on setting up devices or using functionality like the real-time feature for viewing graphs.

For devices being polled from a remote poller, the master server will ask that remote poller to provide the required data. The remote poller then gathers the data and provides it to the master server using the hostname from the Data collectors table, which is still set to localhost. Obviously, the remote poller will therefore not be able to provide the data to the master server unless you change the hostname to the correct resolvable hostname as well.

Time for action – setting up the remote poller system

The following steps describe how to to set up the remote poller system:

1. Log on to the master Cacti system.

2. Got to the **Console** | **Data Collection** | **Data Collectors**. You should see a list of available pollers:

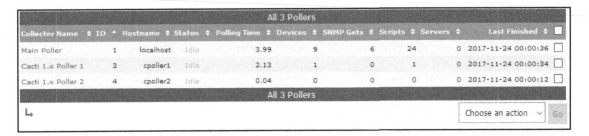

				All 3 Pollers							
Collector Name ⬍	ID ⬍	Hostname ⬍	Status ⬍	Polling Time ⬍	Devices ⬍	SNMP Gets ⬍	Scripts ⬍	Servers ⬍		Last Finished ⬍	☐
Main Poller	1	localhost	Idle	3.99	9	6	24	0	2017-11-24 00:00:36	☐
Cacti 1.x Poller 1	3	cpoller1	Idle	2.13	1	0	1	0	2017-11-24 00:00:34	☐
Cacti 1.x Poller 2	4	cpoller2	Idle	0.04	0	0	0	0	2017-11-24 00:00:12	☐
				All 3 Pollers							
⤶									Choose an action ⌄		Go

3. Select the Main Poller by clicking on the name:

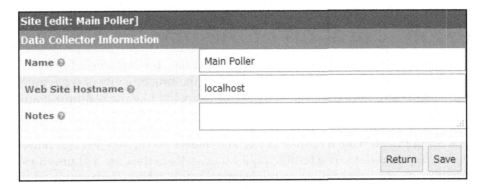

Site [edit: Main Poller]	
Data Collector Information	
Name ❷	Main Poller
Web Site Hostname ❷	localhost
Notes ❷	
	Return Save

4. Note that the **Web Site Hostname** is listed as localhost, which should be changed to the actual IP of the master server. In the example, the master server should be 192.168.44.134:

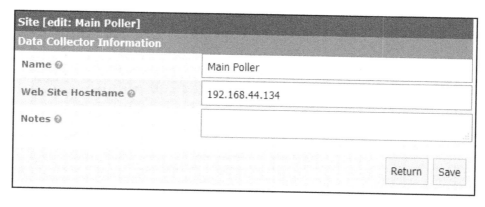

5. Click on **Save** to complete the setup.

What just happened?

You have made sure that the remote poller can communicate with the master server using the correct hostname. This is the final step required for the remote functionality.

You are now ready to add your first devices to the new remote poller.

Adding devices to the remote poller

The final step is assigning devices to the remote poller. Let's have a look on the options we have.

Time for action – setting up the remote poller system

The following steps describe how to set up the remote poller system:

1. Log on to the master Cacti system.
2. Got to the **Console | Devices**.
3. Click on a device which you want to be polled from a remote poller.

4. You will see a field called **Poller Association** with a drop-down box. Here, you can select the remote poller you want this device to be polled from:

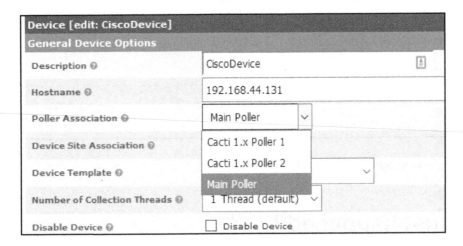

5. Save the device when you're finished.
6. Go back to the device overview, select several devices, and choose the **Change Device Settings** from the drop-down box:

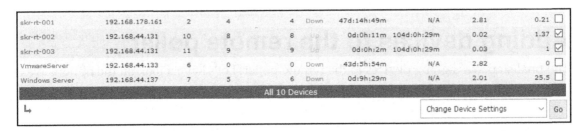

7. Check the **Update this Field** box from the **Poller Association** section and select the poller you want to assign the devices to:

8. Click the **Continue** button to save the new settings.
9. Using the **Data Collector** filter on the device view, you can verify which poller the devices are assigned to:

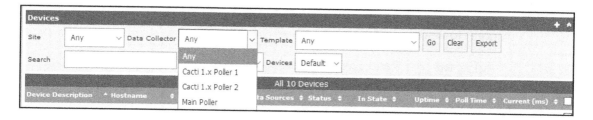

What just happened?

You have assigned your first devices to the remote poller. You have successfully implement the remote poller concept for Cacti 1.x

Further information

This chapter only showed you a brief overview of the new remote poller concept in Cacti. To fully utilize this new feature, you will also have to make sure that you keep the systems in sync regarding your scripts and local configuration files like the WMI user credentials. As your system grows, you will have to review some of the settings, especially the boost values.

The new feature allows you to distribute the load of polling your devices and therefore increasing the number of devices you can poll. Keep in mind that the database and disk drives on the master system are sized in a way that they can handle the additional load each remote poller puts on it.

In case you run into any issues, you should check the Cacti forum or the Cacti GitHub repository for any information regarding your issue and ask for help if required.

Pop quiz – let's test your knowledge about Chapter 14

1. Which files do you need to change on the master system for the remote poller concept to work?

   a) `spine.conf` and `include.conf`
   b) `my.cnf` and `spine.conf`
   c) `include.conf` only

2. Where can you assign a device to a remote poller?

   a) **Device Edit** screen
   b) **Device Overview**
   c) All of the above

3. What do you need to check before being able to run a **Full Sync** on the remote poller?

   a) The hostname of the remote poller
   b) The database connection
   c) All of the above

Summary

In this chapter, you have learned how to set up a master Cacti system and two remote pollers. You have learned how to prepare a Cacti system to become the master server for the remote poller concept. You have also gone through the steps of configuring and setup a remote poller and assigning devices to it.

The number of remote pollers is not limited to these two systems, so you can set up as many remote pollers as you require. With the integration of the boost technology, this new concept of remote poller, implemented with the Cacti 1.x release, as well as the new daemon functionality which has been added with the tholt plugin, will allow you to build a scalable Cacti performance monitoring environment.

With the migration of the Cacti development platform to GitHub, new features and functionality are being implemented every day. This can be seen by the high number of releases being provided by the Cacti team during the past months. During the next few months, more and more of the old plugins will be migrated to the new Cacti 1.x release, including the Weathermap or the nmidSmokeping plugin.

Make sure to stay covered by visiting the Cacti forums at `forums.cacti.net` and the GitHub page regularly.

Online Resources

Cacti website

The main Cacti website provide the latest patches as well as lots of other useful information. It can be reached at:

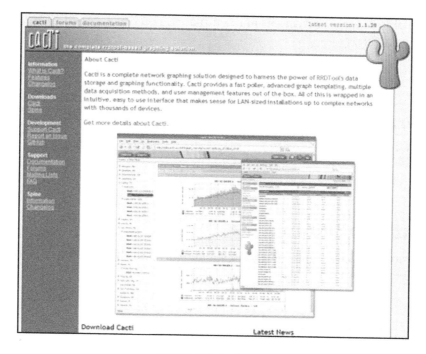

A screenshot of the Cacti homepage

Spine

Spine is a high performance poller which by far exceeds the performance of the original `cmd.php`. You can find the latest Spine version at:

```
https://www.cacti.net/spine_download.php
```

Plugin architecture hook API reference

You can find a list of available hooks provided by the Plugin Architecture and their description at the following page:

```
https://docs.cacti.net/plugins:development.hook_api_ref
```

Cacti documentation

The Cacti community as well as the Cacti developers provide lots of documentation for Cacti, the available plugins and scripts and templates. You can access the Cacti documentation site at:

```
https://docs.cacti.net/
```

Cacti forum

The main source for support and information is the Cacti forum. You can find it at:

```
https://forums.cacti.net/
```

Cacti GitHub page

With the migration of the source code from subversion into GitHub, the development took up speed. You can find it at:

```
https://github.com/Cacti/cacti
```

Cacti bug reporting

If you do find a bug in Cacti and the community in the forums can confirm it, you should post a bug ticket in the new GitHub issue tracker at:

```
https://github.com/Cacti/cacti/issues
```

Cacti GitHub plugin repository

All of the plugins for Cacti 1.x which are supported by the Cacti team, have been moved to the GitHub repository as well. Look at the main repository here:

```
https://github.com/Cacti
```

Howie's stuff

Howie, an active user from the forums, provides the well-known Weathermap plugin for Cacti. You can find his page at:

```
https://network-weathermap.com/
```

RRDTool

RRDTool provides the basis for data storage within Cacti. You can find more information on it here:

```
http://www.mrtg.org/rrdtool/
```

Tobi Oetiker

Of course, when talking about RRDTool, the creator of this and many other userful tools, Tobi Oetiker should also be mentioned. You can find his homepage here:

```
http://tobi.oetiker.ch/hp/
```

RRDTool, Cacti, and time zones

You should always have your Cacti server run in UTC time. There's a good article about why you should do so:

```
http://www.vandenbogaerdt.nl/rrdtool/timezone.php
```

Xing German Cacti group

There's a German speaking Cacti group on Xing.com. Look here for more:

```
https://www.xing.com/net/pri1c981ex/cacti
```

LinkedIn Cacti group

Of course there's also a Cacti group on LinkedIn:

```
http://www.linkedin.com/groups?home=&gid=968927
```

NMID plugins and CereusReporting

The NMID plugins as well as the CereusReporting plugin have their own pages. It also contains plugins for integrating Cacti into an InfluxDB or Bosum environment. You can find more information here:

```
https://www.urban-software.com/
```

B
Further Information

The Round Robin database tool

Cacti uses RRDtool to store and graph its performance data. RRD files store data in a fixed size file using a **First In, First Out (FIFO)** methodology and in order to aggregate data, different **Round Robin Archives (RRA)** are defined within a single RRD file. These RRAs usually consist of daily, weekly, monthly and yearly archives but can be freely defined.

The RRD file architecture

The principal of an RRD file is shown in the next figure. We have defined three Round Robin Archives, one storing 5 minute polling data, one RRA storing 20 minutes (4 * 5 minute polling data) aggregated data and another one storing the hourly (12 * 5 minute polling data) aggregated data.

In this example, the data step is defined as 5 minutes (300 seconds) so updates to the RRD file should happen every 5 minutes. During each update, the data is being written to the first archive. After 20 minutes have passed, the first data set is aggregated and written to the 2nd archive so that it contains an overall view of the 20 minute period. Once a full hour has passed, the first data set is once again aggregated and written to the hourly archive, providing an even broader view.

Each RRA is limited to a specific amount of data points, after which the data that has been written first will be overwritten by the newest data. This methodology ensures that the RRD files do not grow in size beyond their initial state. The disadvantage of this is the loss of detailed data once the RRA overwrites it:

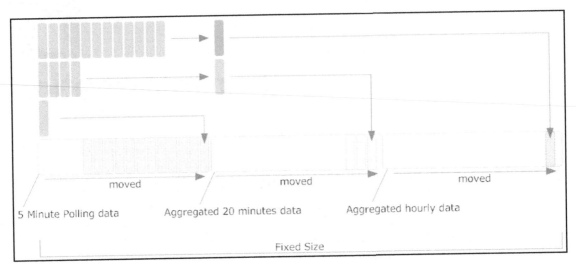

Let us take the example and look at the corresponding `rrdtool` command:

```
rrdtool create test.rrd --step 300
   DS:data:GAUGE:600:U:U
   RRA:AVERAGE:0.5:1:16
   RRA:AVERAGE:0.5:4:16
   RRA:AVERAGE:0.5:12:16
```

The `--step` flag sets the heartbeat in which data is supposed to come in. In the example it is 5 minutes (300 seconds) which is the default for RRD files. This file contains one data source (DS) called data, which is defined as a gauge. Since we don't want to limit the data entering the archive based on a minimum or maximum value, it is set to U. The 600 defined here is the time in seconds allowed to pass between two updates before the specific data point is set to unknown.

The file contains three round robin archives. The first one stores 16 data points, so a total of 80 minutes of data is stored.

The second archive stores 16 data points which are each an aggregated average of the last 4 data polls. This gives a total amount of 320 minutes or 5 hours. This also means that this archive has already lost some detailed information as each data point in it only represent a 20 minute timeslot, but we can view data going much further back

The last archive also contains sixteen data points but this time one data point is an aggregated average of the last 12 polls. Therefore, each data point in the archive represents one whole hour but allows us to keep data from 16 hours earlier.

As can be seen in this example, if you go beyond the previous 80 minutes, you will lose the data granularity as aggregation kicks in.

The default round robin archive definitions of Cacti are:

- Daily (5 Minute Average)
- Weekly (30 Minute Average)
- Monthly (2 Hour Average)
- Yearly (1 Day Average)

As the default polling interval for Cacti is 5 minutes, the daily data will have the most detailed data. Unfortunately, the default amount of data kept for the daily data is set to about 2 days, after which you will lose the detailed information. This can be changed in Cacti, but will also increase the RRD file size significantly.

There are many more options available during the RRD file creation. If you are interested in learning more you will find some links and references in the appendix.

SNMP - the Simple Network Management Protocol

When it comes to network management protocols, the **Simple Network Management Protocol (SNMP)** is probably one of the best-known. It is commonly used in networks and several applications internally support SNMP for monitoring purposes.

In this section, we will only provide a short overview of SNMP because its full workings are beyond the scope of this book.

The Management Information Base

SNMP stores information in a virtual database called a **Management Information Base (MIB)**. The database is hierarchical (tree-structured) and entries are addressed through **object identifiers (OID)**.

Generally, an organization that has an SNMP agent will publish a MIB-Module for their product and this is used on the management station to map the OIDs to human readable equivalents and perform some basic sanity checks on the format of data returned.

SNMPv1

SNMPv1 is the original SNMP protocol defined in the late 1980s. One of the main design goals for SNMP was to keep it simple and easy to implement. Due to this decision, SNMPv1 gained widespread commercial relevance and today most manageable network equipment supports at least SNMPv1.

By keeping it simple on the agent (network equipment) side, their limitations and more complex tasks were left to the clients.

SNMPv1 had 5 core **protocol data units (PDUs)** for getting and setting data as well as sending out alerts. These are

- GetRequest
- GetNextRequest
- SetRequest
- Response
- Trap

The GetRequest and GetNextRequest units are used to retrieve data from an agent but they can only retrieve one data point at a time, so retrieving interface statistics on a large network device required many GetRequests or GetNextRequests to be sent to the device.

With the SetRequest unit, data can be set on the device. This is typically used to change configurations (for example, on Cisco routers/switches), or for sending commands to a network device (for example, ping).

The Response unit is sent by the SNMP agent to the management station as a response to a Get or Set request.

Traps are initiated from the SNMP agent to send immediate alerts to the defined management station. They include information about

- Who is sending the trap
- What occurred
- When it occurred
- Additional information as OID/value pairs

Security

SNMPv1 does not have any encryption and only uses a community string to identify the management station, and even then, it is transmitted in clear-text. As a result, SNMPv1 is a very insecure protocol because SetRequests can be used to reconfigure network equipment if improperly configured.

Modern network equipment allows the definition of access list for requests to the SNMP agent which should be used in order to reduce security issues.

SNMPv2/SNMPv2c

SNMPv2 addresses some of the shortcoming of the SNMPv1 protocol by introducing two new protocol data units; GetBulkRequests and InformRequest.

The GetBulkRequest unit allows a single GetRequest to retrieve numerous OIDs from a SNMP agent without the need to send several GgetRequests. This is particularly useful for retrieving large amounts of objects like a list of all interfaces of a network device.

The Inform unit addresses the unreliability of the Trap unit, which sends a unidirectional trap. In contrast to this, Informs provide a mechanism to send reliable events from the agent to the management station which is then acknowledged with a response so that the notification is confirmed by the agent.

With SNMPv2 there was also an update to the MIB definition, which was enhanced to support more data types like IPv6 addresses, Octet strings and 64 bit counters.

Security

Although SNMPv2 was also supposed to address the security deficits of SNMPv1, it still uses un-encrypted communication, secured only by a community string and access control lists. This is also reflected by the additional c in SNMPv2c.

SNMPv3

SNMPv3 does not add new operations or enhancements to the MIB, but addresses the security problems of SNMPv1 and SNMPv2c. It can be seen as SNMPv2c plus additional security as it allows message encryption and strong authentication of senders.

SNMP support in Cacti

Cacti supports all three versions of the SNMP protocol which allows legacy equipment to be monitored alongside the latest devices.

MRTG - Multi Router Traffic Grapher

You have probably already heard of MRTG, but what are the differences between Cacti and MRTG? MRTG has been around for some time with Version 1 being released in 1995, about 6 years before the first version of Cacti.

MRTG provides the ability to gather network performance data on a scheduled basis and a fast graphical view of network use with historic data for comparison is available.

Both use RRD files to store performance data and also use a web-interface to display the graphs. The major difference between MRTG and Cacti is the feature rich web application that Cacti offers. The whole configuration for the system is done using the Cacti web interface whereas MRTG only offers text-based configuration files.

In contrast to MRTG, Cacti also offers granular user rights management, which allows administrators to allow or deny access to whole graph trees or even individual graphs. This enables Cacti to also be multi-client aware. MRTG itself doesn't have such a system which reduces the ability to use it in multi-client environments as would be needed by network outsourcing centers.

Where to get support?

There are several options for getting support for Cacti or the numerous add-ons and plugins.

Cacti forums

The Cacti forums are the primary source for support, finding solutions or getting add-ons and plugins. The Cacti community is very active, with most developers posting on the forums daily.

You will find helpful HowTos and lots of information on plugins, templates and monitoring different kinds of hosts.

You can find the Cacti forums at `https://forums.cacti.net/`.

Mailing list

The Cacti community also provides a mailing list which is mainly used for announcements. It is also monitored by the Cacti community but less frequently than the forums.

The mailing lists can be found at `http://www.cacti.net/mailing_lists.php`.

Commercial support

Cacti is open-source and the main development team does not offer commercial support for it. There are however a few companies like **GroundWork** Open Source or Urban-Software.com that offer commercial support for Cacti or have specially integrated Cacti versions available.

In addition, some of the plugin developers offer commercial support for their plugins.

C
Pop Quiz Answers

Chapter 1 — Installing Cacti

A few questions about Chapter 1:

Question Number	Answer
1	a.
2	b.
3	c.

Chapter 2 — Using Graphs to Monitor Networks and Devices

A few questions about Chapter 2:

Question Number	Answer
1	c.
2	c.
3	c.

Chapter 3 — Creating and Using Templates

A few questions about Chapter 3:

Question Number	Answer
1	c.
2	a.
3	c.

Chapter 4 — User Management

A few questions about Chapter 4:

Question Number	Answer
1	a,d.
2	a.
3	d.

Chapter 5 — Data Management

A few questions about Chapter 5:

Question Number	Answer
1	c.
2	c.
3	c.

Chapter 6 — Cacti Maintenance

A few questions about Chapter 6:

Question Number	Answer
1	c.
2	c.
3	c.

Chapter 7 — Network and Server Monitoring

A few questions about Chapter 7:

Question Number	Answer
1	c.
2	a.
3	a.

Chapter 8 — Plugin Architecture

A few questions about Chapter 8:

Question Number	Answer
1	c.
2	a.
3	a.

Chapter 9 — Plugins

A few questions about Chapter 9:

Question Number	Answer
1	a.
2	a.
3	b.

Chapter 10 — Threshold Monitoring with Thold

A few questions about Chapter 10:

Question Number	Answer
1	b.
2	b.
3	a.

Chapter 11 — Enterprise Reporting

A few questions about Chapter 11:

Question Number	Answer
1	c.
2	a.
3	d.

Chapter 12 — Cacti Automation for NOC

Let's test your knowledge about Chapter 12:

Question Number	Answer
1	b.
2	c.
3	c.

Chapter 13 — Migrating Cacti to a New Server

Let's test your knowledge about Chapter 13:

Question Number	Answer
1	c.
2	a.
3	b.

Chapter 14 — Multiple Poller with Cacti

Let's test your knowledge about Chapter 14:

Question Number	Answer
1	b.
2	c.
3	c.

Index

Made in the USA
Monee, IL
12 October 2021